Lying Down With Dogs

A Personal Portrait of a Polish Exile

For Jinks

Mark Zygadło

Lying Down With Dogs
A Personal Portrait of a Polish Exile

Foreword by Norman Davies

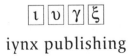

iynx publishing

First published in the United Kingdom by

inyx publishing
Countess of Moray's House
Sands Place
Aberdour
Fife
KY3 0SZ

www.inyx.com

A CIP catalogue record for this book is available
from the British Library

ISBN 0-9535413-7-1

The Publisher acknowledges subsidy
from the Scottish Arts Council towards
the publication of this volume

Typeset in Sabon by Brinnoven, Livingston
Printed and bound by Creative Print and Design, Ebbw Vale, Wales

Contents

Acknowledgements

Before the idea of this story becoming a book, I was already grateful for the help I received from my family and friends on my visits to Poland and the Ukraine. You are too numerous to mention individually, some of you appear in the narrative but many do not. I am equally indebted to you all and I hope some day you will be able to read this in translation.

Tom and Julie Pow, for your enthusiasm and constant support which gave me the confidence to write it. Myrna Kostash, you too *chuk*. Ronald Turnbull, for your clarity. The Scottish Arts Council in the shape of Jenny Brown and Gavin Wallace, without whom this would have taken so much longer.

Other invaluable help from the friends who have had to listen to this story over and over; particularly Jen and Pete Smith from the beginning, Mark Berman for your nit-picking and outrageous suggestions, Joanna Wood for your sound advice and Hieronymus Filipiak for countless translations.

Publishers Liz and Tom Short, a million thanks.

Beata Kohlbek, dziękuję bardzo.

A special order of thanks is due to these people. My cousin, Marylka Jakubowicz for your unfading patience, your inspiration and for being the voice from Poland. My good friend, Roman Hryhorchuk for being the voice from the Ukraine and my guide there. To my wife, Denise, who read everything aloud and cried in the right places. Ryszard Lubaczewski and Leonard Koniekiewicz.

And, to Franz Schubert for the C major quintet.

I am also indebted to the writers of the many books I read while researching Poland's history. Most notably; Norman Davies, Neil Ascherson, Tim Garton Ash, Robert Conquest, Raymond Hills, Eva Hoffman, Ryszard Kapuściński, Anne Michaels, Radek Sikorski and Konrad Syrop. Thank you all.

Note on Spelling

For the sake of continuity I have used local spelling through-
out. Polish language spelling therefore includes its own accents
and letters. In the case of the modern Ukrainian spelling of
placenames, they are the phonetic translation of the cyrillic.
There may be some confusion between pre-war Polish spelling
and modern Ukranian, eg; the city Lwow is later referred to
as Lviv. Różniatów becomes Rozniativ etc. I apologise for this,
the frontiers have moved.

Foreword

by Norman Davies

It is well said that 'the past is a foreign country'. But some past experiences are more foreign than others. They are foreign both geographically, if they happened in lands far away, and foreign psychologically, if the people and cultures which inhabited those lands have since been dispersed. Such is the case of pre-war Poland. Here was a country, which had survived all the vicissitudes of the centuries, notwithstanding the ravages of wars and empires. And here was a multi-ethnic society of many languages and religions, which had lived in tolerable harmony since time immemorial. Yet, in 1939–45, it all came to a sudden end. The eastern half of the country – with which this book is largely concerned – was subjected to three brutal invasions, first by the Soviet Union, secondly by Nazi Germany and thirdly by the returning Soviets. The population was decimated by political purges, deportations, ethnic cleansing, genocide, and the collateral human damage of the Eastern Front. The Catholic Poles were repressed by Stalinism, assaulted by Ukrainian national bands and largely deported or expelled by the Soviets. The Jews of the region were annihilated by the Nazi Holocaust. The Ukrainians and Belarussians were mercilessly attacked by the Nazi occupation of 1941–44, then mercilessly suppressed by the triumphant Soviets in 1944–45. By the end of the fighting, when Eastern Poland was annexed to the Soviet Union, its pre-war society no longer existed.

Families may also contain large expanses of foreign territory. For a variety of reasons, people get separated from their relatives who can quickly become strangers. The mutual incomprehension of the generations can create barriers between individuals who remain physically close. The contrasting geographical and cultural associations of maternal and paternal relations can create gulfs, which are hard to bridge. The task of knowing and understanding one's family is part of knowing and understanding oneself. Yet it is never simple. When one half of the family belongs to 'a vanished world across the sea' it presents a challenge that is doubly formidable.

In reconstructing the life of his father, who came to Britain from pre-war Poland, Mark Zygadło has undertaken a highly imaginative venture. For he is exploring much more than a mere biography or historical narrative. On the one hand, he is recreating the moods and feelings and experiences of his father's life, which had been so different from his own. On the other hand, he is also wrestling with the interactions between his father's tale and the imperfect mechanisms of his own memories and perceptions. Lying Down with Dogs can be recommended both as a fascinating attempt to re-enter a vanished world, and as an exercise in piecing together intangible things, which lie beyond our immediate knowledge. It is a psychological and historical jigsaw puzzle of considerable complexity. But it has been assembled with great clarity, and with acute powers of observation.

Norman Davies
21 May 2001

Introduction

A few months after my father's death I was driven by necessity to record what I could remember of the last trip we took together to Poland. To record it before time eroded the detail and softened the power of his story. I knew when we first mooted the idea that this would be more than a holiday. My father, already in his eighties, was not well and as the preparations progressed it became clear that he was regarding this journey as a farewell visit to his country and family. In the back of my mind were a host of unanswered questions about his past and though I did not plan to interrogate him, I had become increasingly curious about him and about my own connection to Poland.

As we made our way across northern Europe he alternated between dozing in reverie beside me in the car and revealing short episodes about his childhood in America, the family's counter-migration back to Poland and their life in the Polish Ukraine before the outbreak of war in 1939. At times his discomfort over these memories was palpable and it would take him some time to recover the desire to speak at all. Then after a sylvan picnic on our way from Szczecin to Bydgoszsc he spontaneously launched into a detailed account of the day the Nazis came to Lwów where he was a student. His revelations became longer and more and more vivid and he built up, over the course of our journey through Poland to Slovakia, an intense and real a portrait of his own life. There were times of real hardship and danger but in the main, as he would say himself, he was very lucky to have survived a cataclysm. Not everyone was. There is heroism in this story, but not perhaps of the obvious kind. Although those times produced violence and intolerance, they also produced extraordinary generosity and humanity, sometimes in unlikely quarters.

To complete his story, to understand better the setting, it became necessary to take another trip. I went alone this time to the Ukraine, to stand where he stood and in my imagination at least, to see what he saw. This book is an exercise in memory and imagination. Hung upon the framework of our journey are his memories of flight from the invaders, capture by the Red Army and escape to Hungary, and also an account of my own later journey to the Ukraine.

Memory is the raw material of history. East central Europe, politically closed for so long has forbidden its memories, and survivors of that great conflict have had to live with the knowledge that their memory might be their deadliest enemy or perhaps their only place of safety. My generation, which was brought up in post-war Britain but whose family connections are in pre-war central Europe have grown up, until the collapse of the Soviet Union, with at least half their family and half their past in deep shadow. There has been general reluctance on the part of many expatriate parents to talk about the past, in most cases for reasons of loss or displacement but in some cases, shame. It is a great irony that now at the very time when it has at last become possible to talk about their experiences and open a great floodgate of memory, that generation is dying and taking history with them.

Bronek's story is important, it should to be remembered because it represents the stories of so many of his generation and of my own. For every stranger who gripped his hands recognising in him someone else they had been in prison with, fought with, or known before the war, and for all the people I have met, out of context, whose parents had a similar story to his. We are all ripples, dying shock waves of a distant storm breaking on a foreign shore.

LITHUANIA

Königsberg

Wilno

Minsk

DANZIG

EAST PRUSSIA

Bydgoszcz   Torun

Inowroclaw

Posen

Vistula

Bialystok

RUSSIAN
OCCUPATION

Warsaw

Brzesc Litewski

GERMAN
OCCUPATION

Lublin

Bug River

UNION OF SOVIET SOCIALIST REPUBLICS

Kotowice

Vistula

San River

Tarnów

Oświęcin   Kraków

Przemyśl

Lwów   Zloczów

G A L I C I A

Tarnopol

Zakopane

Poprad

Dolina

Stanislawów

CZECHOSLOVAKIA

Różniatów

Nadwórna

Brustura

HUNGARY   Khust

Budapest

EASTERN EUROPE

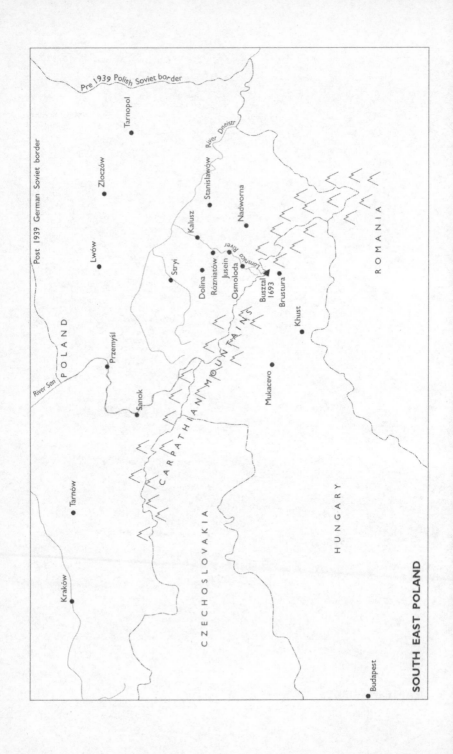

SOUTH EAST POLAND

— 1 —
Departure

I am dozing in the sitting room after supper thinking about my dad. I have my left hand on my cheek with my little finger supporting the weight of my head by the eye socket, just the way I've seen him doze a million times. His hands were like mine, square and flat, but older of course and rheumatic. His fingers followed a sort of dog-leg course to the nail and the skin of their backs was paper thin, purple and bruisy with haemorrhage stains. He took some drugs for his heart, I should know what they were, Amiodarone? He took a load. One of their side effects was to make the skin of his face and hands very fragile. As I think of him I see his head in the same position as mine as I doze, the position in which he died.

White hair. His hair was never untidy; it was the way it grew; he was no great comber. When we were in Poland, each morning after he'd finished washing he would stand in front of me proffering his not too clean comb, 'Now, Mark, please, make me the parting.' I wish I could hear him say it now, I hear it in my head just the way he spoke it. His delivery was always deliberate, Polish accented and usually imperative. The first time this happened, on our first morning in Szczecin, I couldn't understand why he should want me to do his hair, 'My hands shake too much now; you do it.' By the end of the trip, he would present himself just saying, 'Now, Mark...' I would be reading. I found it awkward but touching. He had been so capable all his life and I expected him still to want to be, but he seemed not to feel diminished by having his son comb his hair. I take this as a form of courage, not pretending.

The shape of his head was typically Polish. Standing over him with my comb as he sat to attention on the edge of any of the bed-settees we occupied in Poland, his head looked per-

fectly round from the top. As wide as it was long. As a child
I always wanted a long Anglo-Saxon head like my mother's,
not a Polish head that looked flat at the back. I wanted this so
much I cannot truthfully say what shape my head is.

Now he is gone and there is no physical man to bring my
memories into focus, I think of him as simultaneously young
and old, vigorous and feeble, with the thick black curls of his
youth and the thin white hair I parted for him every day in
Poland. And I think of him in the stories he told me, reluctantly
to begin with, but by the end of our trip deliberately and with
some purpose. They lie over the parts of his life I already knew,
filling in some of the gaps and reminding me how little it is possible to know of someone, yet still know them. And how much
the world is made up of memory. History.

Now that he is gone, his memories mix with my own and in
my imagination his story comes to life, animating the images
of old photographs, fleshing out bare bones and I seem to be
remembering things I never knew.

'When was your last trip, Dad?' We are an hour out of London
on the A12, heading towards Harwich.

'It was with Peter, or was it the one with Mummy and
Peter?'

'Jinks and Pete, wasn't it?' Family names. Everyone except
for Dad calls my mother Jinks, a nickname he disapproved of.
Conversations with him about her were awkward and slightly
formal, he called here, 'Mummy' or 'your mother'.

'Maybe it was Mummy and Peter; I just don't remember very
well.'

We finally agree the chronology of the last few trips including two which Pete, my younger brother, took on his own. My
last was in 1972, when we went as a family to cousin Renia's
wedding in Czechoslovakia. It was also my first. Dad, Jinks,
Pete and I.

'The first time I went back after the war was in 1962, with Toni
Micharowski. Hetman arranged it.'

'Hetman?'

'Yes. Hetman, you remember him. He had the Polish mobile shop.' I knew about the shop of course, but his travel business was new to me.

'Toni and I travelled together to Poland. He went to visit his family in Łódź and I went to Kraków, to Antonina. Then I went on to Czechoslovakia to see my mother. She moved in with Hanusia after she stayed with us in 1958 or 1959.

'I can hardly remember her being with us the first time. How long did she stay?'

'Not long, less than a year I think.'

'Why did she go back?'

'She missed her friends and she never learnt to speak any English, she was lonely.'

'But she didn't go back to Poland; she went to Czechoslovakia.'

'She had nowhere to go in Poland once Father Szczęk died.'

'When did he die?'

'I don't remember exactly, not long before she came to live with us.'

'So you never saw him again, since you left?'

'Not since 1939.'

'What was he like? Father Szczęk.'

He pauses to rub his forehead, rummaging around for the blandest answer.

'He was a good man.'

'He was a priest. Come on, Dad, what was he like?'

More forehead rubbing.

Now, I search through my memory of that day on the road at the start of our journey, what did he tell me then? What did I know already? I have the image of a big man in a black priest's cassock with a thin black belt round an ample waist. He has a fine but heavy face, square.

'He was a kind man, a very kind man.'

'And?'

'Well, he was not rich but he supported a big family. You

know, the priest is always looked after by the parish, in those days they were often the most well off in a community. People were very poor. But, because he had a big house from the church and a bit of land, he brought his nephews and nieces to live with him, to help his brothers and sisters. Antonina and Michał, you know them, they were there, and there were some others you don't know, and later my mother and sister and I, he took care of us all. We were very poor before my mother worked for him. She was a cook in the hospital in Stanisławów and we had nothing. He took us in and we became his family too, he brought us up, Hanusia and I, educated us, everything. Without his help,' he waves a hand over the past, 'who knows? Who knows what would have become of us.'

'How did you come to be in Stanisławów?'

'Ah, Mark, it's a long story and a long time ago; you don't want to hear all that.'

'Well, I do actually; I don't really know that much about you.'

'There is so much I don't remember now.'

I wonder how to get him started.

The concrete road thumps under us with a rhythmic beat. He goes quiet beside me in the passenger seat. Perhaps even this gentle probing is too much. He stares ahead at the road, expressionless, but the age in his face gives him a sad look. He had big sad green eyes, my dad.

'What is your first memory?'

I have asked him about his life many times and sometimes he was persuaded to give a little information but he was habitually reticent, only reluctantly volunteering stories about the time before he came to England in 1940. If I asked about the war, he would say, 'There's nothing to tell; I didn't do anything special. I was lucky, that's all. I survived.'

I once asked him what happens after you die. 'Nothing happens. How can it? You are dead.' No complication, no comfort.

He sniffs in prelude. 'My first memory? My first memory is of standing in the street with my mother in Chicago, watching soldiers marching. I am holding her hand and I press my cheek against her skirt. A band is playing and people have flags. It is very bright, windy and cold. I have to shield my eyes to look up at the soldiers. As they pass by, the sun flashes between their heads into my eyes, on, off, on, off, in time with their feet and the music. The shadow of their heads slides over the crowds of the people watching them from the pavement. Children march along beside them stamping their feet and swinging their arms too high, laughing and shouting. I want to stamp too but my mother picks me up. The end of the column passes us with some children chasing after them. Swirls of dust in the wind follow them to the corner of the street. When they disappear we stand for a while and listen to the band dying away.'

'What was it? Do you know?'

'I know now. It was in 1917 when the United States joined in the first war. I was four.'

He was born in Chicago in a Polish community, a piece of Poland in America. In Europe, at the time of his first memory, Poland did not exist as an independent country until the next year, 1918. In theory it was still partitioned between Germany, Austria and Russia; in practice Russia had collapsed into revolution and what was left of her armies were being pushed back behind her own frontiers and were fighting each other. Austrian soldiers were wandering home having no one to fight and not really wanting the vast empty lands they had conquered in the east. Germany was still fighting on the western front.

Into the big Chicago community of economic migrants from central Europe came, in small groups, the entire younger generation of his mother's family along with most of her generation of their native village, Brzozowa, in Galicia, Austrian southern Poland. The Małczyńskis, his mother's family, were three young men, Władysław, Bronisław and Mieczysław, and three young women, Maria, Stanisława and the youngest, Gabriela, my grandmother.

Gabriela Małczyńska met Józef Zygadło, also of Brzozowa, in Chicago. At the beginning of the twentieth century families sent their younger generations to America to earn money and to avoid the depression and the over population at home. A family arriving first in the city would be the base to which others came, to people they already knew and trusted in this strange land until a whole generation from a village might live in the same apartment house. Zygadłos and Małczyńskis from the same Galician village would thus have been together in Chicago, met, fallen in love and married each other in just the same way as they would at home. Józef and Gabriela married, and in 1913 their first child, my father Bronisław Zygadło was born. Two years later his sister, Anna, arived. In Polish, names are usually abbreviated or changed to familiar forms. Anna, which has many variations, in this family is usually called Hanusia (Hanusha), and my dad, Bronisław was called Bronek.

Gabriela was a seamstress like her sisters. Her plan, once she and Józef were married, was not to stay in America but to work hard and save enough to buy land back in their village. Economic migration was much the same then as it is today, and though the USA was populated mainly by those who never intended to go back home, there were also many who did. Today from Brzozowa the men go to Austria to work as builders during the summer months after planting the maize and oats on their farms, returning in September for the harvest. In the winter they work on their own new houses built with materials bought with Austrian schillings, and make rustic furniture or craft items which they take back to Austria the following year to sell in markets. Their wives and children stay at home, keeping the animals and running the farms.

'What did your father do in Chicago?'
'Not very much.'
'How do you mean?'
He sighs heavily, lifts one hand again, palm up, but turns it over and lets it fall back on to his knee. I think he's going to say

something but he turns away to look out of the side window of the car.

Slowly at first, he tells me the way it turned out for Józef and Gabriela. While she sewed, he drank. And when he drank, he became violent. Bronek looks steadily away from me as he tells me his father's story. His reticence is not suprising, but his memories of this period are not all unhappy. Their household in Chicago included Józef's brother, another Bronisław Zygadło, a schoolmaster to whom the little Bronek and Hanusia were devoted. In the background were all of Gabriela's brothers and sisters with their wonderful names, all with familiar versions: Władek, Bronek, Mietek, Marysia, Stasia, Gabika. The extended family.

In 1922 Gabriela decided that she must leave and return to Poland. They had saved a little money, enough to pay the deposit on a farm, and though he won't say so, it is obvious that they were all relieved to get out of a violent domestic situation. Józef promised to work and to keep sending money to get them started and eventually, when things were better, to come back too.

'She put down a deposit on some land next to my father's family in Brzozowa and they helped her to build a small house. You remember the place?'

'No, I've never been there.'

He pauses and I feel him looking at me, 'Ah yes, it was Peter. You will see when we get there. The house is gone now, but it was a beautiful place. My father's family still lives there.'

This reminds me of the story of Pete helping his great uncle Mietek to harvest cherries in the orchard of his neighbouring farm. I can see them working away on ladders in adjacent trees, chattering all day like starlings at the fruit but neither understanding a word the other said.

He recalls the rolling Galician country and the forests, 'Ach, it's too bad we had to leave it.'

'What happened?'

Again a hesitation, rolling back another stone. The story

comes in bursts as he reviews and probably edits things he hasn't told for a long time, maybe ever.

'We were waiting and waiting for my father to send money, but nothing came, nothing came. Finally things got so desperate my mother had to give up the land and we moved in with my grandmother, her mother-in-law. She and my mother didn't like each other and there was always some trouble between them.'

Gabriela gives Hanusia some chocolate on her birthday.

Józef's mother sees it and asks how can she waste Józef's hard earned money like this, on chocolate.

Gabriela says, 'What money? He never sent any yet.'

'How dare you talk about my son like that. I will write to him today and tell him to send the money to me from now on. You are living in my house after all.'

'I hope he sends you as much as he has sent us.'

'What do you mean by that?'

'If you save it all up you'll have nothing too, like us.'

'Did he never send anything?'

'No, not really.'

'How do you mean?'

'After we heard he had disappeared, I got a letter from him.'

'He disappeared? What happened to him?'

'He moved and lost contact with the family in Chicago.'

'Lost contact?'

Silence.

'What did he say in the letter?'

'Oh, nothing much. Just, you know, what they say in the cinema, "Look after your mother, you are a man now." I was about ten I suppose. And there was five dollars inside.'

He goes back to staring out of the side window. I've stirred up some seventy-year-old mud and it has made us both uncomfortable. It sits between us like another passenger. He turns back to me, shrugs and sniffs, 'That's how it is, Mark. My father gave me five lousy dollars.'

'Not much.'

'Not enough. All my life I have felt the lack of a father,' he looks away. Then strangely, he adds, 'Most keenly.'

'My first memory is of you, Dad.' I hate to have distressed him.

'What?'

'My first memory is of Plas. You climbed the chestnut tree to get conkers for us.'

At the farm where I was born, in Wales in 1952, there was a huge horse chestnut tree growing not quite in the rubbish tip, but hard by it in the corner of the yard. Its great branches hung into the deep shadow it made.

'I did?'

'Yes, you did.'

'Hm, maybe so, I don't remember.'

At the bottom of the big yard which slopes gently down from the house to the road, there is the rubbish tip and the conker tree, a whitewashed stone wall along the roadside, a standing stone by the gate, a mill with a wheel and stone steps leading up the side of it to the granary. There is the gate in the wall with fat round gateposts and there are the people. The imaginary people and the real people. Perhaps we are all imaginaries now.

Two imaginaries reside in this part of the yard. In the tip, Mr Kenny, and inside the right hand gatepost is Tectuwoctu. These gentlemen are my older brother Julian's inventions, his discoveries, rather. He knows them best and however hard I try, they will only speak to him. They are dignitaries; any approach must be respectful and their permission must be sought for certain things. Tectuwoctu must be saluted when entering or leaving, he is the keeper of the gate, but Mr Kenny is a little more mysterious and he is not always at home. This fact always baffled me. I would stand watching Julian in serious discourse with Mr Kenny about the price of milk or the weather, the sort of adult formality that binds us together. Social grooming. Yet I had to wait, I had no conversation, I was still an infant waiting for their attention.

Even with these familiars Julian is shy. He blushes, just as he does with our neighbours as he stands at the edge of the dump calling, 'Hello, Mr Kenny, are you home today?' We wait. Sometimes he received no reply and he would say to me, 'He must be out; we'll come back later on.'

'Where is he then?'

'How do I know? P'raps he's in Crymmych.'

I imagine a man made out of bits of old pram, leaves and twigs shuffling into our local town, Crymmych. Lots of real people in Crymmych look pretty much like Mr Kenny.

In this memory Julian calls as usual, 'Hello, Mr Kenny. Are you home today?'

'—'

'Oh yes, not too bad, thank you. How are you today?'

'—'

'Ha ha, yes very nice, isn't it.'

They go on like this for some time, it's like a phone call only no one has a phone yet.

Eventually Julian conquers his shyness about the request he wants to make. He holds his head a little on one side, scuffs his boots and has an embarrassed smile. 'Please can we get some conkers, Mr Kenny?'

Julian and I are throwing sticks into the tree. I'm three and he is nearly six. My sticks don't even get to the lowest branches and although his throwing is much better we are not knocking any of the conkers out of the tree. My mum must be about, because although that part is blank somehow I know she persuaded my dad to help us. I remember this as being unusual but how could it be? How could I know that? This is my first memory, I have nothing to compare it with. In fact this is the moment to which the rest is added. There is nothing before this. The yard, Mr Kenny, the tip, the conversations are all added later like an overture, in effect this must be the beginning of my life, the opening sentence in my story. From this point on I am remembering.

But, it is also true, looking back through forty-odd years of tangled memories, it was unusual; he seldom repeated this sort of treat.

He throws off his jacket, a khaki battledress jacket, and climbs the tree. He is a spare man of my age now. Fine bones, black curls, a broad brow and nose. He's a Slav, he stands straight up and smiles with his mouth full open. There's a big gap between his front teeth which are long, equine and yellowy. Slavic teeth. I must tell you about his friend, Koskowicki, but later. Bronek is waiting in the conker tree to amaze us.

For a three-year-old whose memories are just beginning, tree-climbing alone is impressive. He hauls himself easily by his arms, his legs kick under him in mid-air like a swimmer or the flower-pot men. In a moment he's gone into the foliage; we follow his progress by his grunts and the twitching leaves. We think we know where he is; I am pointing, clapping. Who knows what I was really doing; now I am excited. This is my birth; all time proceeds from this fantastic moment. The tree with indigestion, a section of foliage suddenly separates from the whole shape of the canopy and shakes violently on its own, letting go its fruit in terror. This is too good. He works his way up the tree like this, grunting and laughing at our cheers. He was a great grunter, my dad; I am too. In old age he became a great sigher. Shall I?

The last image in this my first memory is of his black head pushing through the leaves at the very top of the tree. What made this sight so extraordinary and fixed it so indelibly in my mind?

My time at Plas was short, like one day's memory, sunny and dreamlike. The sounds are of Julian chattering away to his people, of Dad talking Polish to Big Michael, but of my mum's cooing singing voice more than anything else. I was so impressed by the tree-climbing escapade because I hadn't noticed the world beyond her voice up until this moment. In its warm womb there was no separateness and no memory save of the voice itself, and it too has its own story.

My father had no recollection of that event, as I have no recollection of this one. This is his version of the beginning of my life: 'I remember well the day you were born, Mark. A Wednesday. The labour started in the early hours of the morn-

ing. Auntie Mae stayed with Mummy after breakfast while
I went to fetch the midwife. At lunchtime you still had not
arrived, so to keep out of the way, and to keep Julian out of the
way, I took him with me to cut thistles in the field behind the
house.'

The field slopes up sharply behind the farmhouse but rounds
off higher up. It's more of a paddock than a field, too small
and steep at the bottom to be cultivated, but rich and sheltered,
prone to thistles and docks. They can take over a field and are
best cut before they set seed.

It is July, a Wednesday, still and hot in the middle of the day.
I see him with Julian wading in the deep grass. He carries the
scythe on one shoulder like the reaper but he is listening for the
feeble cries of birth, not death. It is too bright and colourful a
day to be morbid. The quilted Carmarthenshire landscape in
the fluttering air; buttercups, clover and cowslips in the grass
and the cool black earth below it.

It makes my mouth water to think of the day I was born.

He swings the scythe effortlessly, lazily, not focusing but
regarding the blade slicing and feeling the sparkle of milky sap
spray up on to his hands. One stroke for every thistle, at every
stroke a death and with every stroke a name. What shall I
name this child?

Names for the quickening, names of the dead. Six million
strokes in the Polish camps. He thinks in Polish. One million
Polish names in Russia. What shall I name this child? Twenty
million nameless strokes in Russia. A girl or a boy? Four with
my own name in Auschwitz, in Oświęcim. How many living?
How many dead? So many strokes, so many names. Can I ever
go back?

It makes his eyes water. The day I was born.

Into his swimming pool of vision, into the middle of the arc
of a stroke, Julian's foot. Julian's big foot. He was the kind of
boy who would put his foot to the scythe or his hand in a flame.
He has become mesmerised by the rhythm, fascinated by the
possibility, his body always a little ahead of his thoughts. Once,

in Kaziek's turkey shed, he put his forefinger into the trigger-guard of a .22 vermin gun and shot the back out of Bronek's best coat; his finger could not resist the possibility. A yell comes from the house. There is a yell from his own throat and he buries the point of the blade in the earth beneath Julian's stupid heel. There is a yelp from Julian who holds his ear; it feels like it has been cut with the scythe. Across the field, following the running man, drifting clouds of thistle down.

'And you were fat, Mark. You were so fat your eyes didn't open for a week.'

— 2 —
Wales

We make very good time on the first stage of our journey and arrive in Harwich with a couple of hours to wait before we can board the night ferry to the Hook of Holland. We follow the ferry-boat sign and find our way to the dock, which is some way from the centre of the town. We go mechanically through the processes of preparation; filling the car with diesel, checking levels of oil and water, tyre kicking. Then we enter the large car park marked out in long queuing lines and find ourselves sitting in the car with nothing much to do.

I ask him about the Polish language and we go through the conjugations of a few verbs but it peters out quickly; my interest and my imagination have been fired by our conversation on the A12.

His face, watching from the foliage of the chestnut tree, opens a sluice and a torrent of memory floods out. From the present, I know that he was the reluctant green man. Bronek, something human tangled up in something vegetable. The vines that wound around his neck strangled and wounded; they did not decorate or conceal. The leaves about his face restrained him, disguised him; he was not the embodiment of the wild fecundity of the untamed natural world, he was a man out of his context struggling with things he does not yet understand, having the familiar sapped out of him and a new alien juice forced into his body. A kind of kidnapping, a kind of rape, another invasion. Like a chimera, he was neither one thing nor another and much later, now in fact, he might have said so. But then, with time, the alien sap rising through him became familiar, it became a family, and his memories started to change. They became like my own, sunny and happy, filled with a simple meaning, a natural one.

Farming in Carmarthenshire at that time, in the mid-1950s was much as it had been before the war. Farms were relatively small with little in the way of spare cash for modernisation. Most farms still had working horses for cultivation and draught work even if they already had a tractor. We were a one-horse farm in those days. Doxie. I remember her plodding across the yard still in her draught harness with Dad sitting sideways on her. Her back was too broad and flat to sit comfortably astride. She moved towards the stable as though still pulling the harrow.

'Why did you start farming, there were surely other things you could have done?' An obvious question I had never thought of asking.

'What's wrong with farming?'

'Nothing, but it wasn't what you were planning to do before the war, was it?'

'No, but the war changed everyone's plans. I didn't plan to leave Poland.'

'What did you plan to do?'

'Well, I was studying to be a vet.'

'Could you have gone back to that after the war?'

'I did, in Edinburgh. There was a Polish college for refugees, all Polish, the staff, the course, everything. The qualification of course was useless in this country.'

'But not in Poland.'

'Probably useless there too in the end because the Russians took over everything.'

'Did you think of going back?'

'Yes, before I was married I thought about it, before I realised that the communists were there to stay and, well, there were some other things.'

'What other things?'

He seems about to tell me, then changes his mind, 'Ah, never mind that now. Once we were married and Michael was born things were different. I had more reasons to stay here. So after I finished the college in Edinburgh, I went to work on a farm in Yorkshire, Northallerton, for a year, then we started to look for a farm.'

'And you found one in Wales. Why Wales?'

'The cheapest land was in Wales.'

A yellow 1930s Rolls Royce pulls into the car park, glides round in front of us and stops in one of the vacant lines marked out for queuing. The driver and single passenger descend from the open front section of the car in huge tweed coats, sheepskin gauntlets, goggles and deerstalkers. They open one side of the bonnet and poke about inside, nodding to each other that the old girl is doing well, isn't she. Then they begin a tour of inspection, checking the shiny drop handles, the leather straps holding the trunks on the back and the skinny chevron-patterned tyres.

'You know all this anyway, Mark. I must have told you many times already.'

'You have, some of it, and I have forgotten a lot. I knew you had been at college in Edinburgh but not the rest of it.'

'Well, it's not very interesting.'

'You may not think so.'

A black 1950s Rolls enters the car park, one of those big ones made to carry royalty, with extra tall windows and a beige-hide interior. Sweeping lines close in the rear wheels and taper to a point at the rear bumper.

'Funny how they put the same design of back lights on a Roller as they did on Landrovers or Austin Sevens.' The black D-shaped pressed metal cases set at each end of the number-plate with a red window on the face and a clear one on the flat side to illuminate the registration number.

'What?'

'The lights.' He hasn't followed me at all; he gives me a genuinely puzzled look.

'I don't know what are you talking about, Mark.'

More Rolls Royces join the two already in line and we watch as the proud owners disembark and compare their prized examples. There's a good-natured bonhommie about it all, the confidence of the extremely wealthy among their own kind.

'Come the revolution, eh, Dad?'

'Don't you believe it. Breshnev used to collect Bugattis.'

Nothing changes.

'All the communists, especially the Russians, make lousy cars.'

'People are collecting Trabants.'

'I don't know Trabant, or Lada. I wouldn't touch it. Or Skoda.' An idea brightens his face, 'Aha, Mark, you know what it means, Skoda?'

'No.'

'It means shame.'

Looking at the collection in front of us, 'What about Zil?'

'Zil is an armoured car for the protection of the politburo.'

Beyond the cars is a hotdog trailer.

'Shall we take a look at some of these and get a cup of tea, Dad?'

'Good idea.'

We walk through the gathering knots of drivers and ordinary passengers like us who have come to admire the cars. I ask a driver in a Norfolk jacket and cloth cap with ear-flaps if they are on a tour. He tells me they are all going to Sweden, to a rally. They will drive up from Bremmerhaven through Denmark and take a second ferry crossing to Sweden. Bronek makes a show of being interested as we look at a sparklingly clean engine, but I know he is not. We detach ourselves from the enthusiasts and wander towards the smell of hotdogs and the Bolsheviks leaning on the counter.

'Look at that, there's Lord Montyqueue of Bewdley dressed as a bleedin' chauffeur!'

'Was it difficult, starting up in a strange country and not knowing much about farming?'

'I knew something about animals from my studies, and in Poland everyone knew something about farming, it was a peasant economy. Your mother had been a land girl during the war and in fact she was keener on the idea of farming than I was. But you know, it's very exciting when you start something like this with nothing. You work hard together and things improve; a family comes and you have the future around you. It was a marvellous time.'

A sip of scalding tea from a polystyrene cup.

'When we bought Plas there was no roof on the house; the cheapest we could get was corrugated iron, so that's what we had. The noise of the rain on the roof the first day it rained was so bad I immediately regretted it. Slates were hard to get even in Wales; there was still so much rebuilding after the war. Farming was simpler then than today. We really were little better than subsistance. The government helped with subsidies and with advice, they were trying to regulate food production, and the marketing boards guaranteed prices for what we produced beyond our own needs. Milk was the best bet in Wales. Yes, there were many things I didn't know. I used to watch my neighbour through the hedge and copy what he did. Sometimes I didn't understand what he was doing, but I did it anyway.'

Another image of Bronek hidden in the foliage.

'Why didn't you just ask him?'

'I didn't want to bother him every day with questions.'

'Were our neighbours not friendly?' I try to remember who they were but cannot.

'Oh yes, people were very kind to us. But you know, we were different, foreign, and sometimes that was difficult. Once I bought a load of hay, our first winter at Plas, and I had to buy in fodder. The lorry came to the gate in the terrible rain and they wouldn't wait till the rain stopped or for me to bring the horse and cart each time. I could only take a few bales at a time. They threw down the whole load in the road in the rain and I had to shift it on my own. We started to argue; they thought I was a fool because I didn't understand what they were saying, so I told them where they could go in Greek, in Latin, Polish, Russian, German and then in English. They told me to fuck off in Welsh and left the hay in the road. It's funny now, but at the time I was not amused. The hay was wet and getting heavier and heavier and afterwards I had to turn it every day till it was dry to stop it going black. They gave me a lot of work.'

Jinks descibed him in those days as a firebrand, often losing his temper especially with the illogical behaviour of animals. Julian and I used to imitate him chasing the cows, shouting Polish oaths that we didn't understand. But I remember him later as a patient man, more readily aquiescent, stronger perhaps.

'I remember the noise of the rain on the roof too; it reminds me of bath night for some reason.' Maybe because the bath was tin.

'Ah, the bath was such a palaver.'

There was no plumbing in the house, but in Wales water is a constant presence. A stream running through a rough area behind the house emerged at the west gable end flowing in a channel constructed on the top of a bank. The mill leat. The mill itself was on the western side of the yard wedged under ash and sycamore trees that marked the boundary of the known world for me. From a cast-iron spout in this bank, near the corner of the house, issued our domestic water supply collecting in a gravelly pool where we washed our boots and played mud games. It was controlled by a tapering wooden bung. When it was removed a curved glassy rope of water hung from the spout to the pool.

On the eastern side of the yard there was also water. The main flow of the same stream ran across a ford in the track leading from the yard through a leafy tunnel to the rickyard. It was dark and cool in here under the trees. When it was dry and hot in the yard and there was only half an inch of water in the ford, in the tunnel it was always cool. In my memory these places have some essential Welshness to them. These out-of-the-sun places where moss and pennywort grow on stony banks; Welsh damp is always there under the surface, like emotion.

This is where Big Michael kills an adder with a pitch fork. This is where I stand watching Julian ploughing the grass with my pram. Starting near the front of the house, he walks back and forth pulling the pram so that the wheels follow the faint track they left on his last pass until the grass is covered in parallel pram tracks. He is talking constantly to someone.

'Ploughing's finished. Oh well, better roll it next, boy.' And he starts at the beginning again. He has been cultivating this field all day. Everyone says he'll be a farmer when he grows up.

We are called to be bathed. Water is carried from the spout, heated in cauldrons on the range then poured steaming into the tin tub. Julian and I bathe together in the wobbly bath on the kitchen floor in front of the range. He's big for his age, he's heavy, and when he leans back against the bigger end of the bath the long sides pull in; when he leans over the side the whole thing twists a bit. He loves this sort of game, taking things to the edge. He watches Jinks and as soon as she turns away, he leans or he pushes and the water level rises to the brink.

'Oh crikey, it's going to spill, man. It's going to spill.' He teases me in a Welsh whisper.

I lean the other way desperately trying to counter the twist, but my weight is insignificant. He keeps an eye on Jinks.

'Look out, man,' a spoonful slips over the side, 'Ooh, Jinks will be disappointed.'

'What are you up to, boys?'

The bath clunks back onto the flags making the water stand up in peaks around us and bounce out on to the floor.

'Boys!'

'What?' Julian is all innocence, his hand surfaces with a sponge in it and he is concentrating on washing an armpit by the time she gets to us.

'There's water all over the floor.'

'Where?'

'Here!' She points at the pool spreading across the flagstones. We look over the side. 'Ooh, it must be leaking.' He looks at me with a straight face.

'Don't be so silly, Julian.' Too late, we are completely silly with giggling.

'Oh, hell. Now we'll have worms in the kitchen.' She goes for a cloth.

'Ooh, werms, man. Weerrmms. We'll have worms in the bath.' And he tries to jam his toe up my arse, 'You got worms, wiggly wiggly.'

I shriek and splash at him.

'Boys! What's the matter now?'

'Mark's got the tickles.'

'No, I haven't.'

'Have you?' Jinks is serious concern. 'I'd better have a look later; it's a while since I wormed you all.'

'I haven't.'

'Yes, you have. You said.'

'Didn't.'

'Did. Now you'll have to take the medicine.'

'So will you.'

'Yeh, but I like it.' And he knows I hate it.

The spilt water from the bath drains away slowly through the cracks between the black slate flags. We hang over the side of the tub and wait for the first worm to show up following the rising water table.

When we're hauled out Mike, the eldest, goes in, sitting on his own in the middle of the tub with his white-blond hair standing on end. Julian and I are wedged into the armchair next to the stove wrapped in towels. Tilley lamp light hissing. While she washes Mike she gives us each a cream cracker. 'Don't drop any crumbs; we've had enough mess for one day.' It's an invitation for Julian.

She turns to Mike. I watch Julian take a bite of biscuit and keeping an eye on Jinks' back he shakes crumbs over the side of the chair. He's calm, as she turns back he smoothly continues nibbling, she smiles, he looks at me, 'Can I have another cracker, Jinks?' After every bite he shakes a few more crumbs over the arm. As she washes Mike we get more extravagant with our crumb scattering; the best is chewing them up dry and blowing the crumbs out, but this is noisy. Julian starts chattering with a mouthful of ground-up bits, letting the words carry the crumbs, 'Can I have another cream cracker, Jinks, this one's gone?'

'Julian could twist you all around his fingers.'

'You too.'

'Mm, maybe so.'

Bronek's stories plunge me into an uncertain world. Like listening to a dream, I sink into a creative state and embellish his very sparse account. To his description of the cold in Chicago watching soldiers in 1917, I add the sun and the dust. I hear the rhythm of their feet tramping through his memory to the sound of a military band and I can't resist the temptation to let his four-year-old legs join in. And later, now that this has become an item of my own memory, I am uncertain of how I first heard it. The event itself is like a distant star whose faint twinklings reach me through time after the star itself has died, or moved on. Review and repetition seem to encourage variation, modification for the sake of a good story, or to make better sense of the present. In this sense memories are cultural; they change as we change, becoming enriched by the present as well as enriching it.

— 3 —
The Road

Szczecin is our first destination in Poland, and is about one thousand kilometres from the Hook of Holland, where we land at 6.00 am, 7 September. Our plan is to get to Berlin the first day, stay over and go on to Szczecin the following day. I grew up with Germany as two countries in a divided Europe. In effect, for me the real Europe existed only on this side of the division, the west, and everything on the other side was dark and inaccessible, somehow inferior and definitely threatening. Berlin, the once divided city, an enclave in the twilight zone, now beckons us. I'm carrying towards it my own message, my own piece of the new jigsaw map of Europe in the shape of my dad. He is after all from this forbidden place, the east.

We speed through Holland and most of western Germany in very good time. Bronek is tired, he doesn't say much and my questions seem to bother him. He sinks into private reverie and even music annoys him, he says it hurts his ears.

'I never liked it much, *La Bohème*,' he says. I know this is a lie. Before I had heard of it I remember him saying how much he enjoyed a performance he and Jinks had attended. 'Don't you know *La Bohème*? What do they teach you at school? All the young artist friends living together in Paris and looking after each other; it's marvellous. All life is there: love, death and confusion. The music, ah – you know Puccini himself said he could set anything to music; the quality of the libretto was not important. He said, give me your laundry list and I'll make you an aria. You must know "che gelida manina", it was Harold Wilson's favourite song.' This was one of Bronek's favourite jokes of the 1960s during some wage freeze.

I thought it was Rossini who said that about a laundry list, but we continue in silence. I had purposely brought recordings I thought he would enjoy, *La Bohème* among them.

He has the ability to retreat into himself, which I am to discover he does a lot on this trip, and I wonder if he is in some discomfort connected with his medical condition. We had postponed our departure twice over the last eighteen months because he wasn't well enough to come. At first we thought there would always be another chance, but as time went on it became obvious that we should go whenever we could. This was his last chance. When I ask him how he is feeling or if he has taken his daily cocktail of tablets, he says yes, he's fine and looks at me as if he can't understand why I should be asking.

As our journey progresses I feel a mounting excitement about our approach to Poland, but I'm also aware that some of it is felt on Bronek's behalf. He however gives no outward sign, he dozes.

'Aren't you excited, Dad?'

'What about?'

'Well, we'll be there soon.'

'Oh. Yes, of course,' and he continues to doze.

We are in a kind of limbo. We have left home but have not yet arrived. The preoccupations of preparation are over with; the checking and double checking of documents and money, maps, addresses, route planning, all that is now in gear and has left a space which I fill with speculative visions of Poland. I often have the sensation at the moment of departing on a journey, that I have forgotten why I wanted to make it at all. I am completely lost and empty and feel as though only the momentum of preparation carries me through departure and into travelling. The hopes invested in it are inaccessible and they may in fact be irrelevant, except as catalysts. Now we are en route, in this mobile limbo with no visible clues from Bronek; his expectations of the trip are as big a question as mine are.

By the time we cross the old Iron Curtain near Helmstedt we are hungry, and Bronek is a little agitated about the time and whether we should call Irena, his cousin in Szczecin. We pull out of the heavy traffic into a service station; this is our first touch of the ground we have been skimming over in a long low-level leap since disembarking at the Hook of Holland.

We find ourselves in a very modern service station, huge but split into lots of small areas on different levels, each with its own feature. Ours is a little fountain and a pink rock in a tiled pool next to our table, which is elevated slightly on a dais. Every effort has been made in the design of this place. Every square inch of the surface, every tiny aspect of the interior has been minutely considered and then overdone. The totally designed environment invariably produces an uneasy feeling of dislocation and alienation. I walk in, gaze at the brightly lit 'traveller's fare' in the 'country kitchen', and exercise an existential choice based on pure indifference. The only genuine reaction is horror at the fantastic cost of completely bland food.

I watch Dad drinking his soup. He has a slow-motion tremor, a wobble, like a violinist's vibrato that he cannot stop. Putting the hot edge of the soup spoon slowly to his lips, blowing and gently sipping from it he wastes half the spoonful. His left hand is at rest on the table, fingers curled under, his thumb pulsates involuntarily against his index finger.

In their wedding photograph they stand shoulder to shoulder in a London street. Jinks is on his right, their arms linked, hands clasped together with their fingers interlaced presenting a joint fist. In heels she is almost as tall as him. He stands with his body square to the camera but turns his head fully into profile to smile at her. She looks straight at the camera, smiling the happiest smile of her life. He has a dark suit in a stylish cut for 1946, double breasted, wide trousers with turn-ups falling perfectly on to his black Oxfords. I remember these shoes on the stone shelves in the back kitchen of the farm, worn well into the shape of his feet by then but resoled and heeled and still in use. Like everything left there for more than a few days they have flakes of whitewash in them from the crumbling landscape of the walls and ceiling.

Layer upon annual layer of fragile sediment smoothing out the roughness of the stone substrate. The constant natural damage, erosion from even the mildest contact and at the foot of these white cliffs and on to anything left near them the flakey debris falls. On to his webbing gas-mask bag and tin hat, his West African Rifles cap with the palm-tree badge and on to his snake-proof boots. The 'back', as we knew it, was the repository for these props from old photos, the residue of other times crammed on to high shelves and cupboard tops. Exotic jewels that we kids proudly exhibited to our friends. There was a desiccated snakeskin coiled up in a Sugarpuffs box; too delicate now to remove. It was inside out and even the skins of its eyes were there, shed with the rest, like contact lenses. An enormous amonite from Charmouth in a canvas bag and the gander's wings. The wings of that terrible bird, now stilled, now eaten, now beaten. Our dartboard hung over the perforated zinc panel in the larder door, scattering more perforations like woodworm flight holes around it, and my white mice lived on the windowsill in a two-roomed appartment. Saddlery hung opposite them in the corner above the end of a long row of turned wooden pegs, from which were suspended all the coats in the world. Beneath them were all the boots and shoes. And his shoes. The wedding shoes.

There they are, firmly planted on a London street in 1946 being photographed, new, uncreased, unscuffed, with Bronek, the new man laced up in them, newly wed. He had still the slimness of army rations and African heat about him, but he is younger looking than his wartime pictures, very young looking for his thirty-three years, and some of the softness of his real youth has returned. He stands very straight with his feet well apart, at ease but not easy, his weight equally divided on to the shoes in a gingerbread-man pose but for his arms, and with his head twisted to the right to look at Jinks. His left arm hangs at his side in the soft curve of the sleeve. From the cuff, his left hand, the one I'm looking at now, was also then made into the same gentle fist, his thumb dished into the crook of his index finger, pushing it forward, slightly proud of the curve of his other fingers.

He sucks in the soup noisily, flattening his lips against his teeth in a grimace. I hear his voice echo from family meals thirty years ago, 'Mark, what a noise. Don't you know how to drink your soup?' He was a stickler for table manners and is disgusted by modern laxity, but, like me, he expected his children to know table manners without ever being taught them. The situation was always worse when we had a visitor and worse by far if they happened to be Polish. Then, more concious of our behaviour in a public context, instead of glossing over any lapse from us he would make an issue of it, embarrassing everyone except us.

We used to get a regular monthly visit from Hetman in his Polish mobile shop, which he drove to the doors of all the Polish families in south Wales. He was a thin, weaselly man, but his meagre appearance belied the extraordinary, exotic and sumptuous contents of his old grey Citroen van. A clash of cultures took place in every gateway or farmyard where he stopped to remind his compatriots of mitteleuropean cuisine. The British at the time were discovering the American dream of deepfreezers full of Wonderloaf, Birdseye and TV dinners. Hetman was our relief, our foreign holiday. He was all preserved meats, pickled vegetables, stinking goats' cheeses, jars of sauerkraut, gherkins, beetroot, rows of limey-looking sausages and bottles of firewater with unpronounceable names on their labels. And I owe him two debts of gratitude.

The first is for Polish sausage. So much of what I enjoy eating is related to my memory of this time; some things, like sausage, I loved then and still do. Other tastes have taken longer to acquire but through them all the flavours of the past flood my senses, harmonics of the dominant note filling out the taste resonating through the past.

The second is for getting me off the hook in a table manners crisis. We sit in the tiny farm kitchen crowding round the table. Round the table were: dad, me on a stool next to him at one end. On my left and on the side of the table sat Hetman then Mike. Jinks presiding at the other end with Pete, still the smallest in a highchair next to her. Julian, already the biggest, and John Giles, only just the second smallest but the oldest on the side facing Mike and Hetman. Hetman has arrived in time for lunch, most of which he has just sold to his hosts. Pork boiling ring, horseradish, potatoes and sauerkraut.

Dad probes Hetman for news of other Polish families, people we may only see twice a year. Multi-functional Hetman, he is travel agent, mobile delicatessen, human newspaper and introduction agency. Through his agency, Poles in south Wales eat Polish food, hear about their friends that live in the next county, send messages to each other, hear about and eventually meet other families and, new to me, they occasionally visit their homeland.

'Yes, Karmen Sierosławska is engaged.'

'Ah, Karmen.' She is the Polish beauty of Cardigan and the only reason any of us will agree to accompany Dad to the Polish church in Lampeter. 'She is a lovely girl. Give them our congratulations.'

Mike looks dejected. The facts that she is three years older than him and has never spoken to him mean nothing. He is in love and has an elaborate fantasy about an elopement to Australia. His disappointment is shortlived though. He transfers his attentions complete in every detail to Anna Gutowska at the next Polish gathering.

'Of course, of course.' Hetman makes a mental note of it.

Having this strange man next to me at the table distracts me. I am fascinated by his yellow boney head, the blue veins at the temples and the mechanical movements of his jaw visible through thin transparent skin. He is a working model of a person, a demonstration of the process of mastication. I have stopped with my fork half-way to my mouth, a hot potato held in mid-air, watching him eat. He stares at the middle of the table just beyond the rim of his plate, chewing his own sausage and listening to my dad's questions and picking up our news. His answers, three words at most, are hoarse whispers, impassive between mouthfuls. As I am watching him the potato slips silently from my fork and falls directly into my lap. Hetman's chewing stops. The ratlike man, he is alert. Without shifting his gaze from the table, or mine from his jaw, we wait. I can feel the wet heat of the potato scald my groin through my shorts but I daren't move, not yet, not until his rhythmic motion starts again. No one else has noticed, and, as the talk continues, I quickly flick the burning vegetable on to the floor.

Julian eats faster than anyone else and has finished his first plate. He sinks into his chair and stretches his long legs right under the table and under Mike's chair. This is a mealtime ritual, and, once developed along well-rehearsed lines for a few minutes, will produce an explosion from Mike and chain reactions from Mum and Dad. It goes like this: Julian's crossed feet push across into Mike's territory. Mike is normally quiet but is very easily riled and will always be violent, never pulling his punches. I can see from Mike's spasmodic jerks above the table that he's kicking or stamping on Julian's feet below. Julian shows no sign of pain or even the slightest interest in Mike; he looks at the stove as though waiting for the next course or another helping. This is exquisitely calculated, Mike, with his cheek full outside his clenched teeth, bouncing violently on his seat, goes into a frenzy of sub-tabular thrashing completely unconscious of catapulting a fork of potato and sauerkraut exactly into the spotlight of Hetman's steady scrutiny.

Freeze frame moments:

As dad's hand is descending palm down, Julian turns back to face Mike, grinning, triumphant.

Mike is still dancing, intent, irate, with no idea that the game is over.

Hetman's jaw slows to adagio, puzzled, *ma non troppo*.

Crash, percussion *fortissimo*, Bronek's hand slaps the table hard. All the crockery lifts and bounces.

This sudden entry makes me jump, and perfectly to Bronek's beat my own next forkful is tossed into the air.

'Boys, Boys.' *Basso profundo. Maestoso.*

'Aaah!' Jinks, *Mezzo soprano.*

Hetman stops.

Agh, I have another potato in my lap.

Fermata.

During the ensuing polyphony I push this one to the floor, it breaks up on impact and I kick the pieces away towards Hetman as best I can. My feet only just reach the ground.

Diminuendo. Poco a poco rit. Fine. Applause from Pete in the highchair.

Hetman gives me a sad look; he slowly turns his rodent head and his attention back to the table before him, newly wiped.

After lunch, Hetman has left and Dad is sweeping the slate flags as Jinks clears the table. I'm trying to read the Wiśniówka label on a wódka bottle. Jinks is defending my elder brothers' performance at lunch. Bronek is furious and disappointed, 'What will Hetman think? He is such a polite fellow.' He sweeps under the table moving the chairs and continues muttering about throwing food. He moves my stool. From the corner with the shopping I watch as the broom clatters about the wooden legs and stops at Hetman's place; it hovers above the fragments of potato, an echo of his gaze at the arrival of Mike's slingshot.

'Oh! Look at that.' More disgust in Bronek's voice. 'That Hetman is such a filthy eater.'

— 4 —
Berlin

We are lost in the outskirts of Berlin with only a map of its centre. I think, it must be easy enough to find the centre of a city, but we end up twice in the same truck park. I look for an English numberplate in vain, then a French one, still no luck. Finally, I choose an Italian to ask directions. I have been in Italy once and I had to ask a lot of directions then too. Next to our car the truck cab is like a house, I reach up to knock on the bottom of the door which opens immediately revealing a worm's eye view of a cross between a very swanky office and a fitted kitchen. The driver of this home-from-home sits on a swivel-chair in a Torino football strip looking like he's ready for kick-off. Glistening gelled-up hair, sparkly nylon kit and a striker's Latin looks to boot. I almost expect him to be a Geordie and my head is uncomfortably level with his feet. I do my best Italian accent for the two phrases I can remember then immediately regret it; he thinks I speak Italian and answers very quickly with lots of sinistras, destras and wild gesticulations. 'Capisci?'

'No.'

He is stunned. He goes through the same thing again, louder and more quickly. 'Capisci?'

What can I do? 'Si, si gracie.'

He looks relieved, 'Prego.' I turn to go back to the car.

'Hey,' he calls after me, and asks me something else I cannot understand.

I take a wild guess, 'Si, Scozzia. Ciao.'

A look of complete bewilderment passes across his face but I'm already in the car giving him a cheery wave. We're lost in Berlin again.

Unter den Linden. We find it of course by asking a German.

Bronek is in his element; he loves cities, the wide boulevards and gracious buildings seem to energise him.

'Go this way, Mark. Here is the Reichstag.' Recently unwrapped. We cruise by it slowly; he concentrates on it for a while, twisting to get a last look then lets it go with a nod and a barely audible grunt. History.

We come in from a flank towards the Brandenburg gate. I'm half-ready for this: I push the Brandenburg concertos into the tape player; dad gets the joke immediately. Seized by a sudden impulse, I steer through a gap in the traffic barriers and, with my heart in my throat and Bronek's protests in my ears, we drive under the arch, through the great gate into the east. I wished to have been at this place when it was unblocked, to have taken part insignificantly; now we make our own hesitant dash, hoping not to attract attention. This is a private moment; to be noticed or caught is the worst thing that could happen. The mere presence of a gateway is an implied invitation or barrier. This one, a barrier for thirty-odd years, bricked up like a taxable window, is now an open invitation, one I can't resist. It is a triumphal arch again, standing for irrepressible humanity, life breaking through the grey monolith. The most exciting political event I can think of.

We stop in the cobbled square on the eastern side of the gate at the beginning of Unter den Linden. We are surrounded by Berliners selling Russian army uniforms, a feature of all the ex-eastern bloc cities. In Prague on the way home I buy T-shirts printed with messages like, 'The KGB is still watching you.' It's almost as though their constant presence is missed. The military and the secret police have become part of the mythology, and now their time is over, we can be nostalgic about the bad old days. Bronek eyes this laundry with interest and tells me what rank they could be. They were all generals in this army.

It is mid-afternoon; too soon to stop. We consult maps and think about looking for somewhere to stay, but Bronek doesn't seem keen on the prospect of looking for a hotel: 'I don't know this city; where should we look?' I don't know it either and I can see half a dozen hotels from where we stand.

I say, 'You know it's only 70-odd miles to Szczecin?'

We head out through the old East Berlin and get lost again. Crawling along in a stream of traffic in a suburb, I lean out of the car window, having first got dad to dredge up some German. 'Bitte mein Herr, wo ist die Autobahn?' This young guy is walking along the pavement at the same pace as we drive. He looks at the car and at me driving on the wrong side and says, 'Right, squire, second left, first right round the church then straight ahead for a couple of klicks and it's in front of you, large as life. You can't miss it.'

I say, 'Christ, what are you doing here?'

He says, 'I live here, don't I.' He's still walking and I'm still crawling along beside him. I must be looking quizzical, wondering why.

He shrugs, 'A woman.' Then accelerates away from us.

It does seem strange to me now that we should have left Berlin only a couple of hours after we got there, but Poland is our destination and any more time spent in Berlin could only be more complicated, looking for hotels, telephones and all the time wishing we were on our way. For myself, I know I can go to Berlin any time and this short visit could not have been better or more appropriate. For Bronek leaving was easy; I think he was in Poland already.

We thread our way through the traffic jams between East Berlin and the Autobahn, and, without my prompting, he begins to describe the situation in Brzozowa at the time of Józef's disappearance, the time of the lousy five dollars. How, with the knowledge that nothing would ever come from America and the impossible living arrangements, Gabriela realised she would have to find some kind of work which solved both problems at once. But his description veers more and more into Polish history.

At the time, the mid-1920s, Poland was settling into the shape it was to keep until 1939. It was a country reborn from the partitions and out of the territories recently won by Piłsudski and the Polish Legions.

The identity of Poland and the position of her frontiers is a complicated subject, especially for us island dwellers, because, unlike Britain, it has no natural boundaries at all to the east and west. The extent of the territories occupied by the countries of central and eastern Europe have constantly varied according to the relative strength of the neighbouring powers.

The Commonwealth of Poland, which included the Grand Duchy of Lithuania, achieved its greatest size in 1648, when it included all of the Ukraine as far east as the wild plains, White Russia (Belarus) to within 300 miles of Moscow, and as far as Riga along the Baltic coast. The wild plains was the lawless area around the north-western shores of the Black Sea, which was home to the Cossacks. There was no definite border there, but it was itself a sort of frontier, an edge. On the western side of Poland the border was further east than it is today; Prussia occupied what is now Polish Silesia and Pomerania, and many Polish towns such as Wrocław and Szczecin were then Prussian. At this time Poland was at the height of her power and influence; a country of singular religious toleration, which accounted for its enormous Jewish and Armenian populations by the end of the nineteenth century, it also included the Eastern Orthodox and Uniate Churches of Russia and the Ukraine, Catholicism of the Slavic Poles and Protestantism from Germany, all enjoying equal rights of worship under a secular elected monarchy. This is the period that romantic Poles of Bronek's generation hark back to as their glorious past. To the time when they defeated the Teutonic Knights at Grünwald, and when they banished the Turks and Tartars from the gates of Vienna and Europe for ever. When the university of Kraków was as great a seat of learning and philosophy as Vienna or Prague.

By 1772 Poland's power had declined in relation to its neighbours to the extent that the country could be carved up between Prussia, Austria and Russia in a succession of partitions, until 1795, when she ceased to exist at all. She was caught between the hammer and the anvil.

Between 1795 and 1918, 123 years, Poles kept their identity and their country alive in their imagination and memory until the Treaty of Versailles at the end of the Great War re-established it in reality. Its shape was still undecided and it took until 1923 at the Treaty of Riga to finally stabalise her boundaries.

Gabriela and her two children came back from America in 1922 into a very exciting, if a little uncertain, climate: the realisation of Polish hopes, a new country. There was an atmosphere too of radical political change. Peasant and worker groups, organised at the turn of the century in reaction to the oppressive policies of the partitioning powers, were transforming themselves into political parties. Estates were being divided and peasants emancipated into farmers.

'Do you think your mother came home then because things were improving in Poland?'

'It could be; I really don't know. Certainly, there was the opportunity to purchase land for the first time, but times were still very hard. I never knew her to have any interest in politics: she was very old fashioned. And, you know, the situation in Chicago was...' he shrugs.

'Yes,' I try to keep him going, 'and how did you get to Stanisławów?'

'Mark, I must have told you this.'

'You haven't.'

The Autobahn has its own momentum, its own pace, and we slip back into this as into something familiar.

'It's not a complicated story. We couldn't stay with my grandmother any more; she was also poor and even if she had wanted to help, she couldn't. So, my mother looked for something else to do. I don't know how she got the job, maybe the government were advertising or something, but she became the cook at the hospital in Stanisławów. It's in the Ukraine now, Ivano Frankivsk. This part of Ukraine, Galicia, was Polish in the time of the Commonwealth, then Austrian during the partitions. After the first war, in about 1920, not long before we went there, Piłsudski won this area back from the Bolsheviks. In fact he went as far as Kiev but he couldn't hold his position there and very nearly lost the war.'

'Do you remember that?'

'We were still in America, but everyone followed the latest stories in the newspapers.'

Poland was in the strange position of having been a national force on the winning side in the war but of having no country. The principle of the Polish state had been agreed by the allies but there was still argument about where the boundaries should be drawn. Meanwhile, a relatively large and victorious Polish army was returning home from the western front into the amorphous new country, surrounded as it was by defeated and exhausted neighbours. Piłsudski took the initiative while the nationalists were talking their heads off in Versailles, gathered these armies and proceeded to push back the frontiers as far as he could. It was not difficult; his main thrust was to the east to reclaim the old commonwealth lands occupied by the Russians or recently vacated by the Austrians. He expanded rapidly into Lithuania beyond Vilnius, into Belarus and the Ukraine. He initially encountered little or no organised opposition in the Ukraine and quickly reached Kiev. He hoped to make a deal with Ukrainian separatists promising them a sort of independence with allegiance to Poland, the kind of offer he himself had refused from Germany, but they also refused it and soon his overextended position became untenable. The Red Army burst through the Polish lines in Belarus, overrunning central Poland. One piece of over-ambition was now matched by another; the Red Army quickly overextended itself, allowing the regrouped remnants of the Polish cavalry to perform the classic military manoeuvre of attacking the exposed Russian flanks, charging across the direction of their advance and cutting off the army from its lines of supply; snatching a famous victory from the jaws of defeat.

Though Piłsudski was a socialist, he believed that Poland should be as large and variable as it was in the eighteenth century. A commonwealth. In a way he was right; a small country surrounded by these major powers would never last very long. And it didn't, twenty-one years only, until 1939.

'Piłsudski did the best he could; he won a great victory, but it was an unfinished job and no one liked these boundaries. There were too many Russians in Poland, too many Poles in Germany, too much of Poland in the east probably, and the Polish Corridor along the Wisła to Gdańsk dividing East Prussia from Germany. There were bound to be problems and once those bastards Hitler and Stalin got together there was no hope.'

I have to do another steering job.

'Yes, yes. But what about Stanisławów?'

'Stanisławów?'

'You were telling me about it. When did you go there?'

'About 1925 I think. We lived in one room at the hospital; mother's pay was terrible and we had nothing. That was a miserable time. My mother was all the time looking for another job. The greatest piece of good luck in our lives was the day she saw an advertisement in a newspaper for a housekeeper to a village priest.'

'And that was Father Szczęk?'

'Yes, Michał Szczęk. From the day she got that job, everything in our lives changed. We moved to Różniatów, his village, and he looked after us as if we were his own family; in fact we did become part of his family. He sent me to school and later on to college. He looked after the sons and daughters of his brothers and sisters too; you know Michał and Antonina, we were all there together before the war. I told you this already.'

'Where were they from?'

'The Szczęk family came from the Nowy Targ area, south of Kraków. You remember, we stayed with Michał in Czarny Dunajec last time we came. He is dead now, of course.'

'Did he stay there during the war, or leave too?'

'He stayed.'

'How did he survive? He was with you in Lwów, wasn't he?'

'Yes, we were at the college together. He and Antonina went back to their families in Nowy Targ. I think Michał had to work somewhere; he never told me about it. Antonina, she...' he tails off here.

'What?'

'What?'

'Antonina, she what?'

He doesn't answer but looks out over northern Germany, flat land, heavy sky.

In the next half hour he nods off and wakes at short intervals, hardly changing his position at all. His head drops slightly as his eyes close and lifts again when they open. We are travelling through a landscape that is less and less cared for; fields give way to open areas of heath with tall white grass heads and dark-green bushes. When Bronek jerks out of his somnolence with, 'This is the old frontier checkpoint,' the neglected look of the frontier hinterland falls into place. We pass by some concrete sheds and bunkers already overgrown.

'Maybe they have built something new further on.'

The character of borders changes with the political climate and this one is not as important now, from the German point of view at least. We go through the new German checkpoint quickly and without fuss, immediately joining a queue that stretches across no-man's-land to the Polish side. Bronek starts to fidget nervously. The day is disintegrating like our speed and fatigue is overtaking us. A fine drizzle brushes the windscreen and I think, this must be a lowering sky. It is getting dark, wet and the road is losing definition. Crepuscular muddy light and broken muddy margins. Vehicles come towards us hissing on the filthy road, their lights unnaturally yellow, intensifying the grey murk hanging over Poland. We inch forward to the rhythm of the wipers, the ululating whine of their motor and Bronek's agitated sighs. Though we cannot see it yet, we are edging towards it; the closer we get the more nervous Bronek becomes, and the more exasperated his groans.

We wait in limbo, our momentum lost, with a strange feeling of uselessness, hopelessly immobile in a machine on the road. The white lines and road markings don't read properly seen at rest, they are over-elongated and made of uneven porridgy bandages pasted together on the road with unsettling dribbles of paint trailing from the ends. The texture and filth of the surface should be invisible in the smear of speed, but all

now is uncomfortable detail. The apprehensive atmosphere of
a waiting room invades our creeping cocoon, but there is more
than just this buried in Bronek's restless grumbling, an anxiety
too disturbing to be kept still, it increases with every inch.

On a family visit to Poland in 1972, we were stopped on the
way home at the border between Czechoslovakia and Austria.
We had a broken windscreen and a boot full of unauthorised
exports. Items bought with foreign currency rather than vouchers. At the police checkpoint dad couldn't find one of the insurance documents and became frantic in his searches for it. The
police eventually lost patience with us and marched him off to
be interrogated. In those days there were amazingly thorough
regulations about the most trivial things. We had every Pfennig
of our small change counted as we entered East Germany and
counted again when we left. We waited for what was in fact
only half an hour, helpless and trying not to be frightened. The
foreignness of the place and the severity of the atmosphere was
intimidating. He re-emerged all smiles and relief having found
the papers folded into his passport.

The next hurdle, customs, was actually the one we were all
worried about. Inside the country we had been a little blasé
about how we bought things; now all the bravado has disappeared and we are very quiet as the officer asks where we have
been and what we are taking out of the country. He opens the
back of the car, which is full of luggage, camping equipment,
gifts and so on. On top of all of this is a wet tent which has
started to smell. His head recoils as the wave of hot damp stink
hits the back of his throat. He unslings his machine gun and
for a minute I think he is so offended by the tent he is going
to shoot it. Instead, he muzzles his way through the layers of
luggage. His gun clinks on a bottle of wódka, prods a card-
board box containing national dress; like a sniffer dog it inves-
tigates while he studies our papers in his other hand. Finding
no officially cancelled vouchers for the things his gun uncov-
ers he barks something at Dad. He shrugs nervously. We've
been caught; I can see it. There is a long pause while the young

officer and Bronek stare at each other, both faces perfectly
blank. The officer's size is acutely accented by the Russian-
style hat, whose wide top curves up at the front above the shiny
black crescent peak. He looks down at Bronek, hard faced but
his skin is fair and smooth stretched over jaw and cheekbones;
his eyes are long incisions. But it is he who is caught, I see
this now, by the apparent neutrality of his captive. Bronek
seems smaller than usual, more compact in contrast to this big
youth. Very slowly the officer's chin demurrs to one side, his
lips part, he inhales and I see Bronek's eyebrows flinch, but it is
already over. In one movement he presses the vouchers against
Bronek's chest, no longer interested in the paperwork, slings
his weapon back on his shoulder and retrieves the bottle from
the boot. Neither man speaks; Bronek closes the boot against
any further duty and with a nod they separate. He is muttering
to himself as he gets back into the car. Jinks leans over the seat,
'What did he say, Bronek?' He doesn't answer for a while until
we are moving.

I was driving then too; he beside me looking a long way
ahead into Austria through the broken windscreen.

He sniffs, 'Huh, bloody Russians.'

'Czechs, weren't they?'

'Russians.'

'Aah hell,' Bronek explodes, disgusted. The griminess of the
Polish border control infuriates him. We turn into it finally
and are directed by a policewoman into one of the streams of
traffic lining up beside a series of temporary buildings. They
look like lorry backs with windows cut into them. The spaces
between, now full of cars, are a greasy wasteland of oily puddles and nastiness. We pitch and yaw through this shite.

'Look at her,' Bronek is out of control, he can't stop himself.
'Look at her,' glaring at the policewoman. 'Look at this bitch.
Who does she think she is?'

'What, Dad? What are you talking about?'

'Look, she even has a gun, she must be a bloody Russian.'
He is venomous. She stands beside the car unaware of the man

staring at her through the closed glass of the window. 'She's not Polish anyway.'

'Hey, come on, Dad, she's just police; they all have guns.' He is suddenly embarrassed, self-conscious of his outburst, which took us both by surprise. He rubs his forehead side to side into his hand, his fingers spread up into his hair and he groans but his anger won't leave him.

'I don't know, I don't know.' He stares ahead through the windscreen and the drizzle at something I cannot see, some distant Poland, the Poland of the heart. 'This is a filthy shit.' He cannot bear his shame, 'We are entering Poland by the arsehole.'

Pope John Paul II held a child in his arms on his first visit to his native Poland after becoming pope. He asks her, 'Where is Poland?' She is confused by his question; it doesn't seem to make sense to her and she cannot answer. He places his hand on her chest, over her heart. Poland is here.

At the window we hand over our passports and follow their progress through the dingy truck, creeping alongside in the car; at the other end of it they are handed back to us and we are waved on into Poland. To get back to the road to Szczecin we have to cross a fairground of moneychangers and bootleggers, a free-for-all of little kiosks lit by low-grade electricity, by the kind of lamps that burn rather than shine. Very dodgy-looking guys in black-leather jackets hang about. The market economy. They could be car dealers. All the way through Germany we have been overtaking Polish vehicles towing trailers that carry the smashed-up wrecks of western-registered cars. They get delivered to the frontier and bought on arrival.

Bronek doesn't recover any good humour in the miles between the frontier and the city; the day caves in to a gloomy evening, the premature darkness and heavy cloud perfectly suit his mood. He continues to stare ahead through the window groaning and sighing, or rubbing his forehead.

'All right, Dad?'

I have yanked him out of somewhere and he seems to look through me for a moment recovering the present, then shrugs, 'Yes, of course.'

'Will you navigate?'

We have back-to-school nerves. Our journey is focusing, dropping down through the layers from country to city, to street, number, flat and person. We are about to arrive.

The rain stops and fragments of a luminous deep-blue sky appear between the heavy black clouds as we get to the outskirts. Bronek wrestles with the map guiding us towards the centre. It is dark, an autumn evening by the time we get to the centre of Szczecin and start looking for Irena. The main streets are well lit and there are people still shopping.

We stop at a small row of shops in a street that has the right name, Kaszubska, but the numbers are all wrong. They start at 29 on the corner with the main road, but we are looking for 27. Puzzled, Bronek says, 'I just don't remember exactly,' looking into the square across the main road, 'here is the church but where is 27?' As we stand at the corner staring at the numbers on the wall, scratching our heads, a man addresses me in Polish. I know he's asking if we are lost but I can't answer him properly, 'Tak, tak, prosze.' Yes, please, is the best I can do to hold him there while I call to Bronek, who has gone on to 31 and is talking to himself. 'What's going on here, how can the street numbers start at 29, what kind of a number is that?' The stranger gives Bronek the simple explanation, on the other side of the square the same street carries on, and he offers to take us there. He's a middle-aged man, tall, thin faced with a fur hat. He and Bronek fall immediately into conversation. All the Polish conversations of my childhood, never understood, flood and echo in this one. They talk like old friends, Dad's face lights up, his mother tongue is wagging in his head.

In the terrible winter of 1963, I was taken by Mum and Dad to an interview at a school in Reading. On that day the whole of the Thames Valley was submerged in the thickest fog, so thick that when we finally got to Reading in the dark and fog with a failing dynamo, Dad had to walk in front of the car to guide it. Like everyone else that night we looked for a hotel and, like everyone else by that time of night, we were too late. Everywhere was full. As we listened to another apology from a receptionist in surely the one hundredth hotel, a foreign-looking gent, in trench coat and black beret, took Dad by the arm, 'Excuse me, serr, you are Polish, no?' Like a torrent, Polish gushes from him; a wave washing over us. The Polish solution. We follow this man into the fog, Mum and I behind watching these two chattering away, shoulder to shoulder, their heads bent towards each other, laughing Polish laughter in a pea-souper all the way to his house.

He touches the front of his hat as though to lift it as Bronek thanks him for his help, shaking his hand, and he waits on the corner of the street as we get back into the car. He points across the square, his briefcase dangling under his outstretched hand, and makes big sweeping circles with the other. He mimes, 'Go round then turn.' Bronek translates.

Opposite number 27 is a bar; half its patrons are on the pavement drunkenly cheering our arrival, a foreign car. There is another complication with numbers, this time with suffixes. The whole grey concrete monolith is 27. At one end a plaque says 27b, at the end where we are parked another says 27c.

'Oh, what's the matter here, where is 27a? How can the letters start at b?' He remembers from the last visit that the same thing happened, he tells me to stay with the car, he will look further down the street. The overflow from the bar is still shouting and laughing. I am the lone sentry. Very lone.

It slowly dawns on me that this isn't drunken heckling at all, it is getting more insistent because I am ignoring it. Two young men sitting on the pavement with bottles of beer are telling me something about the car, they point at it and shake their heads, make single clapping gestures and mime a key in a lock.

The car is clapped out? It won't start? We have made a connection now and a miming game starts across the width of the road. I dig for some Polish words: the car is good, it's okay.

'Tak, tak, dobry samochód.' But they wave their hands, 'Parking strzeżony, zamkniecie.'

No parking?

'Nie, nie.' One of them does a strange furtive dance around a car across the road, bobbing up and down behind a Polski Fiat 126. His mates are laughing and shouting advice at him and giving me a commentary. It gets more and more obscure. He does: driving the car, shaking his fist, counting money.

I'm lost, I spread my hands, I'm sorry, *nie rozumiem*, I don't understand.

In the middle of this pantomime, a Lada pulls up beside me. Alexander Solzhenitsyn gets out and asks me something in what I take to be Russian. This is becoming a farce. He tries again in German. I ask if he speaks French.

'Oui.'

Enfin. He wants directions to a street and I get out my map for him. I ask him if he can translate what the crowd over the road was trying to tell me. There is a short and dismissive exchange across the street; he thinks they are drunk and they think he's interfering in their entertainment. I'm a little disappointed too.

'They say, lock up your car in a protected car park; it's not safe here.' Then, ' Sell me this map, how much?'

I want to keep the map but so does he and I have to remove it, almost forcibly, from his grasp. He looks incredulous when I say I need it.

'What for?'

'Because I am a stranger here.'

'No, I am the stranger here.'

That's true, 'Where are you from?'

'Romania. We are going to Germany.'

His car is full of cases and bundles; he is going to Germany for good. He is almost there.

Bronek returns with another stranger in tow. A tiny but very fierce-looking old man in a packamac with a terrier on a lead and a plastic carrier bag. The Romanian retreats to his Lada at the sight of this fearsome dwarf, or is it Bronek? He drives away.

'What did the bloody Russian want?' Bronek is excited and
I am too tired to argue with him.

'He was Romanian. He wanted the map.'

'What map?'

'This one, of Szczecin.'

'Did you give it to him?'

The little man shakes his head and starts telling Bronek how
dangerous it is everywhere, how everything gets stolen, better
to have nothing at all. He delves in his shopping bag and produces a black knobkerry, 'I had to use this only the other day.'
He also says he knows Irena and the answer to the riddle of
the missing 27a. I am posted sentry again and they disappear
round the corner to the back of the block. The entertainers
across at the bar have lost interest and I'm left to take a look at
Szczecin for the first time.

Szczecin is a new city and an old one, a Pomeranian Baltic
port and a modern shipyard in the long estuary of the Oder
river. From outside Irena's block, most of what I can see is
post-war concrete in the Soviet style. Big slab-fronted buildings with shops on the street level and acres of regular apartment windows above. Often there is a heavy cornice moulding
at the skyline, rather like a piece of furniture. It's not unlike a
lot of bad 1960s housing in Britain; the difference here is that
these residential blocks line the main streets of the city, and
they give a monotonous and neglected impression as much of it
is starting to crumble. But later we discover some excellent new
apartment buildings in the centre of town and much evidence
of regenerative building. There is a raw and exciting feel to this
town; like all ports it feels busy with maritime history and commerce and the people have an open humour and confidence,
they talk easily, looking straight at you. I like it.

It became Polish after 1945 but from the tenth until the partitions of the eighteenth century, Pomerania had been on the
fringes of Polish territory, becoming variously: an independent
duchy, Polish in the twelfth century, part of the Holy Roman
Empire, Brandenburgian and briefly even Swedish. After 1772
it was in the Kingdom of Prussia until the German states

united. After 1945, with the newly positioned frontiers, Szczecin found itself in Poland, whose centre of gravity had been moved west, gaining the territories of Silesia and Pomerania from Germany. This necessitated the repatriation and resettlement of 4.5 million Poles into these western and northern areas and the expulsion to Germany of about 2 million Germans. In the east the situation was similar, half a million Ukrainians and Belarussians were returned to the Soviet Union, and about 2 million Poles were brought back to Poland from the east. During the war 1.5 million Poles were deported to Russia, to the slave labour camps in Siberia or the Caucasus, from which the great majority never returned.

The new administrative area or voivodship of Szczecin in 1950 had a population of 510,000 of which 70 per cent were resettled from other parts of Poland, from areas like the Ukraine, which had been lost to the USSR, and the rest were repatriated Poles from Germany, Russia and elsewhere. Among the resettled was Irena.

— 5 —
Szczecin

Irena is Bronek's cousin. She is widowed and lives alone on the fifth floor of the apartment building that took us so long to find, the one I had been standing outside keeping watch on the car. She welcomes us weary travellers into her tiny apartment. Into a 25-feet square floor area is squeezed: an entrance hall, bed/sitting room, kitchen and tiny bathroom with truly prehistoric plumbing. She has filled it with the minimum of necessary furniture but even this leaves almost no floor space at all. With three of us in the flat, things are going to be pretty intimate.

As she starts to prepare a meal for us I can tell from her tone and the answers Bronek is giving that she's not very happy about something. He explains that as we have arrived a day early in Szczecin, she has not had time to prepare us a special meal. Like all Poles she is very particular about food, not only about the preparation and presentation, but its significance as a measure of hospitality. We have deprived her of the chance to welcome us in the way she had planned and this has upset her. Despite this, during our stay she happily forces food on us at least three times a day and has a very special way of being offended if we don't eat everything with enthusiasm. This is great hospitality but very disconcerting. She watches us closely while we eat, often without eating with us. When I ask her if she isn't hungry, she half-turns away with her eyes shut as though eating with us would be too impolite to think of. It's a very Polish expression this, resignation but with a touch of the duck's back. That's life but it doesn't bother me. I think of it as the Polish shrug. I have seen Bronek do it all my life.

Their tense conversation continues through the preparation and into the meal itself, long accusations accompanied by lots of tut-tutting and staring out of her window in pain. When she looks away, he looks at me. I can see he thinks the whole trip is a disaster. This is our first day. Then, with a sigh, she starts again. Polish is a beautiful language; it is sung not spoken, particularly by women whose clear voices swish and slide through so many soft-sounding, shifting shapes. It would be a nightmare if you had a lisp. Poor Bronek, I'm thinking, what can he have done? He looks at me when he can without appearing to lose concentration. A slight shrug and an imperceptible raising of his eyebrows. In one lull he says to me, 'You know, Mark, I am a complete failure.'

'Is she still cross about the meal?'

'Oh no, much worse.'

At first he won't tell me what he has done to exercise Irena to this degree, but eventually he caves in and explains that on his last trip, three years before, Irena asked him to send her a tube of Germolene when he got home. He never did and now he must pay. This simple ointment so easily obtainable for us is a very valuable commodity to Irena; it is her panacea. She ascribes miraculous healing powers to it alone among all the other more available creams and uses it for the most unlikely ailments. She makes him pay a little more until we convince her that we will phone home tomorrow and get some Germolene flown out. Dad is subdued all evening. I try to cheer him up a little with one of my famous Germolene jokes, but he will have none of it.

'Mark, this is a very serious matter,' is all he will say that night.

Irena has a mixture of great generosity and the irresistible urge to wound you with your own guilt. This latter is most potent when least expected, adding to its effect the element of surprise. You're having a nice time, everyone is happy, then suddenly you're covered in Germolene.

We discovered one positive application for her black art: haggling. I went with her to buy some amber from a street trader who, though hardened through years of illegal back street dealing under the noses of the KGB, was no match for Irena. She gave her the same treatment she gave Bronek the night before, now known as the Germolene rub. I felt sorry for the woman and a new respect for my dad.

Back at her apartment we study the necklaces I have bought with her help. She's a little disparaging about them. Amber is not what it used to be apparently, and to prove it, she produces a long golden string of clear beads, uniformly light coloured and startlingly beautiful. Mine are dull and look overcooked in comparison. Amber really isn't what it used to be. Before I can stop her she has taken a pair of scissors and cut the string.

'Take half for your wife.'

'Irena, I can't do that. Tie it up again, it is too beautiful to cut in half.'

She ignores me. She rummages in her sewing box, carefully removes two beads from the length, almost two metres, and ties a button on to each end.

'Please, Irena. It's too good.'

She catches the beads in the middle and lets them hang, adjusting them until they are equal.

'Dad, tell her.'

And she cuts the string.

She is Bronek's first cousin, the only daughter of Gabriela's sister, Stanisława. Stasia, as she was known, also returned from America before the Second World War, but Bronek seems reluctant to tell me whether Irena was born in Chicago or here in Poland. We are discussing the family tree and I am trying to draw a diagram of it in a small notebook. Some of the families were so big that I have to devise a lateral and a linear system for reading the pages. Though not an infallible guide, the number of children in a family of that generation seems to be an index of their fortunes.

In the case of Gabriela, my grandmother, there are only two. Stasia, only one. Maria, six with her first husband, then at least one with her second, but contact was lost with her during the war because her second husband was German. At some time in the 1960s that family appeared again in France. Dad received a letter from Bronisław (Schulz), who was a grandson of Maria and her second husband.

Mietek, the youngest of the three boys, had no children but stayed in America. Uncle Bronisław had a family of six who have become completely American. Władek, the oldest, had three and also stayed.

Irena and Bronek, prompted by my interest, find themselves remembering details of their lives, their families, their names and bits of history from the 1930s. Irena is unfailing on names and numbers of children and their nationality. We work our way through their generation and their parents'. I probably miss most of the detail, though Dad does his best to keep the translation going both ways while I fill in the names on the diagram. At her mother's place Irena's commentary stops abruptly.

'No brothers or sisters?' My questions continue to run on at the same pace.

Silence. Without looking up I draw in one vertical line under Stanisława and write Irena below it.

'What was her father's name?'

Bronek doesn't translate this. When I look up at him he is frowning at me. Irena answers my question.

'Józef Małczyński.'

I start writing, but something is wrong here, this is her grandfather's name. I look at Bronek again wondering if Irena has misunderstood me or has made an extraordinarily frank admission. He shakes his head indicating I should not pursue this. I have already written Józef Mał…into my diagram. The half-finished name is staring from the page making paralysing accusations.

He looks over my shoulder, 'C…Z…Y…'

'But.'

'Yes, Małczyński. When there is no father you put the grand-father as legal guardian, like the father.'

We go quickly to the rest of the family. Maria, oldest of the girls, first marriage to a cousin of Gabriela's husband and so also has a family named Zygadło. Her second husband was the German, Schulz. The second son of the first marriage, Władek, has a family in Poland who we are planning to visit next in Inowrocław.

'This is like the begats in the Bible.'

Next, Bronisław Małczyński.

'You remember Basil and Natalie in Brooklyn. My mother's brother Bronisław married a Russian, Helen Gaber, in Chicago. They had six children, the youngest of them was my cousin Natalie. I knew them all but it was Natalie who kept in touch. She found me after the war through the Red Cross; that's how we kept in contact with the family left in America.'

'I wondered how they fitted in.'

I do remember Basil and Natalie. We arrived late one evening at their daughter's house in Brooklyn. My wife, Denise and I had driven across the States delivering a car from Los Angeles to New York and the only contact address we had there was Natalie's. Bronek had not seen her since 1922, when she was a tiny baby. We had difficulties finding the house in the numbered streets, they didn't run continuously, like the streets in Szczecin, and it took us a long time on a dark March evening tracing a street that was broken into half-a-dozen sections, sometimes only one block long. Eventually we found the little wooden terraced house near an elevated railway in an ancient and neglected corner of Brooklyn looking on to the Upper Bay. This could have been an old fishing village that the city has overtaken. Did things like that happen in New York?

I rang the bell and the door was opened by a large girl in her mid-twenties with a long cigarette held near her mouth between two chubby fingers.

'Oh hi, you must be Mork and Mindy, how are you? Come in, I'm Carol la Torre, do you like Spanish? I like Spanish, I'm restyling my room.' One long statement.

Do I like Spanish what? The only Spanish I can think of is the black liquorice lace rolled round a pink sweet we used to buy from the Post Office in New Moat. David used to ask the same question, 'Do you like Spanish? Let's buy some Spanish.'

As she turns to lead us into the hallway I notice that her hair is full of sparkling fragments and there are smears of what looks like wet Polyfilla on her hands and clothes.

'Don't you like Spanish? Everyone's doing it.'

Spanish dancing? She leads us straight into her room on the
ground floor. 'How d'ya like it? Spanish.'

Most of the room is taken up with an enormous carved
rococo bed in colonial Spanish style. It's black and monstrously
overdecorated with swirling foliage, fruit and poultry. The
headboard is an orgy of cherubs in attitudes of Isabeline rap-
ture: dancing, playing musical instruments standing on one
chubby leg, that sort of thing. The two at the top are balancing
a couple of pigeons on their heads. It's a fantastic piece, worthy
of the Big Top.

'Yes, I like Spanish.'

'Yeah, Spanish is good. I'm just doing my ceiling.' She takes
a handful of glitter from a plastic tub and throws it upwards,
'The stucco's still wet, I just did it. The glitter sticks to it.' It's
true. There are glittering patches on the grotesque ceiling, and
on our heads and shoulders after a few more throws.

'Hey, Carol. Who was at the damn door?' A big male New
York voice from upstairs.

'Yeah, yeah, we're coming.' She turns to us with another
handful of glitter, 'Better go meet Mom and Pop.'

Natalie was typically Polish: a square woman with high
broad cheeks and blue eyes, her long black hair could have
reached her waist but she kept it coiled up on top of her head
under a ghastly nylon wig. She was very much like my grandmother, Gabriela, her aunt, and had something of my father
about her too. Gabriela had the same long black hair, always
worn in a bun, but no awful wig. Natalie married Basil la
Torre, an economic migrant from Sicily and Brooklyn wide
boy; they have at least six children and, when we were there,
three grandchildren. In profile he reminded me of the Leon-
ardo cartoon of a old man whose nose seemed to have been
pressed down hard on to his upper lip. He had that punched
look, but in his youth he must have been something, a regular
Marlon Brando. He was immediately attractive, sitting in his
vest and braces waiting for pasta to be served. He always took
his shirt off to eat and from the front of his vest you could read
the last week's menus.

He asked me once which was my favourite pasta, 'Mork, I make great pasta. Hey Natalie, do I make good pasta or what?'

'Get outa here, Basil. You make the best.'

'See? What'd I tell ya? So, which pasta?'

'Lasagne.'

'Lasagne? Hey Natalie, he says lasagne.'

'I heard him.'

'So, lasagne. Okay, I take tomorrow off.'

'Off what?' Natalie laughs to herself.

'I take tomorrow off to make lasagne.'

'Hey, Basil. You retired five years already with a heart condition; you don't work nothing. What you going to take tomorrow off?'

'Natalie, it takes all day to make a lasagne, I gotta take it off.'

'Off what?'

'Off nothing, I'm taking it off, okay?'

The next evening we sat down to the lasagne, this was to be our last night in Brooklyn and the lasagne their parting treat. Basil took longer; the pasta itself was made the evening before and layed out overnight and he spent most of the next day preparing the dish. He shooed us out of the house so as not to be disturbed in his kitchen.

That lasagne was unforgettable not only for its exquisite taste and texture but because it was part of an unforgettable evening. Basil is dead now; he did have a heart condition which he treated by drinking strong coffee all day, eating huge helping of deserts, fatty meat and stinking cheeses, all with great relish.

I will always remember him as the man who knew Al Capone; here's the story.

We sit around the table, Basil and Natalie stripped for action. Basil to his usual vest and braces, or suspenders as he calls them. Natalie in a pink nylon shift and theatrical wig. We sprint off the blocks, conversation is minimal, we are concentrating on the rich delight of the pasta. It is delicious; Basil really does make the best lasagne and since then, all lasagne I eat is measured against this one. When our first hunger is sated and the pace slows to an amble, Basil starts to reminisce about the days when he met Natalie.

'Yeah, when we was courting, Natalie and me, wasn't I the best dressed-guy in Brooklyn? Hey, Natalie, wasn't I the best-dressed guy or what? Natalie, get away from that refrigerator. Wasn't I?'

'Yeah, yeah, Basil.' Natalie's huge body is quivering by the fridge, she could be laughing silently, 'Yeah, you was a good-looking guy. So what?'

'Dressed, Natalie, dressed, I said dressed. I'm talking clothes.' But he sticks his chin out, 'Sure I'm a good-looking guy.'

He is a good-looking guy. A great-looking Italian, what else?

'Basil, why don't you shut up and eat something.' She has played this game before, 'You spend all day making lasagne, now you don't eat it.'

'Hey, I'm eating already.' He takes a mouthful in demonstration then gets back to the story, 'I used to run a bowling alley on Flatbush before the war; everybody used to go there.'

'Yeah, just to take a look at the best-dressed guy.' Natalie's laughter sounds like a horse whinnying in the distance.

'That's right,' he is serious. 'That's right they did. Every cent I had I spent on clothes. Clothes, hey, I had some great suits. Soots, I got a whole closet full of soots right here in this house. Shirts,' he says, shoits. 'I got such shoits!' The rapturous expression is left to hang in the air. He tells us some awful joke about a depressive with a stomach upset who puts a gun to his own head. To me the punchline is all confusion, did he die, mess himself or just change his shoit?

'I also have a closet of shoits. Yeah, it was difficult to get good shoits in them days. You want to see it?'

'Come on, Basil, he don't wanna see no lousy shoits.'

I did want to, but their game was too fast for me. My mouth is full of lasagne and the sound I make is not understood by either of them. By the time I've swallowed it he is already on to shoes, ties, coats, hats.

'I could get all this because everybody comes to the bowling alley. Everybody who is anybody that is, not just anybody.'

'Whadaya mean, "everybody is anybody," Basil?' Natalie is shaking again.

'Hey, Natalie, people came, all right. People who was somebody.'

'Somebody, Basil. Somebody? They was nobody, they was trash.'

Basil considers this during another mouthful of lasagne, 'Yeah, you're right, Natalie, Brooklyn was full of hoodlums. Everybody was into some racket. That Alphonso 'di' Capone, I knew him before he went to Chicago. He was a bum.'

'Basil, you going to eat that lasagne or what?'

'Yeah, yeah.'

After supper Basil plays the huge electric organ that takes up half the sitting room. Natalie takes up the other half laying beached on the floor in her nylon shift with her arms spread out wide. Presently she groans her way through to the kitchen, opens the fridge door in the dark and pulls up a chair. I find her there spooning ice cream from a gallon tub; she is all vanilla coloured in the glow.

'You like ice cream? Taste, it's good.'

'Natalie, I told you already. Get away from that refrigerator.'

'Aah...Shut up, Basil, you're full of shoit.'

On a clear windy day we take a walk, Bronek, Irena and I, from the castle down the steep incline to the broad dock. Moored alongside, next to the road almost, is the *Dar Młodzieży*, the gift of youth. She is one of the family of Russian ships, the largest sailing ships ever built.

As we descend to the river, dad gets quite excited, 'I know this ship; she was in the tall ships race last year when they came to Milford Haven. *Dar Pomorza*.'

When we get near enough to read the name he is disappointed that it is not after all the same ship, but her sister. This is typical of Bronek; he attracts obscure coincidences. He and

Pete had gone to Milford Haven to see the boats taking part in the tall ships race when they put in there. Seeing a Polish ship, they go aboard and present themselves to the captain, for a chat. That evening, the officers and some of the crew not on watch turn up at the house by taxi, armed with the ship's rations of rum and wódka, and present themselves to my dad, for a chat.

We climbed the gangway of the *Dar Młodzieży* next to the grey steel slab of her side, hopeful of the same kind of reception, but at the top our way is blocked by a sailor who has very strict orders. So we climb down again and Irena buys us an ice cream in consolation.

— 6 —
Picnic

When we leave Szczecin for Inowrocław, Irena loads us up with what she calls a little picnic. We set off in the late morning through the wooded landscape of northern Poland. It's a clear warm morning and we are in good spirits for the journey. We head towards Bydgoszcz through the rolling northern plains, passing villages strung out along the road. About midday we bypass the slightly bigger town of Piła, 'Ah Piła,' Bronek's memory is jolted, 'this used to be the frontier with Germany between the wars. Piła was on the German side at the bottom of the Polish Corridor.'

'Strange idea, the Polish Corridor.'

He works backwards through Polish history of the twentieth century to the origin of the idea, if it can be called that. It is really a compromise resulting from a lot of conflicting ideas, interests and promises.

Against a background of the partitions, which was a long period of relatively little change, the beginning of the twentieth century saw increasing international awareness of the plight of Poland. The Polish question. The creation of a new state of Poland had wide support in the world due in part to the efforts of the famous pianist and freelance diplomat Ignacy Paderewski, who used the platform of his musical tours to inform the world of the growing nationalist feeling in Poland, and the repressive regimes it existed under. The question of where the new Poland should be in the amorphous topography of central Europe gave rise to serious political divisions not only among its foreign supporters, but even among Poles themselves.

Before 1914 there were two distinct camps: a strong right-wing national democratic movement, modelled perhaps on the

German example, led by Roman Dmowski; and a larger left-wing socialist grouping of several parties but with no single leader. Both were committed to rebuilding Poland, but their visions of its form were quite different.

Dmowski's nationalists saw a relatively small, Catholic, ethnically Slavic Poland. His support came from the conservative upper classes, the Catholic Church and he also sought support from Russia. His great fear was German military expansion, his hope was to persuade the Tsar to grant autonomy to Poland within the Russian Empire in exchange for military help against Germany. He believed this would be the first step towards independence.

Things were different on the left wing. The biggest group was the Polish Socialist Party (PPS), formed in the Russian partition before the turn of the century. They were outlawed and after many of their leaders were arrested they fell eventually under the leadership of Józef Piłsudski. His vision of Poland was old fashioned and romantic, along the lines of the commonwealth of the eighteenth century. Piłsudski saw the coming revolution in Russia as the opportunity for a new Poland, gathering from the fragments of a disintegrating Russian Empire territories lost to it in the partitions, and forming a federation. He aligned himself with the Austrians later as Russian repression increased before the revolution.

There were other groupings too: Rosa Luxemburg's Marxists, who had no interest in Polish nationalism; Jewish groups, which were Zionists, orthodox conservatives or, most significantly, the Bund. This was another international Marxist movement but formed in Russia, Lithuania and Poland. It was to become one of the founding groups of the Bolsheviks. Jewish history in Poland is important and complicated, but at this time it did not play a role in the rebirth of the country. Their extermination later on Polish soil and in Polish consciousness is a difficult subject that Poles share with all perpetrators of the Holocaust, and incredibly, anti-Semitism still exists today in Poland, in places where one supposes people should know better. Despite the huge Jewish population at the beginning of the twentieth century, as a group they had no particular interest in Polish nationalism, apart from the extent to which any of the other political groups threatened them. Not surprisingly for a country divided and occupied, Poland's welfare depended on events in the partitioning powers, and among these Russia was pre-eminent. In 1904 Russia embarked on an unpopular and unsuccessful war with Japan, which exacerbated the already difficult economic climate at home and in Poland. Cracks were starting to appear in the Empire, and the Tsar, rather than trying to woo the support of the populace, became more and more the repressive tyrant. Demonstrations against unemployment, low wages and impossible working conditions in Poland as well as in Russia were crushed with pitiless violence. Bloody Sunday in St Petersburg not only presaged the revolution in Russia but sparked off a revolution in Poland, and from 1905 for the next few years the left, which now included the peasant parties, was in open insurrection. During this period, questions of allegiance within the left wing became divisive. The internationalist Marxists saw these events as the beginning of a world revolution and finally split with the PPS and joined the group around Rosa Luxemburg, becoming the Polish Communist Party a few years later. The rest, under Józef Piłsudski became more partisan and more terrorist. Although the revolution started in the Russian section, it spread to all regions of the Polish population in the form of school boycotts, peasant demonstrations, and demands for suffrage as well as armed stuggle.

Piłsudski, seeing that he was making little headway in the Russian sector, moved his headquarters to Galicia, in the Austrian partition, and began to organise a real army instead of bands of guerillas. The Polish Rifle Brigade started in secret but grew very quickly and soon was able to offer its services to the Austrian army to fight against the Russians. When the First World War started in 1914, Piłsudski set off to fight with the heroic Polish First Brigade. Actually they saw little action at the outset because the Germans were there first.

During the years of the First World War the Polish question became more important on the international stage. The promises and threats made by the protagonists, Austria and Germany on one side and France, Britain and Russia on the other, varied according to how the war was going at the time. America came out in support of independence for Poland with access to the sea before it even joined in the war. The idea of access to the sea was to become one of the significant questions about the shape of Poland in the later negotiations and was resolved by the creation of the Polish Corridor.

In 1917 Russia collapsed into revolution, leaving a military vacuum on the eastern front into which the Austrians and Germans flowed into Lithuania, into Galicia and the Ukraine. Success emboldened them to demand that the Polish forces fighting on their side make vows of allegiance and accept the prospect of being a client state to the new German Empire. Not surprisingly their offer was rejected. Piłsudski was imprisoned and some of the Polish legions from the eastern front crossed the lines into Russia, fighting their way north against both sides, to the Baltic and thence by sea to France to re-form against Germany on the western front.

The war in the east ended in a way that no one anticipated. The atmosphere of revolution in central Europe was contagious. The enormous primitive areas recently annexed by the German side seemed empty and were impossible to govern; they were roamed by autonomous partisan militias, bands of little more than brigands. These were not the expected spoils of victory, and the exhausted, hungry and demoralised soldiers of the Austrian and German armies mutinied and started to go home. In the west the prospect of continuously fighting over a few yards of soil at such an appalling cost in human suffering became insupportable, and once the Americans joined in, the numbers could no longer add up.

Suddenly, there was room for Poland in the space left by the deserting armies. Piłsudski seized the moment. Not waiting for the outcome of the peace negotiations at which his rival Dmowski was expounding at length on his vision of the new Poland, Piłsudski put his dream of re-establishing the commonwealth into action. He started carving out as much as he could of the lost territories, winning back by force Galicia, much of Belarus and Lithuania in the east. In the west, Silesia from Germany and some of Bohemia from Austria. These victories soon proved unsatisfactory, though at the time they gave Piłsudski the ascendency, and Dmowski's star began to wane.

The fixing of the frontiers and therefore the final shape of the new Poland was not decided by the Treaty of Versailles, though the existence of Poland was. Even after Piłsudski had done as much as he could by force, some of the rich industrial area of Silesia was annexed by plebiscite and a region of East Prussia was lost by the same process.

The Polish victory in the war with revolutionary Russia in 1920 was important not only because it temporarily saved the new Poland from another period of occupation and allowed her to establish at last something resembling a country, but because it finally discredited the idea of international Marxism. When the Bolsheviks broke the Polish lines and dashed westwards across its heartland, the battle cry was not so much imperial expansion as world revolution. They threw military strategy away supposing that the communist revolutionaries of the pre-war partitions would flock to the Red Flag starting a chain reaction across the whole of Europe. Instead they discovered that even in socialist Poland, patriotism or nationalism was stonger than communism. The next time they came, in 1944, they came with no such illusions.

It is hard to describe the shape of Poland in the interwar years. Not reminiscent of anything, it doesn't follow natural or former boundaries except along its southern edge, and, if anything, only reflects the fashion in which it was made. Like spilling water on to a flat surface, the wet edge is pushed out from the centre where the inner pressure is greatest, and expands fastest where the resistance is least. In this way Poland spilled into the Ukraine as far as Kiev, haemorrhaged into central Lithuania and Belarus. There were adjustments with the Russian campaign and the plebiscites, but at last in 1922 the ragged bloodstain dried for a few years into the map of Poland.

In the north there were two peaks; in the west, the Polish Corridor to the Baltic at Gdynia, north-west of the free Port of Danzig (Gdańsk); and in the east, in the area around Wilno (Vilnius), an important old city in the commonwealth era and now the capital of modern Lithuania. Between these was the scoop of East Prussia and the coastal part of Lithuania, which, for this short period, was independent. From Polotsk near Vilnius the frontier ran due south through Belarus, through the Ukraine to the Romanian border at Chocim. From here it ran roughly west along the Hungarian and then the Czechoslovak borders as far as Silesia and from here north to the Baltic. Superimposed upon a map of modern central Europe, roughly half the land area of pre-war Poland is to the east and outside its modern boundaries, and similarly, in the west, not quite half of modern Poland lies to the west of the pre-war state.

Down the middle of this shape, this butterfly wing, runs the Curzon line. This was a provisional eastern boundary for Poland proposed in 1919 by the British Foreign Secretary, Lord Curzon, in the discussions about the shape of the new Polish state. His suggestion was not taken up at the time because Piłsudski and the Polish legions had already gone far beyond it. Lord Curzon's proposal is remembered because it was more or less the line through the middle of Poland which Hitler and Stalin agreed should be the borders of the new partitions in the non-aggression pact of 1939. Half to Germany, half to Russia, again.

Since leaving Piła we have been driving through forest, along the base of a square trench cut into the deep vegetation that covers the undulating terrain in luxurious profusion. Occasionally, from the road, through a break in the bushes lining its edges, we are given glimpses of the interior of the woodland. It is open and airy at its floor with a high canopy above. From our moving perspective, the long trunks of oak, ash and pine seem to dance by each other under the stable cover of their collective roof; those further off chase along, keeping pace with us overtaking the trees next to the road.

'Lunch, Dad?'

'Good idea.'

This looks perfect and I turn off the road on to a sandy track and go about half a mile into the wood. Sunlight slants down through gaps in the top cover and the air is still and warm. 'You don't need to go so far, Mark.' But I can't resist the bumpy track winding between the trees, it draws me deeper in. We pass several perfect-looking clearings with grassy banks in patches of sunshine.

'Here, Mark.' I don't know why I don't stop.

The track becomes less distinct the further we drive into the wood, a pair of faint ruts only. The apparently endless forest before us gives me a ticklish feeling of both excitement and fear. Ahead the growth is denser and the atmosphere damper.

'Why you don't stop at one of these places back there?'

I have had to stop at a division in what is left of the track; its failing identity divided now in indecision. We halt and look across its groin into the unmanaged darker recesses. The ceiling of foliage is lower, in places descending into thicket, and it is opaque admitting only the coldest light as far as the black ground.

'Now Mark, why don't you turn round?'

'Good idea.'

Facing back towards the road, the forest immediately reassumes its former welcome. Our Little Red Riding Hood car bobs along the path in and out of the trees.

We stop in one of the clearings, spread out a rug and I unload Irena's little picnic. From the top of the carrier bag, strained against its contents, I pluck two beer cans.

'Na zdrowie, Dad.'

'Cheerios.'

We wander around in circles for a while, reluctant to sit again after the morning in the car. My hands tingle with the texture of the steering wheel and my legs and back itch from prolonged contact with the car seat. We stagger this way and that, peering behind bushes as though we have lost something, but never straying too far from the car or from each other.

I miss my wife Denise's ordered mind; she would know we needed a walk and a pee before lunch. I know it but I need to be told. We are alike, Bronek and I, in this respect, despite having the insight, our lives seem deliberately abandoned to chance or direction from outside, as if knowledge alone is not enough.

Eventually, in protest against my conscience, I lay on the rug in the sunny patch I have found and shut my eyes voluntarily for the first time since leaving home.

I am driving with Dad in the little red car towards a fishing village on the left side of a long inlet; a fjord. Tall cliffs rise out of the sea on each side and the road runs along their base at sea level towards the village hidden in a cove ahead. It is a beautiful sparkling day, light reflects off the blue water, and above the cliffs on the opposite shore the fields are green and fresh in the sunlight. I notice that the level of water has risen and started to cover the road. We keep going but I am alarmed. I can no longer see the road at all, the surface looks the same over deep water as it does over shallow and now it stretches unbroken from one cliff to the other. I look ahead wondering what the cause could be. Across the whole width of the fjord is a huge tidal wave. It is perfectly straight; at the point of breaking, a pure white shining crest is being whipped off the top as it rushes through the air. The ends of it are shattering against the cliff walls on either side and the spray flashes in the sun almost to the full height of the rocks. We are drawn by the undertow and we float away from the cliff to the middle. Helpless, I watch the wave approach; it is beautiful in every detail. Exquisitely formed ripples glint over its rearing face, a dazzling vapour-trail peals off the crest as it thunders relentlessly towards us.

I am roused from my reverie by the sounds of Dad unwrapping the neat newsprint parcels Irena made of our lunch. Polish sausage, chicken legs, tomatoes, gherkins, slices of rye bread.

'Look at this, Irena is not so bad you know, Mark.' This is

praise indeed from Bronek, not usually given to it. He continues unwrapping; fruit, pastries twists, 'Ah chrusty, my mother used to make this, you remember?'

'I think chrusty are in my recipe book.' I bought a Polish cookery book in Szczecin, which I now fetch from the car and we chat about the merits of Polish cooking. Bronek remembers other dishes he was fond of in his youth, but he seems most enthused by memories of nocturnal feasts prepared in the forests of southern Poland on hunting or hiking expeditions. A campfire, people singing and the crazy góralski dance of leaping through the flames.

'Did you do that?'

'Of course, what do you think I'm not going to?'

'No, I can see you leaping with the rest of them.'

'Bigos, you know bigos? We used to make this in the woods.' I look up bigos in my book. The preparation doesn't look very outdoor to me and I show him the book.

'Not like this,' he says. 'We made it with everything you could find in the woods. Mushrooms, fruit, some rabbits or something like that. This is the kitchen recipe.'

We are helping ourselves to the spread of treats before us. Seeing it all laid out I wonder at how she packed it all in the carrier bag. We set to heartily making appreciative grunts and noises about the quality of the sausage and the gherkins, the beef sandwiches.

'I thought Irena said it was impossible to get good meat, it all went for export.'

'Irena will always find the way to get what she wants; you saw her with the amber trader.'

We continue with the chicken legs and blood-red tomatoes the size of apples, still enthusiastic but a little daunted by the task ahead. As time goes on we become more thoughtful and have less to say; there is still half of Irena's little picnic uneaten. Soon we are completely silent, determined. A dull gloom descends on the wood and I can feel her presence eyeing our meagre progress. She would be sitting there with her hands in her lap, closing her eyes and turning her head away with the

Polish shrug. I look across at Bronek; he feels it too. The food has gone solid in his mouth; he is staring into the trees his face is packed but his jaw has stopped working: he is dry. When I catch his eye he gives me a sad smile; he looks so much like a demented hamster I start to laugh. He has so much food in his mouth he can't can't keep his lips shut. Pressure of the hysteria rising in me is too strong to suppress and I roll over in painful silent giggling, infecting Bronek at the same time. Incapable of holding it back, laughing and spitting up mouthfuls of Irena's little picnic, the relief is tremendous.

Later, when our aching bellies and cheeks have recovered a little, I take a photo of Dad sitting in this paradise holding a sandwich. It looks like any normal picnic.

Flight

Sitting in this paradise after lunch, Bronek starts telling me about the invasion in 1939. 'You know, many times since those days before the war, I wondered how could we have been so blind to what was happening around us.'

Poland was expecting war and trying to prepare for it with their meagre resources but according to Bronek, they were facing the wrong way and preparing for only half of the war that arrived. The old habit of facing east towards their traditional enemy, Russia, hoping and trusting that Britain and France would deal with Germany, left them exposed and unprepared for the attack from the west when it came on 1 September 1939.

After the war it was generally thought that Poland was ill equipped and the army old-fashioned and unprepared. It was only partly true. Compared with the German army, it was antiquated and the image of the Polish cavalry charging with sabres drawn against Panzer tanks has stuck in everyone's minds whether it happened or not. However, at the time there was no army in Europe that was a match for the Germans. When they struck at Poland from three sides, from Germany itself, from East Prussia in the north-east and from Czechoslovakia in the south, with the highly mobile motorised infantry and the Luftwaffe, which was practically unopposed, softening up all the targets in advance of the ground forces, the speed with which they overran the country shocked everyone. The same was to happen in 1940, when they turned west and overran Belgium, Holland and northern France in a few days, obliterating the British Army in the process.

In the east, against the Red Army the Polish army had already proved itself effective. The terrain is mostly flat, but the distances are greater, over which the roads and communications are poor. In these conditions a large cavalry and light infantry could move quickly and survive with the minimum of support, and this is what the Polish army was designed to do.

In the west however, the situation was different. The Blitz-krieg tactics of the modern German army were impossible to resist for long on their own. Despite this, for the first week of September there was strong resistance, but at the same time plans were made to evacuate the remnants of the army and the government to Romania.

The Polish Ukraine, though initially invaded by the Nazis as far as Lwów, was already allocated to the Soviet Union in a secret protocol of the Non-Aggression Pact between Hitler and Stalin, signed by von Ribbentrop and Molotov on 23 August, a week before the outbreak of hostilities. In the terms of this agreement the Soviet Union would gain all territories east of the Curzon line, which today roughly marks Poland's eastern border, and Germany all of Poland to the west of it.

I imagine these two black dogs, these self-invented leaders, discussing the fate of Europe. Hitler and Stalin, if only they had kept their real names: Mr Schicklgruber and Mr Dzhu-gashvili. Could they have created such powerful myths or been so kitsch?

'Mark, you know what is the V2 rocket?'
'Yes.'
'During the blitz in London, there would be the explosion followed by the sound of the rocket arriving...'
'What?'
'They flew faster than sound. The Nazis came like that to Lwów, before we were expecting them. They say the Golden Hoard was the same, when news travelled at the speed of the galloping horse, they could arrive without warning.

'When they came to Lwów everyone started to leave, run-ning east to get away from them, streaming out of the city until the roads were black with people. My unit was not mobi-lised. Perhaps because it was mostly students, reserves. Maybe because there was no time. There was a strange lull after Lwów fell. Instead of the harsh treatment you would expect from an invading army, the Nazis seemed to be doing nothing. There were no arrests, no imprisonments of local government and no rounding up of the young men. It was a strange time, unreal like the heavy calm before the storm. We know why now, but then, we took the opportunity to leave while we could.

'I went with my friend Mietek to his family, who lived near Tarnopol, a town about eighty miles east of Lwów. Mietek had a bicycle and we found another one for me in an abandoned house on the road out of the city. People were leaving everything except what they could carry. We thought bicycles would be a good idea but later on we found the roads were so clogged it was difficult to keep riding. People were carrying bundles and suitcases, pushing carts and prams with their children in them. There were cars, lorries, ponies and even ox carts, but most people were walking. In those days people walked more; anyway walking was the best in those crowds, even our bicycles were a nuisance.

'Of course I wanted to go back to my home in Różniatów but that seemed too dangerous. We thought it likely that the Germans were there already, it being to the south of Lwów and close to the Czechoslovak frontier. His home seemed the safer option, being to the east and away from the invaders, so we decide to go there first until we could find out more clearly what was happening, and I would try to get some news from Różniatów. We talked about going to Romania; it was supposed to be neutral and we had heard that the Polish government had gone there. But, if the news from Różniatów was good, I would go home first.

'We had trouble from the outset keeping together in the crowds, our bicycles seemed to draw us in different directions and I lost him soon after we left the city. I didn't worry too much because I knew his family and where they lived; we had arranged to meet there if we got separated along the way.'

On my own in the crowd in the afternoon, there are still too many people to ride. It is dusty and hot and the black coats of the walkers are becoming grey. A silent march advances between an uneven avenue of shivering poplars, a grey stain leaking out from the city into a harvest landscape.

Not far into the first morning, not far away from the city I notice a few bundles abandoned by the roadside, luggage flung down, worthless treasures too heavy to carry any further. How quickly value is forfeited from the least important, attaching itself finally only to life itself, and how quickly everyone recognises this. The sight of the first article cast aside starts an avalanche of agreement on the embankment below the road. And beyond this, to harvesters working in the fields, how do we look? Carrying our goods from the city and throwing them down into the fields. Are they gifts? Another harvest.

Seeing their incomprehension, their separateness from us on the road, it occurs to me to take the bicycle to the foot of the embankment and pedal through the cornstubble beside it. It is rough going and I worry that I will soon have a puncture but the feeling of freedom from the gloomy press makes me optimistic. My new speed freezes the procession into a static crowd, silent and trapped between the margins of the road and elevated on the embankment, statuesque. They are mostly Jews I realise, bearded men heavy in their black coats, gloomy escapers wading away from the unspeakable. So resigned is their expression, my feeling of adventure seems to me improper, sacreligious almost, as I push hard against the pedals speeding into the wind.

The road forks. It is the second morning. The left hand goes east towards Tarnopol and Mietek's home, and the right hand, south towards Stanisławów and mine. I stop at this junction for a while pretending to wait for Mietek but really it's because I can't bear to make the decision to finally head away from home. The longer I wait for him the more I worry about my mother and sister in Różniatów, the more I want to go south and the more certain I am that the Nazis will be there already. If I don't go, am I abandoning them? If I do, will I be endangering them? My reason screams at me to go east, my heart screams south. I turn and cycle east unable to stand still any

longer, feeling as though I have put off the decision. The
crowd has divided and thinned along these roads and the going
becomes easier.

In the evenings people stop and descend to the fields. They
gather wood and light fires to cook and keep themselves warm.
The nights are already cold and as darkness falls crowds gather
around the fires. I stop at one. It is quiet; tonight there are no
góralski leaping through the flames, this is not a hunting party.
Children are crying. Already we are hungry. With the heat of
the fire on my face and the chill of the night at my back, I stare
into the flames and it dries my eyes. Someone tells a story. A
mother sings a Yiddish lullaby. Yellow sparks in the air. On the
road, still a steady slow march.

In the morning my cycling is stopped by a group of armed
men. They have been watching the crowd from woods near
the road. Four or five Ukrainians, partisans perhaps, armed
with hunting rifles and shotguns. One grabs the handlebars
and stands astride the front wheel. He says nothing, he's the
tough guy. He's waiting for the leader to speak, but the leader
is watching the crowd; like a scavenger he is concentrating on
the slow-motion flight of the quarry. I wait too, astride the
frame and also holding the handlebars. I am the juvenile separated from the herd, easy pickings. We are like actors new to
our parts waiting for stage directions.

'The bicycle.'

'No.'

On cue the tough guy pulls the bars towards him; I am
jerked and dragged. How many of the fights I had at school
started like this: threats first, pushing and shoving, mockery
for being the recipient of the church charity, the poor kid, the
swat, the orphan, the American.

'What good is a bicycle in the woods?'

'What good to you in this crowd, or if I shoot you now?'

'I need to get to Tarnopol, quickly.'

'So do they.' He tips his head contemptuously at the crowd,
'They won't get far. The Bolsheviks are coming.'

'What?' How could the Russians be coming?

'Yes, Polak.'

I don't believe it, 'Where are they?'

'They are coming, don't you worry. And then you'll be going.'

'And you'll be starving.'

'Not us, Polak. We are going this way.' He points west, against the flow. 'You would do better to come with us, you are running the wrong way. All the way to Siberia.'

I look back at the road, at the line of black robes and beards, 'Join the Nazis? I don't think so. You know what they say, "If you lay down with a dog, you will get up with fleas."'

'Better with a dog than the bear.'

They let me go, pushing me and the bicycle over. It was not yet war but still a school brawl. Later, things would have been different. I cycled on less like an adolescent than an old man, sitting upright and heavily in the saddle, pushing the pedals slowly down. I should have asked them more questions. I travelled all that morning rhythmically rehearsing them; where were the Russians and what were they coming for?

There had been no anti-fascist propaganda from the Russians in the days before the invasion, and no promises of help or protection. They were our traditional enemy, we always distrusted them and now I am certain I am pedalling towards as great a danger as I am fleeing. Cycling across the remains of Poland, a shrinking strip of unknown width, in a curdled mixture of urgency and reluctance. An abdominal hollow replaces the levity and optimism of the previous day, blurring the normal control of my limbs. They feel weak and irresolute. I don't immediately recognise this as fear. When I do, it is with slow detachment, my head as dislocated as my limbs.

'I met the Russian army the same afternoon and all the questions were answered. I had covered many miles since my encounter with the Ukrainians. The crowd on the road had thinned a little more and I could cycle on it again. I thought I might get to Mietek's home before the Russians, if all went well, but somewhere near the town of Złoczów I met them in a village. I don't remember the name; maybe I never knew it.'

Elongated villages of painted wooden houses, picket fences
and conical well canopies of fading red, yellow and blue batons
at the roadside. A stork's nest on every telegraph pole and
roof. Grey haycocks in the yards, golden wheat stripfields and
brown-skinned peasants. Harvest time. A black column of
ants. A cyclist.

I dismount in the centre of the village thinking I might spend a
little of the money I have on some bread or even a beer. In the
open area before the church I prop up my bicycle and look for a
shop. I don't notice the few men in unfamiliar uniforms until I
emerge again with half a loaf of bread. A counter-column from
the east is claiming right of way on the road. From behind I
see the occupant of a motorcycle side-car, the herald, heading
back towards Lwów waving the line of refugees off the road.
It advances like a ploughshare steadily folding the approaching people on to the grass at one side. Dark-blue smoke from
his overheating engine envelopes the receding machine, rising
around a red flag, limp at the stern of the gondola.

An open lorry pulls up in the square and a ragged column of
a dozen boys trots after it, lining up rather awkwardly under
the shade of some trees. An old woman stands silently in front
of them, her head on one side, with a screw of paper in one
hand and a lump of black bread like a stone on the other. In
the act of tearing a piece of my crust with my teeth all notions
of hunger and welcome disappear and I start to run back to
my bicycle; my only thought now to get out of the village as
quickly as possible, even less certain of whom I should fear.

I feel the shot, the physical jolt of an electric shock, and my
body reacts leaping sideways before I hear the report from the
rifle and understand it.

'Sniper!' In Russian.

No one knows where. They are not entirely welcome after all.

I find myself in the narrow space between two houses cowering with a handful of people, my heart bashing against my
chest. I look myself over to be sure that I was not the target,
and spit out the bread I still have clamped between my teeth.

A Russian voice, out of sight, shouting on its own is cut by a second sharp crack. Fire is immediately returned by the squad in the square. From our alley I can see the walls of the church fizzing with tiny erruptions.

'In the tower, in the tower. Oh Jesu Maria save him.'

The intensity of the shooting gradually fades and then stops entirely but nobody moves. Dust drifts, hanging in the air. A sudden flurry of running feet, then another.

Someone shouts in Ukrainian from across the square, 'Are you there?'

A rifle shot, a single whiplash, 'Tak!'

He is still alive. A cheer is immediately drowned in automatic fire; they have brought up a machine gun and it roars steadily below the irregular clatter of rifles. The plaster and woodwork of the tower begin to break up under the hail of bullets throwing splinters and grit into the air, only abating when their magazines are emptied and they have to reload. Surely no one could have survived in there. My ears are ringing and they feel like cold pebbles on the sides of my head. We wait, time concentrated in the hissing silence.

'Dobrze, jeszcze raz,' Good, once more. A Polish voice.

Nothing.

'Prosze Pana!' Please.

Crack, another shot.

Yes, he is still there. I am seized with a silver shard of excitement and I cry out with the rest of them. There is shooting everywhere now. We have taunted the beast with our cheering; it has been stung by the sniper, a wasp on the bear's nose. Firing approaches us like a wave and we all retreat, falling over each other down the alley to the backs of the houses into a labyrinth of fences, small barns and wood piles. I'm so frightened I hear myself giggling. Someone pulls me by the shoulder of my coat to the back door of a cottage and we crawl inside and lie down. We press ourselves against the floor and the walls to stay clear of the windows, and against each other to feel safe. The wave passes, shattering the windows and thudding on the walls outside like the battering of clubs, finally leaving us with a paralysed silence. We wait, not daring to move.

After a long time the sound of voices outside breaks the spell and we start to untie ourselves. Someone says they have gone. A knot of villagers gathers. There is silence and no sign of the Russians but a persistent thought nags me: where have they gone? Why have they gone?

From the distance comes a bumpy sound, like thunder a long way off. I had never before heard the sound of the shell in flight, but I guess what it is immediately. We cram ourselves back into the little house, many more of us, and stand in the small kitchen pressed together by the table, by the stove, by the remains of a meal. With our faces turned up we follow the whirring flight of the shells and the crashing impact of their arrival all around us and we pray. We pray with our eyes open.

One morning in Poprad, Slovakia, where Bronek's sister, Hanusia, lives now, I am woken at about 5.30 a.m. I am sharing a sofa-bed with Bronek in Hanusia's front room. She has a two-roomed flat in a 1960s block. She is completely blind but lives alone and manages with support from her daughter, Renia, and her grandchildren, who have a rota of visits and jobs they do for her. I am woken by movement at the foot of our bed, a sense of alarm makes me fully awake immediately. Against the faint grey light of the window I see Hanusia's shape in difficulties over the rearranged furniture and our thoughtlessly placed belongings. Her map of the flat is suddenly out of date. She knows where everything should be and her hands, searching for familiar landmarks, collide awkwardly with chaos, with another layer of darkness. I am caught, an unwilling spectator, my sight useless and my presence confusing. She swims a kind of low-level breaststroke across the room, her hands like antennae exploring the darkness before her. Her reconnaissance is slow but thorough; each encounter is followed by detailed examination. Sometimes there is something she recognises, a pause as she records its new position in the room then a salute, a slight raising of her hand. When she finds her table shoved against the window, she checks all the objects on it, sweeping her memory over it. Strange objects she interrogates, turning them over and over in her hands until she knows them. At the wall she reaches her destination, opens a cupboard and withdraws something I cannot make out in the darkness, something small that her hand goes to automatically and she retraces her steps between the obstacles to the kitchen without incident. I doze, groping in the dark for familiar forms, drifting up again to the eerie sound of a monotonous whispering. In the kitchen doorway a dim silhouette of Hanusia sits with her rosary, muttered prayers hang about her in the whispering air. Fragile sound and diffuse light vibrate and emulsify, thickening the half-tone, half-light homogeny of this moment. She draws together her threads at the start of the day, re-creates the medium for her daily swim.

In that little house we are all praying. In this place where you cannot fit another person there is room for God, even in hell there is room. We are praying when a shell passes through the roof above us, shaking plaster and whitewash from the ceiling down on our heads. We are packed so tightly in the room, the air full of dust. I look at the lumps of plaster on the table, and I pray too. I pray out loud with the women clutching their children to them, faces buried in their black skirts, with the old men who pray to themselves, and with the atheists like myself who are alone. We make a continuous buzz, comfort and menace against the approaching shells, praying to avert chance.

When the pounding stops we come out to see what is left of the village. In the sunlight we look like statues, white with the plaster dust, or like the dead, colourless and empty. It is the beginning. The Russian front has passed over us a dry rolling breaker; we surface choking in the drowning dust, casting about for something to cling to.

'The sniper? I don't know. Maybe a child, man, woman, old or young. I don't know. Ukrainian, Polish, who knows. A resister, alive or dead. Surely dead by now.'

I found Mietek's family easily. I knew the village and I kept out of sight by riding only on the paths and alleys that ran behind the houses. I was concerned that Mietek had not yet arrived but his family were glad to have news of him, and we all hoped he would arrive soon. In the meantime they hid me at the end of the garden in the summerhouse, an open-sided wooden construction, most of which sheltered the year's supply of firewood, but at one end there was a sun room and a small workshop with a loft above where I waited for Mietek and considered what to do. Instinct and experience of recent occupations seemed to have engaged automatically. Somehow we all knew what the dangers were, that it was best to keep our presence secret, to hide, be invisible. To be unaccountable. At the beginning of the war, in the first few days this was relatively easy, but as time went on, as the invaders built up their records, it became more and more difficult. The typical Russian combination of bureaucracy and thuggery would reimpose itself.

I am lying on a pallet in the summerhouse loft considering that war will be more a matter of patience than fighting when Mietek arrives.

'Ah, Bronek. You are here already. You made good time.'

'What happened to you? Did you meet the Red Army?'

'Yes, they took my bicycle. After that I seemed to be swimming against the stream. Everyone turned round and started to go back to Lwów.'

I tell him about the partisans and the shelling.

'How terrible. Weren't you frightened, Bronek?'

'Of course. I thought I was going to die in that house.'

'But you didn't; that makes you twice as alive.'

'"Still alive," will do for me, Mietek.' He is a natural adventurer and I can see he is disappointed to have missed something exciting, but I wonder how he managed on his own. We had many student adventures together in Lwów, he and I, and although he was always fearless, where I might hesitate he would not, he was never very keen to venture forth without some company. He would rather stay at home than go alone.

We stay in the loft during the first few days and come to the house for a short while at night when no one will see us crossing the garden. The Russian plan, as we all expected, is what used to be called Russification. Now it it has some newly styled Soviet term, but it means the same and involves the segregation and movement of the populations until their new territory is peopled with only those prepared to call themselves Russian. Mietek's mother is German and is suspicious of everyone around her. Poles, because, although it is the Russians who have invaded this part of Poland, it is somehow equally the Germans' fault and she fears a kind of referred reprisal for the Russian presence. Russians, because of her Polish husband and family, which she fears they will separate her from, repatriating her and deporting them, or worse. Ukrainians, because they have another axe to grind with the Poles and it's not clear who they will support. And Jews, because she may be seen as a Nazi, and Jews that are communists are suddenly becoming powerful.

We know that we cannot stay long; our presence endangers the family and raises the tension his mother feels. But we find it impossible to get news from Różniatów, now certainly occupied by the Red Army, and, despite the danger, Mietek is reluctant to leave his family. The autumn is beautiful, the days are still hot and clear and in our loft we can pretend to ourselves that we are safe, and pose no threat to those who know we are there. Finally it is Mietek's grandfather who nearly brings disaster on all our heads.

From our loft late one afternoon we hear a commotion from the house, someone shouting and his mother cries out. Before I can stop him, Mietek dives down the ladder into the workshop and makes for the door. I hear him stop, hesitate a moment, then bound back up to the loft.

'Shit, they are coming. Get this ladder up, quick.'

We are crouched over looking at the floor, listening to the militia poking around the workshop below us. Tools are moved, cupboards opened and shut and boxes scraped across the floor. Below us a man grunts alone in the effort of his search for something, something not someone. People cannot hide in boxes or behind cupboards. I mouth the silent question to Mietek; he raises his eyebrows in return and opens his hands. We are a few feet above the head of a Russian boy, or maybe a man from the village, a neighbour? Strangers to me, but Mietek, as he tries to see through the rough boards of the floor, could be squatting above a person he has known all his life, a school friend perhaps, someone he has played hide and seek with before. A chill runs through me: it could be someone who knows this summerhouse. I look at him drilling the floor the other side of the ladder. We are not ready to be caught and I count to a hundred. Ready or not, here they come.

Someone shouts from the direction of the house, 'Found anything?', in Russian.

'Niet.'

'Come on, let's go.' And the grunter leaves the workshop. Mietek and I don't move for a long time. Then, in the failing light his mother comes across the garden to us and takes us back to the house. As we cross the garden she says, 'One of our friendly neighbours reported to the police that my father-in-law had a shotgun.'

'Who, who reported it?'

'I don't know, Mietek. It could have been anyone. And your grandfather is so stubborn.'

'What happened, have they taken him away?'

'No, but they beat him.'

'What?'

'Brutes, beating an old man like that. Filthy brutes.'

The old man is tougher than he looks. When we get to the house Mietek's father is trying to clean him up and we help to wash him and put him to bed. Slowly his confusion clears and he recovers himself.

'Have they gone?' Mumbling through split and swollen lips.

'Yes.'

He beckons to his son, Mietek's father, 'That fooled those bastards!'

'What? What do you mean, Tatuś?'

'Thought I'd tell them where the gun is, did they? They'll have to do better than that.'

'Are you mad? They could have killed you.'

'No, no. I have fought these bastards before...'

'I know, Tatuś, but that was 1920. Why didn't you give them the gun?'

'Because one day I'm going to shoot one of them.'

He breaks off here and we sit in silence in the wood. The warmth of the day has returned and we are feeling soporific after Irena's feast. After a while he sniffs as though to banish his memories. He says, 'Mark, it's a long time ago but Russian foreign policy never changed since Ivan the Terrible.'

Bronek turns to me, 'You know where the gun was hidden? In the woodshed. Mietek and I found it and buried it later that night.'

How heavily history lays upon Poland. I look down between the blades of grass at the earth beside me in the wood, Polish earth. Ivan the Terrible, Commonwealth, the partitions, Bolsheviks, Nazis, Soviets, they all seem to lie obstinately on this soil, refusing to sink, resisting decay and assimilation. They are features in the landscape and the ground must rise around them before they will disappear. Ivan the Terrible is still there, covered in ivy and eroded into a less monstrous form, but present. Somewhere I read with reference to Polish history, 'The past is never dead; it isn't even past.'

We pack up, leaving a pile of food for the birds and still take with us enough for another picnic before we get to Inowrocław. Back on the road Bronek doses beside me in the car listening to Chopin, a mazurka.

'Poland and France,' he says without opening his eyes, 'Natural allies.'

I picture him pedalling his bike below the road full of refugees in 1939, a practical solution typical of him. Then I remember him in about 1960, sitting bareback on Mike's black pony under the sycamores at the top of the yard by the lane gate. On the point of leaving to fetch the cows from the top fields, he had seen Mike leading her to the stable and decided he would rather ride than walk. It is full summer. Betty's coat is oily black; she's fat as a barrel but she's beautiful.

'She needs some exercise, Michael. She is fat.'

Mike squints up at him excited to see him on her back, 'Do you want the saddle?'

'What for?'

Her tail flicks at the irksome flies, patches of her skin jitter independently and she stamps occasionally to dislodge them from her legs. The reins hang in slack loops to the bit rings, but she stands while Dad rubs the moisture from his brow. He looks at it on his palm before replacing his cap, shuffling it back and forwards over his sweaty curls to settle it straight and level on his head. He smiles at Mike, rubbing the sweat from his hand on to his thigh with one forward stroke to his knee, he sniffs with his lips compressed, gathers and turns Betty at once and they trot away from us into the shade of the lane. Leaning back slightly to soften the ride, he urges her through a patch of deep mud at the lane end where the ditching is shallow and clogged, and the ground is poached twice a day by the herd of milking cows. Her shoes clatter against stones suspended in the porridgy mixture, hooves plunging deep into it, a messy and stumbling dash through the mire. Always reluctant, Betty, but she goes for him.

'Hey,' Mike is incredulous. He runs a few paces after them towards the gateway and shouts, 'Hey, I just finished grooming her.'

Horse and rider stop on the far side of the mud on a light-grey bank in the track where it's dry. They are dappled by sunlight in a green tunnel of trees. Her legs are caked above the knee and hock and her heaving belly is spattered. She is panting, exhilarated, her head is up, ears forward and her whole body pulses back and fore with her breathing. She listens to Mike.

'What you say, Michael?'

'I just bloody groomed her.'

Dad looks at his boot and considers the thick splashes of mud on it. He raises one hand with his fingers spread out and his thumb curved back. Palm up he gestures towards the muddy ground between them. He says something to himself or to Mike, but I cannot hear him from where I am. In the middle of turning her away again he stops and calls back to us, 'Aha, Michael.'

'What?'

'You close this gate.'

— 8 —
Prison

By the time we were leaving our cousins in Inowrocław the pattern of our trip was beginning to emerge. During the time spent staying with relations, Bronek would take over, deciding what we did day to day and how long we should stay in any one place. I was 'off duty' as soon as we arrived anywhere and fell in with whatever he wanted to do, or I spent the time getting acquainted with cousins I hadn't met before.

At the very first stop, in Szczecin, we departed from our schedule. We arrived a day early, so the final effect of staying a day longer than planned only brought us back to our original timetable, but thereafter it became normal to stay at least a couple of days longer in each place than we had allowed for. This was going to lengthen the trip but we were both delighted to do this. For me, the excitement of meeting his family, my family, was irresistible. The indefinable family attraction, especially between near contemporaries, fascinated me and seemed to be enough, even when language was a problem, to inspire the most diverting escapades.

For him, the opposite situation obtained. He was lingering over his farewells. He was not overt in this, certainly he would have denied it, genuinely believing that the acknowledged fact of this as his last trip made no difference to the shape of it. He was never sentimental intentionally. He would never have said, 'This is my last trip. I have come to say goodbye,' but sometimes in his eyes, I saw him taking his last look. In practice it was not usually right at the end, but at some time near the end of each visit. Once in Kraków it was caught in a photograph. Sitting at the supper table with Antonina and her family, he is saying goodbye with a glass of wódka half-raised in a toast to some other thing. And again, as we crossed the Tatra into

Slovakia, sitting on top of the world with Poland behind us now and an echo of his future ahead, the ghosts of his previous crossings release him for the last time. As a spectator, I cannot know what this entails, but this story is a guess at it. It's a speculation of what I might have felt if I was in his shoes.

To me, an account of my diversions in the clubs and bars of Inowrocław with my new-found cousins would be amusing, if I could remember enough to relate. But in truth, the pleasure of these moments is best savoured at the time and forgotten quickly, it would make doubtful reading. The same, with some exceptions, is true of our excursions to local beauty spots and places of interest. They were in the main beautiful and interesting and can be visited freely.

Our drive from Inowrocław to Warszawa is beautiful, a bright, fresh, early-autumn day. Cousin Leszek guides us out of town in his Wartburg. He is very proud of it and never misses an opportunity to tell me that it has a Golf engine. He opens a back door inviting me to look inside. I inspect the back seat and the black-velvet cushions he keeps on the rear window, 'Look, Marek, it has engine of Golf.' He does driving actions, 'You know Golf?'

I find myself looking for a Golf engine sitting in the back of the car.

'Golf is good. Wartburg is good too.'

I follow him for quite a distance out of town along the road to Włocławek and Płock until Dad and I begin to wonder if he will take us all the way to Warszawa. He stops finally on the gritty shoulder of a long straight stretch in the wide landscape. We pull in behind him and get out. He walks towards Bronek with his arms and his hands open but looking down with his head tilted a little to one side. As he embraces Dad, I see he has been crying already, 'Uncle, Uncle Bronek.' He clings to him for a long time, then to me and I can feel the sobs shaking him, 'I am sorry, I am sorry.'

We follow the Wisła most of the way to Warszawa, driving through open flat farmland and the birchwoods that border the great river, Poland's trading artery. It's clear and warm in the middle of the day. Bronek is quiet until it's time to stop for lunch. He suggests we find the place where he stopped with Pete on their last trip, a place where the river spreads out as wide as a lake. Through the trees I glimpse the silver of the water and turn off into the woods for our second silvan picnic. It's not as comfortable in these woods as in the forest between Szczecin and Inowrocław. A new birch plantation, the trees are still young and close together and planted right to the water's edge. We perch on tree stumps beside the river, which is indeed like a lake; it must be a mile wide with no perceptable current. There are buoys far out marking the navigation channels.

'Mark, you remember Leszek's father, Władek? He was a marvellous chap. He was General Sikorski's driver.'

Władysław Sikorski was a soldier and politician of the period between the First and Second World Wars. In 1920, in the war against Russia, he distinguished himself and in 1922 became Prime Minister. He remained in high office until 1926, when he resigned in opposition to the coup and the dictatorship, as he saw it, of Marshall Piłsudski. After the invasion of 1939 he became Prime Minister of the Polish government-in-exile in France, and after 1940 in London. Had he survived the war, the outcome of the Treaty of Yalta may have been different, but tragically, he was killed in a plane crash in Gibraltar in 1943. It was he who organised the Polish division in the French army, recruited mostly from the migrant worker communities in France and attracted the refugees, like Bronek, who had escaped from Poland after the invasion, who needed a focus and a way of getting home. It didn't turn out that way for many, but it provided hope, that essential thing.

I have only the isolated memory of arriving late in the evening at Inowrocław on my first trip, finding their flat and seeing the name, Zygadło, on the door. This time when we arrived, only Anna, his widow, was there to greet us. She had Bronek laughing and joking in the first minutes. She put food on the table to welcome us in the traditional Polish manner: sliced tomatoes, sausage, bread and tea. Dad says, 'Uncle

Władek was as crazy as she is, the two of them together...' He closes his eyes and shakes his head.

Władek Zygadło was the second son of Maria Małczyńska, my grandmother Gabriela's sister. Maria also married someone with the surname Zygadło, who was related in some way to my grandfather, Józef Zygadło, a cousin perhaps. This marriage took place in Chicago.

Remembering our last picnic, I asked him to finish the story he started a few days ago: his flight from Lwów and crossing the Russian front to Mietek's home. He was reluctant to get started and the details are hazy. He and Mietek were arrested in the village; the circumstances and the reason are lost.

'We were not safe there, we knew it but we could not decide what to do. I wanted to go home but it was very difficult to find out what the situation was there. Mietek was at home and he wasn't safe, so I ask myself why should it be any different for me at Różniatów? We also tried to find out what happened to the army or to any resistance. It was impossible. We thought our best plan would be to try to get to Romania. Mietek delayed; his mother tried to make him go. Anyway, we were arrested before we did anything.'

They were held for a few days in the cells at the local police station, then moved to a bigger prison.

We are collected by the militia in a lorry, a sort of prison bus that tours around the villages every day or two collecting prisoners like us. It takes us to Tarnopol and dumps us in the main square in the middle of the town, in front of the town hall. I knew Tarnopol slightly: it is a pretty town on a lake. Two years before we had been camping there in the summer; now we stand in a huddle in the enormous expanse of the square, with the prods of our captors in our backs pushing us towards the town-hall doorway. A last look at the cafés and stores under the limes across the square, and at the statue of Mickiewicz in the gardens next to the town hall and we are inside the building.

They line us up in the echoing hall and check our names against a list. This is serious; lists are serious and I am frightened. Reading from the same list our names are called in groups of two and three and those called are immediately taken by the guards into one of the many dark corridors that lead away from the hall. My name is called before Mietek's. He smiles, and I go with another prisoner upstairs to what must have been an office. It has been stripped bare of all furnishings and is now a prison cell occupied by about a dozen other men. No orders, no instructions. The door is shut behind us and we are locked in.

I soon discover this is a transit prison, a collection point, and that something else will happen to us. Part of the character of the place is determined by this fact: no attempt at anything to sustain life has been made. There is no bedding, no heating, very little food and only rarely is anyone ever let out of the cell. It is distinguished from other Russian prisons only by the fact that they are not working us to death. They probably do not want many to die here; it's too inconvenient in the middle of a town. But people do die. People always die. They die in the cells from hunger, sickness and the cold. They probably die elsewhere in the building for other reasons.

When the prisoner who carries the water to our cell is called out and doesn't return, I volunteer to take his place because at least I will get some exercise and some fresh air. I have to carry out the shit too. It's a stinking job; the whole place smells of shit. They have no reason to make our lives comfortable, where we are going will definitely be worse.

On my trips to the water station and the cesspit in the yard in the first weeks I see that the prison is filling up. Faces watch at all the windows around the courtyard and the pit is filling faster than it drains away. They are rounding up more people every day; no excuse is needed. Polish nationals, Ukrainian separatists, known or suspected anti-communists, fleeing soldiers, intellectuals, teachers, professionals of any sort, the educated, the uneducated, criminals, looters and the unfortunate. Anyone between the ages of sixteen and sixty not prepared to at least call themselves Russian. And there are those who have no idea why they are here: they were denounced, reported, informed upon, suspected. Not knowing of what or by whom. And there are those here by mistake. It is all a mistake.

In each of the rooms there is a slow but regular turnover of people. Prisoners would be called out and often do not reappear. If this is intentionally meant to demoralise us, it is certainly effective. They could have been released, they could have been sent on somewhere else, they could have been questioned and returned to a different cell and of course they could have been killed. Occasionally someone is returned to our cell; sometimes they have been beaten, sometimes not. Both equally intimidating. A tortured body flung back into the cell tortures everyone else in it with the fear that they will be next. The one that returns unharmed arouses the suspicions of those around him into wondering what information he has passed on to avoid the beating. The less anyone knows about you, the less they can tell if they are questioned, and the less you know about them the better too; you can't inform if you know nothing. This reduces us to apprehensive silence and a feeling that one's fellow prisoners are just as dangerous as our captors.

In the mornings, occasionally, new prisoners would arrive to replace the ones that had been removed. One morning there was a face I thought I knew. An older man, probably in his fifties, Ukrainian and obviously cultured. He seemed familiar to me when he arrived but I couldn't immediately remember where or how I knew him. It took me a few days, slowly asking careful questions when no one else could overhear, to discover that indeed I did know him slightly. He was from Lwów. Actually, I need not have been so cautious. I found he had a healthy contempt for our jailers and what I took to be caution on his part was a kind of amusement at the furtiveness of my approaches. He later admitted also to the feeling that he had met me previously, but for him this was not unusual: he was a professor at the gymnasium and thousands of young men's faces must have seemed familiar to him.

'So you are Bronek.' Something in this revelation amused him. Now that we had established something in common, other things seemed to fall into place and trust grew up

between us. He was a good friend of the family with whom
I lodged in Lwów. I would have seen him, probably many
times at parties or bridge evenings at the house, though I could
not remember ever having spoken to him. The family were
very sociable and often held parties or musical evenings with
a small band and dancing. Bridge was also fashionable and
played regularly once a week. They were clever, fashionable
people with many interesting friends: artists, musicians, intellectuals. The conversation was always witty and it was very
exciting, part of the social circuit of the town, and we, Mietek
and I, were fortunate to be included. They were wonderful to
us, we were like part of the family.

'There was another student, was there not?'

'Mietek.'

'Yes, Mietek.'

'He was here too.'

'Here? Oh no, what happened to him?'

'I don't know. We were separated when we arrived weeks
ago. He may still be here.'

Humanity, supressed during the weeks of imprisonment,
shocks me. Our lives have already been reduced to the single
matter of survival, all other normal activities irrelevant. I realise with alarm that I have not thought of Mietek or of his
fate for some time and I sense the flood gates behind which I
have locked most of my life. I have built a second prison inside
myself.

'I am sorry Bronek. We will not talk of such things. I am
Oleksandr Kozachenko, at your service.'

'He was a very unusual Ukrainian, and the more I came to
know him over these weeks in Tarnopol the more exceptional
he became. In Lwów too he would have been unusual. The
society of the town was Polish bourgeois, and in general they
and the Ukrainians were not on the best of terms. Ukrainians
saw Poles as invaders, and there was a tradition of resentment,
despite the centuries they had been there. Poles, on the other
hand, looked down on Ukrainians as peasants and primitives.'

Occupation began under the Piast dynasty of Polish kings in the fourteenth century, when the territory of Ruthenia, as it was then known, the western Ukraine including Lwów, was annexed to Poland. The eastern Ukraine at the time belonged to the Grand Duchy of Lithuania, Poland's eastern neighbour. At the end of the sixteenth century a marriage united Poland and Lithuania and founded the Jagiellonian Dynasty and the Polish Commonwealth, thus incorporating the rest of the Ukraine. In all this time the Poles and Ukrainians had not successfully integrated because of the rigid social structure of feudalism. The peasant economy of the region had been over-laid with the Polish land-owning class, and as larger cities developed, professionals, government officials and the officer classes of the army were often imported from Poland.

There was little open hostility, but a sort of class system had developed that disadvantaged Ukrainians.

'Bronisław Zygadło; delighted.'

'I heard about you often from my friends.'

'My landlord?'

'Landlord. The words landlord and Polish have an unfortu-nate association in the Ukraine, my friend. Better to call them your hosts. They were not typical Poles, or typical landlords, I imagine.'

'I never had any other, so I cannot judge.'

'Very well said, my friend. Please excuse my remarks about Poles. I was bullying you. The truth is I have the habit of making fun of my Polish friends; it is surprisingly easy and my contribution to redressing the historical imbalance of my country.'

'The country is neither yours nor mine at the moment.'

'True. For you, ignominy. For me, terror, starvation and death.'

'Ignominy?'

'For the Polish snob, what greater ignominy can there be than domination by a people he considers vastly inferior? By barbarians.'

'We will starve and die too, if we do not die from our wounds first.'

'Your Holy Wounds. Yes, you Poles are prodigious fighters, but you are too often martyred.'

'This is a vinegar poultice.'

'I see you are a student of poetry as well as medicine.'

'A veterinary student.'

'Are you educating the beasts?'

'Curing them, hopefully.'

'You can cure bacon, my friend, but you cannot educate pork, however hopefully you try.'

Our conversations saved me. He reminded me of Lwówian life. He talked about the graceful house I had stayed in and the beautiful city, the Ukrainian pearl as he called it. To annoy him, I would insist it was Polish, but we agreed about its beauty. And he teased me about the stories of my adventures with Mietek that he had heard from my hosts. The gentleness and affection of these most childish games was a bulwark against fear and the monotony of every day. He did water duty with me and I gladly did his work. He was too frail, an aesthete with white, soft fingers incapable of manual work, but it was worth it for the opportunity of conversation.

'I hear Madame renamed your dog, Bronek.'

It was considered the height of fashion to keep a boxer: it *had* to be a boxer. In the Lwówian evenings we would stroll in the parks and squares, smoking and walking with dogs.

'I hope she still has him.'

'Let us hope she still has him, my friend.'

Our rooms had been on the top floor, the former servants' quarters I suppose, from the days when a larger staff lived in the house. We were independent if we chose to be but had an open invitation to join the family if we wished. I loved this time; everything was new and exciting, very different to my home life in the country. I began to see what a great privilege it was to be a student, what a charmed life we led and how lucky I was, with my background, to have it at all. My mother could

never have paid for it; to her this was an unattainable dream.
But I complacently took it for granted. I found it all very easy,
very comfortable, and I believed that my life would always be
like this. Up to the very last moment I believed things would
never change.

'How did you hear that?'
'My friend, you are famous. I beg your pardon, your dog is
famous for relieving her of a rather tiresome guest, by relieving
himself, as it were.'
'Oh no!'
'Oh yes, sir!'
'Then, that is why we never played bridge with her.'

Once, when I came home after the day at college I could hear
my dog whining to be let out. I ran through the hall and up
the first flight of stairs hoping that I wasn't too late. I swung
round the first turn in the staircase and collided with Madame.
She and another lady were coming down from the salon. It
was a large hall with a grand staircase winding up three floors.
There were wide landings and an open rectangular space in the
middle, the full height of the house lit by a lantern window in
the roof.
'Ah Bronek. Such a hurry.'
'Oh, Madame. Please excuse me, I didn't see you.'
'Evidently. Now Bronek, this is Pani X, we shall be playing
bridge with her on Sunday.'
Sometimes I would partner her if her husband was busy or
if he thought the game would be dull. I looked at her guest and
wondered which of these it would be on Sunday.
'I am delighted to meet you, Pani. I look forward to our
game.' I bow over her hand.
She is a very elegant lady in a large flat-brimmed black hat.
Slim, with an amber necklace over black lace. I can still hear
the dog upstairs. I don't want to appear rude by leaving too
abruptly, but the longer I leave it the harder it is to get away.
Madame explains in agonising detail who I am and where I go

to college, then, 'Is that your dog I hear, Bronek? He sounds a little anxious.'

'Yes, yes, he can hear my voice, please excuse me.' I race up the stairs to the top floor. The poor dog is howling by this time and scratching at the door; I have to push it open against his weight. He is a good dog, full of energy, little more than a puppy. He still gets excited to see me after a day on his own.

But today the excitement and the pressure of his bladder are too much for him; he wants to come bounding out on to the landing but he is hardly able to move his back legs, they are paralysed in a rictus of restraint. It is too late; there is no hope of getting him out into the garden. He comes groaning towards me letting loose a stream of urine, tailstump wagging his rear end and broadcasting a zigzag hose trail. There seems to be gallons spreading out across the woodblock floor of the landing and revealing a definite slope from my doorway towards the centre. I try to block its approach to the edge of the stairwell but there is so much of it and, oh God, the damn dog just keeps pissing. I stand against the balustrade trying to push him back towards my room and sweep away the tide with my feet. He thinks it's a game now that he has relieved himself, and sloshes around in the shallows.

I can hear their light voices in the hall below me, laughing, chatting and making much too slow a descent of the last flight of stairs. The dog's urine is relentless. As I push some away on one side, a snake of it curls behind me and sneaks over the edge into the chasm. I block this leak as quickly as I can but a short dribble is falling through space towards the moving black target. I will her to stop or hurry on, change course, but there's something inevitable about their deliberate strolling pace and this descending string of amber beads. A short burst of golden tracers shatters on the outer ring. The target, hit, breaks off its progress from corner to corner of the oblong tiled field, twists and slowly elipses. Her white, amber beadframed chin appears from behind it and I duck away from the edge, still sweeping at the pool with my feet.

'Bronek, is the skylight leaking?'

A few days later I met Madame in the garden. I was about to take the dog for a walk. She sank down to his level, held his head under his jaw with one hand and with the other stroked him from his brow back over his ears. He loved this and would stand still for it, only occasionally smacking his jowls. Very matter of factly she said to him that she has been considering the naming of pets. 'As you live at the very top of the house and you're obviously a very bright sort of dog, shall we not call you Skylight from now on?'

A few days later, war started.

A few days later, I was in prison.

He shifts awkwardly on his tree stump. 'Mark, my arse is numb. And if we are going to get to Warszawa this afternoon, we'd better move.' My arse was numb too.

In the car, I ask him about the Professor.

'He was Professor of History actually, at the gymnasium in Lwów I think, or maybe at a college, I don't remember exactly. He was a true scholar and he loved to discuss Polish history and literature. I had to revise my opinion of Ukrainians as uneducated people. But, most astonishing was his memory for poetry. It's not an exaggeration to say it saved my life in prison. The poetry. Not from some attack, or being called out for transportation... or worse.' These absolutes are mentioned without emphasis, casually.

'No. How could it? But from the loss of all hope. The atmosphere of suspicion, crammed in that room with all these people I dared not speak to, and waiting for what I was sure was going to kill me, one way or another, had just about destroyed me anyway. Some people could cope with that; I could not very well. I was weak, was frightened, I had just about given up. But he didn't care about any of that. He despised the Bolsheviks and made no secret of it, refusing to be frightened by them. He believed he had been denounced as a known anti-communist and he also knew the likely consequence of his arrest would be deportation to the slave labour camps in the Caucasus or possibly even in Siberia.

'I won't last long, look at me. Even if I was as young and

robust as you are, my friend. I am an academic; worse, I am an intellectual. In peacetime these thing are valuable, but now...I won't last long with them.'

He was older than most of us in the cell, if that makes a difference, but he seemed not to fear this prospect of hardship and suffering. He viewed the inevitable calling of his name with amused confidence. There was no mistaking him. He was right: he wouldn't last long.

'Live in here, my friend,' he would tap his temple with an index finger, 'like a monk,' and change the subject.

A few weeks earlier, even if I had spoken to him over a glass of champagne at one of those parties, as a Pole I would probably have looked down on him, a Ukrainian. But now, he toasts me with thin soup, 'Na zdrawie, my friend, and long life to you,' as though he has some secret, some power to realise this benediction. And it's impossible to see him as anything other than admirable.

'You and I, my friend, we are not so different. We were both misfits.'

'Certainly you Ukrainians have no business being so well educated.'

'We both had no business being where we were.'

I compounded my own feelings of inferiority with the knowledge that I never had a useful father, and that my education was being paid for by a priest. A fact I kept to myself as much as I could, but I felt like an imposter among my contemporaries.

'Imposters?'

'Education makes us all equal.'

Most of my fellow students were the wealthy sons of landowners and professionals, confident of their right to the wealth and position they enjoyed. I was not, and from the privations of the prison, that distant life of one month previous took on a gaudy glitter; my euphoria of the time now looked empty and unconvincing.

'Prison has made us equal, Oleksandr.'

'And ignorance imprisons us.'

He is thoughtful a moment, 'Of course, you are familiar with the works of Mickiewicz, my friend?'

'Of course.' This is fraudulent; I learnt poetry by heart like everyone at school but I cannot claim to be familiar with any of it.

And then he astounds me for the first time with his memory.

Mickiewicz's importance to Polish literature and consciousness cannot be understated, for he was the father of Polish romanticism in the nineteenth century and the originator of the idea that the partitioned land of Poland was anthropomorphised as the body of Christ. This pure and spiritual place, scourged by its neighbours, was sacrificed to atone for the sins of its invaders. Bearing in mind that he was writing from exile in Paris at the time of the partitions, when Poland existed only as an idea in the minds of the romantics, it isn't such an outlandish notion. And for him, it wasn't just a literary metaphor, he dedicated his work to the resurrection of the Body. The idea took hold in the moribund country to the extent that the Catholic Church crowned the Virgin Mary, Queen of Poland. Mickiewicz died during the Crimean War in Constantinople while trying to raise a Polish legion to fight the Russians. During the period of the partitions, the end of the eighteenth and the whole of the nineteenth centuries, Polish legions fought in other armies all over Europe. They had a strong allegiance with the French revolutionaries and fought with Napoleon in the disastrous Russian campaign in 1812.

At night sometimes, against the boredom, fear and the cold we huddled together on our patch of floor and buttoned together our coats to make a tent for warmth and privacy. We talked about many things, always in a whisper. In every subject we discussed he fascinated me, for he knew Polish history and literature, the classics, painting, he was extraordinary. Our situation seemed to sharpen his passion, increase his longing for this sort of freedom, and he opened a trap door from beneath our tent. Through it we wandered at night in defiance of the terror to which we were subjected. And his resource seemed inexhaustible.

But our time was not. The routine of the questionings, disappearances and the occasional beating gave way to a more regular routine. Twice a week an officer came with a list. He called names and the named, in twos or threes, departed immediately and never returned. I could only speculate when it first started about what became of those whose names were called, but even here, on the inside, real news seeped in. It came with new prisoners in fragments, in shreds like a torn paper. Deportation. It came clinging to their clothes, the fresh smell of the outside disfigured into the hard smell of mud, fear and railway tracks. Through the solid stone, information came like the cold of the dying year, chilling us with the alternatives. Deportation, the best we could expect. The worst, a short walk to some quiet place. A quiet place to dig a pit.

'History is rapacious, my friend.'

Our tent, though it could never protect, was a refuge. Our time runs out, sand falls through the glass neck from one invisible reservoir to another. Lives are torn by gravity from the cell and slide gradually to the vortex and disappear. We cling to Mickiewicz, Oleksandr invoking the Polish bard to suspend us a few moments longer over the void below, filling up the space with words. He is determined, stretching the days to weeks with his prodigious memory, gelling the flow of time.

Mickiewicz is exhausted and we turn to Słowacki and to Homer. My school days come back to me as I recite the passages we learnt by rote. Long thought useless and forgotten, they well up to surface, breaking before me line by line, stanza upon stanza, an advancing wet edge.

I walk into my parents' bedroom. Dad is recovering from an appendectomy. He is reading.

'Do you know Homer, Mark?'

'No.'

'No? Incredible. You should read *Iliad*; it is a fantastic

story. I had to memorise parts of it when I was at school. He describes everything as it happened, in detail and all in verse.' He offers me the book, 'Read this part about Helen.'

I take it; sitting down on the bed next to him, I look at it. 'I can't read this, Dad, it's in Greek.'

'What? You don't read Greek either? What do they teach you in that school?'

'Zygadło, Bronisław.'

The only name today. The inevitable. The one I have been waiting to hear has taken six weeks to be called. From autumn to winter, the seasons have changed and the waiting is over. It is dark, it is evening, it is winter.

That our names should have been called before his memory gave out was unthinkable. After Homer he had recited from Taras Shevchenko and Ivan Franko, Ukrainian poets, independents, rebellious national heros resisting the inevitable, holding back the flood, and not until they succumbed, would we. At the same time I had feared this enchantment. For him to exhaust what he knew by heart before his name was called would be defeat, we would be left on the field of our glory with nothing. With silence and with waiting.

And between us, who should be the first?

'What is the word without the heart, my friend?'

When it comes, the sound of my own name mixes shock with relief, affirming the pattern woven by professor and poet.

— 9 —
Oskar

Watching others leave, I had distilled this moment into one question: train or walk?

An eastbound train packed with people in open trucks. How well is the machinery of peacetime adapted for war: town halls as prisons, goods trains to remove the unwanted audience from its theatre. Or the walk. I don't think of the pit and its machinery.

I cannot look at the professor. I cannot meet his eye, but I hear him muttering as we haul ourselves to our feet and I gather my coat around me. I have had weeks to contemplate this leave-taking, but I still cannot think of what to say to him. The moment I have been expecting every evening still finds me unprepared. In the inner prison world superstitions are invented privately around every aspect of our narrow lives. There are places of security, places of danger, secret rituals surrounding the few meagre hopes we have left. I only have one: to delay the inevitable. Any preparation for my departure would have only hastened it.

The guard has me by the shoulder; I am weak with fear and do not know how to resist.

'Serwus, my friend. I will catch up with you on the next train.'

'Do widzenia, Panie profesorze.' I can think of nothing except how he will need my help.

How he will have to struggle alone tomorrow morning carrying the water from the basement to the cell. He will be kicked and punched by the guards because he will be too slow climbing the narrow back stairs and spill some of it, and I will not be there to protect him.

'Goodbye, my friend.' He taps his temple as though reminding a school boy to do his homework. He pats my shoulder and

I am pulled through the door into the corridor before we can shake hands. The door shuts on my last sight of him lowering himself to the floor again.

I descend the main stair with two guards, in a free-falling state of fear. For all its bleakness, I had unwittingly begun to regard the cell as a kind of home. Being torn from it now, I feel regret and longing for its relative security. I am falling in steps, in flights, towards a dreadful abyss, an open grave. There will be a group of prisoners already waiting in the hall or in the street, we will be formed up in ranks and given orders to march. We will be taken to the railway station. We will be marched beyond the station. We will be loaded into trucks. We will be marched into the woods, or a field. The train will wait for hours, maybe days. We will be given shovels and told to dig. Then the whistle will sound, like a scream.

My legs are weak on the last steps, my knees are unreliable, we turn the last corner into the grand hallway I last saw the day we arrived. It is empty and quiet but for a small knot of people near the doors, two more guards and a Pole, another prisoner. They must be in the street lined up and waiting for us already.

Do we nod an acknowledgement? A few words in the echoing space? I don't remember. What could we say? Time is suspended and we are empty of all natural words. Alone. My life dangled over this void for the last weeks in the office, but we filled it up with Mickiewicz, blocked the leaks with Homer and Franko, deadened the echoes with Słowacki and Shevchenko. At the calling of my name they have evaporated leaving the residual, the crystalline question: train or walk? Symmetrical, endlessly repeatable. Pure.

Two prisoners only, strangers, looking at each other while they wait. Are they the first of a group being gathered?

From some deep recess comes the faint rhythmic clicking of iron on stone. An officer. The guards prepare their attention. A tight constriction grips my throat. His measure is perfect, a martial pace, a relentless march in two time. I try to discern from these portents some intelligence of the decision he surely carries. More of a march than a walk, I think, and I chant in my mind the names of the stations between Lwów and Różniatów willing a train to emerge from the corridor.

The officer consults his watch, taking time. He is young and clean faced, my age, a Muskovite lieutenant with the power of life and death over us. What is he waiting for? He removes a cigarette from a crumpled pack; it is not time yet. I wonder about those left in the cell, about Oleksandr. How long before his name is called? We all share the same dilemma. Train or walk.

At an invisible signal, the doors are unbolted and swing open. The officer puts the cigarette between his lips and, squinting through the smoke, makes shooing movements at us.

'Out, out.' In Russian.

'What's happening?'

It is a solid-black night beyond the doorway; a flood of heavy cold air streams in from the square and chills us all. The soldiers push against our confusion, our hesitation.

'Out!'

We are shoved backwards over the threshold. I try to make out if there are already others in the street, my eyes are still unaccustomed to the darkness but I sense that all is still: the square is empty. Something is wrong; where is everyone else? In the bright lighting of the doorway the Russian lieutenant points theatrically at his watch, pressing two straight fingers with a cigarette between them against his wrist until he has our attention. From the darkness outside we watch him intently.

'Six o'clock curfew.' In Russian.

He takes a pace backwards and the doors scrape shut squeezing the yellow light to a thread. Through the thickness of the doors I hear one of the guards chuckling and the retreating click of the lieutenant's heels.

'Six o'clock what?' I don't understand Russian very well.

'Curfew.'

Curfew? Are we free then? We are out, standing in the dark square in the centre of Tarnopol, so wide the other side is lost in the night. It is cold and we are frozen.

'Curfew, six o'clock?'

'Yes.'

It takes a moment for us to realise what this means.

'Bastards, it is six o'clock.'

I stare at this stranger and suddenly he is my companion.

'Come.'

We start quickly away from the main doors, beating down the rising panic and the temptation to run, heading left along the front of the town hall towards the dim light of the gardens and a huge bronze silhouette. Mickiewicz, nothing to say now, he is cold and mute as we approach. I realise I have taken hold of my companion by his elbow, urging him on.

'Don't run.' He shakes me off, 'Calm down.'

Are we free? Released into an occupied town centre at curfew time. If we are caught we will be re-arrested. We could be shot, or we could be put back behind this wall, a hundred feet away in a different world, still waiting.

'Why?'

My companion is not so innocent.

'It's a game.'

'What?'

'It's a bloody game: they see how far we can get.'

'No.' Bladder panic.

We turn the corner into the street that runs up to the railway station; it is dark and deserted, trying to not run and run at the same time.

'I don't believe it.'

'Oh yes, sir, it's a bloody game for them.'

Rapid footsteps running behind us, a shadow has detached itself from the statue and is suddenly very close. Now he grabs my arm and we are off in a coat-flapping dash.

'Jesus Maria, who is that?' he turns without slowing.

A single man, a civilian, waving, hissing at us, 'Wait, don't run.'

'It's only one; there's only one of them.'

'In here.'

In a doorway he removes one shoe, picks it up in one hand and hides both behind his back.

'What are you doing?'

'Quiet!' a free finger to his lips.

But our pursuer keeps his distance. Back to the wall and looking the other way, very quietly he says, 'Zygadło, Bronisław?'

Nothing. Shock.

'Pan Zygadło, I have come to meet you. I saw them release you and I have followed you here.'

'Who are you?'

'It doesn't matter. If you wish I can keep you one night only, if not...' he shrugs.

'Who are you?'

'Please ask me nothing. But if you want my help we must hurry. It is curfew time.'

'And him?'

The man looks quickly into the doorway then back down the street.

'Tell him to put on his shoe. Follow me but at a distance. If you are stopped, I will ignore you.'

'He is a Yid.'

'Yes, I know.' We are walking half a block behind him, when he turns a corner he leaves us alone for minutes until we turn too and look for him in the next street. My senses concentrate on the unknown and the invisible. The streets, an uneven series of dimly lit islands floating in profound blackness. The man ahead appears briefly as he passes through the looms of light and sinks again into obscurity.

'He may turn us over to the NKVD.'

'Why should he?'

'I don't know. He is a Jew.'

We turn another corner.

'How did he know me?'

'Are you a Jew?'

'No.'

'Well...we may be lucky.'

'You don't have to come with me if you don't like it.'

'It's too late for anything else.'

'What is your name?'

'Milan. You are Bronisław.'

'Bronek, yes.'

We are led through an archway to the rear of a shop, an alimentary. The man is silent indicating our way by reluctant gestures to a small chamber lined with shelves. Another cell, a cold store for meat in better times, now all but empty. On the floor in one corner are a roll of blankets, half a loaf of black bread and a small bottle of wódka.

'Please, excuse me.' He points to these extreme offerings, shrugs with his palms open and his eyes half-closed. 'I thought there would be only one. Maybe later I will bring something more and another blanket.'

'Thank you.'

'In the morning I will let you out early. Please get away from here quickly and say nothing to anyone about this.'

'Why are you doing this?'

He looks at us in turn, our breathing clouds the freezing air between us. He hesitates.

'I owe you this kindness. Now, please, ask me nothing more than this.'

Across Mare Street from the the end of our road in Hackney was a delicatessen. A small family business owned by a short, rolly-poly Pole called Oskar. He usually sat in the back corner of the shop behind a counter on a high stool, doing paperwork or carving salt beef for the meat counter. Over his glasses he watched the commerce of the shop and simultaneously carried on conversations in Polish, Yiddish or English with customers, his family and the telephone receiver which was permanently wedged under his ear. He saw everything.

I was a regular visitor to Oskar's and became friendly with the family in the way that people do in pubs and shops. I wonder now how much I had casually told Oskar in conversation about my dad's background. It wasn't much, if anything at all; I'm not even sure he knew my name. One day, when Bronek was visiting me, I took him to the shop. He was on his way to Poland, flying out the next morning. As we walked in, Oskar looked up from his meat, saw Bronek and dropped his knife.

'I was in prison with you.' He climbs off his stool, presses himself past his wife and through a gap in the counter. 'I was in prison with you, sir.'

'Oskar.' His wife.

'But I know this man.'

Oskar is in front of him now wiping his greasy hands in his apron; they look flayed, raw, but he keeps kneading them, torturing some ingrained memory out of their flesh.

'In Russia...yes, yes, you remember? In the war, 1939.'

Bronek laughs nervously, 'No, I'm sorry.' He thinks this could be some kind of joke.

'You don't remember?' Incredible, 'You don't remember? How you don't remember?'

We are all stunned by the sudden volume of the question. It is not a joke; it is a hard and highly compressed piece of history.

'I am sorry, I...'

'No, no, I am sorry. Please,' Oskar collects himself; he is embarrassed, 'but I am sure I know you.'

'I don't think so.'

'Yes, I am sure of it. I don't forget. I know you; I am sure we were in prison together.'

I can see the discomfort behind Bronek's shrug; he smiles at Oskar for my sake but he would rather just leave the shop. He looks around at the laden shelves and bulging cabinets of food. Every corner is stacked, hung, piled up. I brought him here to buy some sausage, I thought he'd be excited by a Polish deli at the end of our road.

'But you were in prison?'

Bronek sighs.

'You were.' Now it's a statement; Oskar is sure of this at least.

'Yes...I was in prison.'

'You see, you see.' Oskar turns to his wife, 'You see, I knew it.'

'Oskar, leave the gentleman alone, won't you.'

'Alone? What alone? Why?'

'Perhaps he doesn't want to think about that.'

'But I know this man already. Don't you know me, I am Oskar.'

'I am sorry, I don't remember.'

Facing each other, their old eyes set they privately review memory's mugshots.

'Where?'

'Where?'

'Yes, where you were in prison?'

'Oh...Dolina and...'

'Not Dolina, no. Somewhere else.'

'In Tarnopol.'

'Tarnopol, I know Tarnopol, but I was not there in the prison.' His certainty wavers now. 'But, you look like someone...' holding his hands up to Bronek's face, 'I could swear...what is your name?'

'My name?'

'Yes, sir. Your name. I am Oskar.' Removing a hand from his apron, he extends it towards Bronek, 'How do you do?' Very formal with his best English accent.

'Bronisław, Bronisław Zygadło. Very well, thank you.'

'Good, good.'

Their hands clasp over this ritual and they smile slowly. But Oskar reels him in, he draws Bronek towards him and holds his elbow in his left hand.

'So, Tarnopol, eh?'

'Yes.'

'The Ukraine now.'

'Yes.'

'A transit camp?'

'Yes.'

'Temporary prison.'

'Yes.'

'What?'

'What?'

'Yes, what. What was it?'

'Oh...the town hall.'

'A town hall.' He shakes his head and smiles releasing Bronek so he can wave his hands in the air, 'They use anything those bastards. The town hall because they lock up the councillors, a school because they lock up the teachers and the children. Sports grounds, factories, they don't need any of that any more.'

'Oskar!' His wife.

'Yes, yes. I know, I know.' He reins himself in again, 'We were held in a school before...before leaving.'

'Oh.' Bronek non-committal. He covers his mouth with his index finger, not taking the bait.

'Near Pinsk.'

Bronek looks at me with his eyebrows raised. He's telling me it's time to go.

'Yes. And you, what?...After the town hall?' Oskar doesn't think so.

'After the town hall?'

'Yes,' Impatience. 'Yes, they send you east?'

'No, I was never in Russia.'

'No?'

'No.'

'Then why you are not dead?'

'Not dead?'

'Yes.'

'I am not dead.'

'Yes, you are not. But why not?' He enumerates with his sausagey fingers, 'You are in the transit camp. You don't go to Russia, and you are not dead. Why?'

Bronek shrugs, desperate for a simple answer, 'I don't know, I was lucky.'

'Lucky. How lucky?'

'Ah...I was helped. Somebody helped me.'

'Somebody helps you?'

'I was lucky.'

'Somebody helps you.'

'Yes.'

'You were lucky.'

'Yes, I was.'

They stare at each other; the shop stares at them, waiting. Bronek sniffs, compressing his mouth. I recognise this as a prelude to departure, on the exhalation he will start his goodbyes and thank-yous.

'Who?' Too late.

'Who?'

'Yes. Who helps you?'

'Ah,' Bronek raises his hands in front of his chest, palms open, showing Oskar something invisible, something round, 'it's a long time ago. It's a long story.' He has wound his past into a tight ball, an unpickable knot.

'Tell me.'

'I don't think so.'

'Yes. Tell me.'

'I am sorry, not today.'

'Yes, come,' he indicates a door at the back of the shop. 'We can sit down with some wódka in the store.'

Bronek shivers.

'Thank you, but some other time.' He looks at me; it really is time to go. He holds his hand out to Oskar, 'I am delighted to meet you; you have a good business here.' It's almost a question. Oskar grips his hand, bodily.

'Yes, yes, good enough.' Shrugging off the change of subject and pulling Bronek towards him again says confidentially, in his ear almost, 'I was lucky too, you know.'

'Yes. We are lucky.'

'Why should a Jewish shopkeeper help you? How did he know who you were and that you would be released that night?'

'I don't know why. There are two possibilities, but I am not sure of either of them. It's possible my mother came to the town and arranged it, but she never said so. I know she came to plead with the authorities, perhaps she bribed them. Perhaps she persuaded them in some way she would rather not tell me.

She told me she had brought food and some clothing but I never received any of it, and she was not allowed to see me. The only other explanation I can think of is that this man was related to a student at my college, someone I had helped. If that is so, how he knew I was in prison is a mystery.'

'Who?'

'Who?'

'Yes, who was the student you helped?'

'A Jew, a student.'

'A friend?'

'No. I had no Jewish friends. At the college there was something called the Jewish bench. Have you ever heard of that?'

'No.'

'Most of the students were wealthy sons of Polish gentry and professionals, rich kids. The rest were a few misfits, such as myself, some had scholarships, some people from the army and a number of Jewish students. They kept themselves apart from the rest of the students, they usually worked together in a special part of the laboratory or class at what came to be called the Jewish bench. So in general, the Jewish group of students was referred to as the Jewish bench. Most colleges and universities had them. Anti-Semitism was very strong in Poland, especially among the gentry and the nationalists, but everywhere.

'The wealthier students formed themselves into cliques, which I suppose I was on the periphery of, but I never felt very comfortable in their company even though I envied their status, their class. I changed my mind about that later.'

'What do you mean?'

'Well, later on, in the war, I saw some of these people in a different light. But even at the time, this incident with the Jewish student made me think.'

'What happened?'

'It was an accident of the alphabet. In the laboratory classes we had to work in pairs to perform experiments. In a class at the beginning of a term there was a list of the students who would be working together. I was at the end of the Polish list because my name began with Z. The Jewish bench had a separate list and, naturally, they came after the Polish list. My list had an odd number so I found myself without a partner and the professor asked me to pair with a spare Jewish student, which I did. After the class, one of the Polish students, a member of that smart clique came to me with some advice. First he asked me if I liked having a Jewish assistant to help me with my work. Then, when I wasn't as amused as he thought I should be, he told me I didn't have to accept a Jewish student as a laboratory partner, I could refuse and work alone or ask to have a Polish partner. No one could make me work with a Jew. He puts his hand on my shoulder, you know, the patronising bastard. I thought, why should I do what he wants? That son of a whore always had his own way. So, I refuse him. There was a very nasty row and I was not very popular with the smart set after that, but they were mostly stupid anyway. Rich and stupid.'

I ask about his own anti-Semitism.

He says, 'No, I didn't particularly like the Jews, but I had nothing against this fellow. He was polite and I worked well enough with him. He was quiet but all the Jews at the college kept themselves apart. I found myself defending him by accident, spontaneously, because an overbearing oaf was telling me what to do.

I say, 'Do you remember Oskar's?'

'Who's?'

'Oskar's, the Polish deli on Mare Street?'

'No. What is Mare Street?'

'Where I lived in London. You must remember Oskar's.'

'I don't remember.'

'I took you there once, before you and Jinks went to Rome or somewhere. Oskar nearly fell off his stool when he saw you.'

'What? Why?'

'God, Dad. Don't you remember? He kept shouting, "I was in prison with you, I know you, I know you."'

'Ah, him! He was a very excitable man.'

'Were you in prison with him?'

'Who?'
'Oskar.'
'Oh...maybe, I don't remember.'

— 10 —
Warszawa

I always experience a frisson of excitement as I approach a city however I travel, but approaches by road are special. Even if the roads are new and perhaps built on legs, as they often are these days, there is no disguising the rawness of the edges of a city. The ragged way the countryside gives way to the suburbs as they spread outwards from the centre, engulfing the older order of farms and villages. Cities never recede again, shrinking back towards their hearts, leaving the countryside like a tide ebbing away from the rocks and pools of a shoreline. It is a non-reversible change, a chemical expansion at a fundamental level. With Warszawa, the case is heightened by the relative primitiveness of the surrounding countryside, horses and carts are still a hazard on the roads and the condition of the roads themselves, though improving all the time, is inconsistent, ranging from the too smooth blacktop of the newly repaired sections to cobbles and potholes of the rest.

We make our approach through a dry afternoon in the suburbs, along a road that runs in from the north beside the Vistula. When we are below the Old Town and the Royal Palace we take a random right turn into the city. We manage to extricate ourselves from the traffic and come to rest outside the National Art Gallery in the centre of the city. The big open space and the unfamiliarity are intimidating; we need to collect ourselves, buy a map and generally get our bearings. My excitement is tinged with disquiet about the safety of leaving the car: everyone has warned us about car theft in Warszawa. It could disappear and be across the border into Russia in two or three hours and the police will be unhelpful, obstructive even. Since that first night in Szczecin we have always left the car in guarded car parks, but even that has seemed risky at times.

I deliver the car into the hands of a couple of very doubtful-looking characters in a caravan on a muddy demolition site. I pay them. They fill out a form with the details of the registration, the make etc., in duplicate. They put one copy in the safe, the other in a drawer in an old office desk covered with cups of tea and the remains of a kiełbasa supper. 'Dziękuję. Do widzenia.' That's it; no receipt, no evidence. I walk away with no proof I ever owned a car or brought one into Poland, let alone to this particular part. But so far the car has always been there in the morning and I have developed some trust in this system.

Coming back through Paris on the last leg of this trip, we met a Dutch couple at Pete's flat. They were finishing their journey by train with a small holdall of all their worldly goods. Travelling light, I thought. Not initially it seems.

They had gone to Gdańsk with a nice Volkswagen Golf GTI towing a sailing boat. When they arrived they had put the boat into the parking strzeżony at the marina and gone on to meet their friends who lived in Gdańsk. In the evening they all went out in the car for supper at a restaurant and left it parked on the street. After the meal they emerged from the restaurant to find that the car had been stolen. In the morning he went to the police to report the theft of the car and she went to check on the boat. She arrived at the police station shortly after him to report the theft of their boat. The marina parking had boasted all sort of security devices, cameras and dogs, but they denied any knowledge of the vessel or the owners. The police refused to take statements from them unless they employed an official interpreter, which cost them, and then made them wait all day in the police station on some spurious pretext before they would finally acknowledge the crime at all. Needless to say, there was no chance of recovering the vehicles even though they made it clear they would be prepared to offer a reward. A bribe.

I look at my old car. Who is going to want to steal this? It's right-hand drive. Imponderables. I leave it anyway and we go shopping.

We spend five days in Warszawa. This is a city with a memory.
A city with a history. Like any capital in the heart of Europe,
the successive tides and storms of politics and history have
eroded and periodically destroyed it, but none has been ruined
to the same extent as this city. And no previous destruction
was so complete, so thorough as that of 1944. The story of the
Warszawa uprising should be well known; I didn't know it.

We spent a few days in this city before Bronek told me the
story. We were visiting the Łazienki Palace in the city, one of
the few buildings not demolished by the retreating Germans
when the Russians arrived in 1944. The guide points to holes
drilled in the base of the walls of the palace. Bronek explains
later that these holes were drilled all around the base of the
entire building to take the dynamite which was to blow it up,
but for some unknown reason the charges in this building were
never set and it was spared.

'Of course you know about the Warszawa uprising.'

'No.'

'Mark, what did they teach you at school?'

'Not that.'

So he tells me.

'There was a totally secret army in Warszawa, in all of
Poland actually, during the Nazi occupation. It was called the
Home Army. It was controlled from London by the Polish
government-in-exile but communications were difficult. Many
messages were sent through the BBC in code, there were people
with transmitters and couriers moved across the lines, but you
can imagine that it was not easy. The most extraordinary part
is that a huge highly organised army existed underground,
even with their own bomb and weapon-making workshops.
After the Russians came over to the Allies' side, there was also
a Polish army in Russia made up of the hundreds of thousands
of Poles that had been deported to slave labour camps at the
beginning of the war. Those that had survived, that is. As it
turned out, this army was really subordinate to the Red Army;
its allegiance was to the Soviet Union.

'In 1944 the planned strategy of the Home Army was to rise

up in advance of the Russian front as it pushed the Germans back, and liberate Polish towns before the Red Army got there. The idea was that Poland should be liberated by Poles rather than invaded by Russians.

'You see, it's a very dangerous thing to have a "liberating" army in your country even if they are supposed to be your allies, and especially if they are Russians.'

'This idea did not work. The units of the Home Army were not recognised by the Russians and, even where their actions were successful, they were arrested or ordered to disband once the Russians arrived. Many of them were imprisoned or even executed as anti-communists, but some of the units managed to stay undercover once the Russian front had passed them. The Russians set up a provisional government in Lublin, a Russian puppet of course, and announced that they no longer recognised the London government-in-exile as representing the Polish people. They made it very clear from the outset what their intentions were for Poland. From Hitler they had got half of Poland already, now they were going to take the other half themselves.

'In Warszawa the Home Army prepared to liberate the capital when they knew that the Red Army was near enough. Even though the plan had not worked in other places it was thought to be even more important for the capital to be freed by the Home Army to establish the legitimacy of the goverment-in-exile. When they heard the Russian guns approaching Praga, on the eastern bank of the Wisła, the order would be given for Warszawa to rise, push out the German garrison and hold the city. The uprising was only meant to last for a few days. The Germans were retreating and were not expected to defend Warszawa.

'When they heard the sound of the Russian artillery in Praga the orders were given for the uprising to begin. It was August 1944. Instead of lasting only a few days they had to fight for three months with no food, no ammunition or medical help. Those Russian bastards stopped their advance and waited for the uprising to be crushed. They let the Germans bring back their panzers and those tiger tanks, the automatic ones controlled by wires from the panzers. And they brought back huge reinforcements including Ukrainian conscripts, who were worse than animals. But even so, it took them months of street fighting to force a surrender. All this time the Red Army waited; they gave no help at all, they even denied the Royal Air Force permission to land on Polish soil anywhere in their occupied territory, which was only a few miles away on the other side of the river. It was nearly impossible to fly in weapons, medical supplies or food all the way from the nearest allied territory, Italy, without stopping to refuel. Some did get through but very few. Stalin said that the uprising was a criminal adventure and refused to recognise it as a legitimate military action.

'When the Home Army was finally defeated, Hitler ordered Warszawa to be completely destroyed leaving not one stone on another. That's why the whole city was blown up, the Royal Palace, the medieval market place, churches, palaces everything. Then they left and the Russians walked in. Warszawa and Poland on a plate.'

Two years later, I met my cousin Marylka in a café in Kraków. I didn't know at the time how difficult it was for her to meet me that day.

'How is your father?'

'Mark, please, I cannot talk about it: it upsets me too much,' and she runs for cover to a ladies' toilet door at the back of the little cafe. I know that her father, Edmund, has been ill for some time and she is staying with her parents. He has recently been brought home from hospital. When she comes back I say, 'Marylka, please talk about him if you would like to, if it would help. I have been through this, I am going through it. Really, I would be honoured.'

'Mark, thank you. No, we must talk about something else. Tell me about your work.'

It's an order, but we talk about the Warszawa uprising.

I tell her that I hadn't known the story of the uprising, even when I went there with Bronek. I knew about the city's total destruction but I hadn't known that the Red Army had been sitting on the other side of the Wisła watching as the uprising was crushed and the city was destroyed. I say something like, 'They just sat there while the Germans did their dirty-work for them.'

'It was not so simple, Mark. Who told you that?'

'My dad.'

'Uncle Broniu was a great romantic, like all exiles.'

'How do you mean?'

'Your father left Poland before all this happened. From the outside it is easier to see things in black and white, he can feel more tragic about it, more sentimental.'

'I wouldn't say he was sentimental; he hated sentimentality.'

'He may have hated it but he was Polish and an exile. Poles are romantic; it's in our blood.'

'Is that the same thing? Romantic, sentimental.'

'I don't know, Mark. Both are probably unrealistic. When you are away from something you only remember the good things; it's natural. He had a beautiful memory from nearly sixty years ago, but so many things have happened here since then. The Poland he knew has gone.'

'Except from the memories of the ones that are left. Anyway, does that mean it's not real?'

'Mark, my father is a Jew, not much younger than your father. They are from the same country but their memories are not the same. How could they be?'

'Is the Poland he knew gone, too?'

'There are not many left who remember it. How many Jews do you think there are in Poland today?'

'I don't know.'

'Yes, it is gone; of course it is gone.'

'Anti-Semitism hasn't gone, Marylka. There are neo-fascists in the university; I've seen it with my own eyes.'

In the university hostel where we stay in Warszawa, the walls of the washrooms are daubed with graffiti. I ask Bronek to translate some that appears below a picture of someone's face looking up out of a toilet pan. There is a Star of David on his forehead. I'm alerted to what it might be by the presence of a swastika in the same picture. He looks at it for a moment, 'You don't want to take too much notice of that; it's too stupid.'

'What does it say, though?'

'It says, "If you are constipated, imagine there is a Jew in the toilet."'

'It's our history. Our history is tragic. I hate it too.'

'Well, is it untrue what he told me about the Warszawa uprising?'

'True? What is true? Probably for some of those who fought and for those who died there, it was true. You die for something; it gives it a kind of truth, does it not?'

'And now?'

'Now, it is thought that the uprising was a mistake. It shouldn't have been started when it was because the Red Army had no possibility of getting to Warszawa when the Home Army expected them. The orders were given too soon. The Red Army advance had been halted quite a long way south-east of Warszawa, and by the time Bór-Komorowski, the commander of the Home Army, realised the true situation, it was impossible, or he did not want to countermand his order. The uprising had already begun. There was too little equipment and ammunition for a sustained campaign; its success depended on a rapid victory, and without the threat of the advancing Russian Army this was impossible.

'It was a rebellion of the most extraordinary bravery and courage. Even children took part as couriers and guides through the sewers and basements of the city, but without the Red Army or some other relief, which was denied them, it was hopeless.'

This is not the picture I have at all. 'That's very interesting, but...'

'Mark, you sound like an American.'

'An American?'

'Yes, when Americans don't agree with you, they don't say

you are wrong, they say you have an interesting point of view.'
She is laughing at me.
'I don't feel very American.'
'Do you feel very Polish?'
I was beginning to feel very awkward.
'Not very, but pretty sentimental.'
'You shouldn't worry about sentimentality; the world is made of it.'
'What about the rebuilding of the city after the war, is that a sentimental exercise?'
'It's difficult to say it is any one thing. The city had to be rebuilt because 90 per cent of it was destroyed. The great churches and palaces, everyone wanted these to be restored. They are our past, our culture. But they were not only precious pieces of history, you know. In the uprising they were the battlefields. Sometimes the front lines ran through the nave of a church, or sometimes the Poles had the basement of a building and the Germans had the roof; battles were fought for days on staircases, in kitchens, in the theatres, even through the halls of the Royal Palace. We lost it; yes, with the help of the Russians, we lost it. Now, I think the rebuilding was the last action in that battle, but fought this time against the other enemy, during their occupation.

'Something like this has many aspects. If you ask a younger person, someone of our generation, what they think it means, the rebuilding; they will probably tell you what we already discussed, that it was a way for Poles to re-establish something of their past and that it has the symbolism of the country rising from the ashes of the war. It is a demonstration of the power of people to overcome the worst defeats. This is all good communist propaganda. Then there is the element of defiance; the communists say it was against the Nazis and, by extension, against the west. Westerners say it was an act of purely Polish defiance against the communists. If you ask the older people of Warszawa, they often tell you it is nothing compared to what was destroyed. What has been rebuilt is nothing to be proud of; the old Warszawa is gone for ever.'

Among the rebuilt palaces of the centre of the city, is the
Ujazdowski. Once perhaps the Warszawa residence of the
Ujazdowskis, it now houses a variety of different independent
bodies. There is a theatre group, a literary society and a very
fashionable restaurant, which occupies most of the ground
floor. It is here, on our second evening in Warszawa, that
Marylka takes us for supper. The approach to it is so unlikely
as to make her suddenly uncertain of the way. We turn off
the main road at a major crossroads into a smaller side street,
which is also the entrance to a roadside café. Its clientele,
sprawling outside the building on wooden 'A' frame picnic
tables, get used to us coming and going trying to find our way
to the palace.

'I am certain it is this way; I have been here so often, but I
don't remember it like this.'

I agree that it looks unlikely; the road becomes an unlit
track heading into the wooded park. We try going down this
several times, a little further each time then going back to the
junction again for a kind of reassurance. We try another street,
but Marylka is sure it's wrong, I swing the car around in the
road and we head once more down the track past the café, into
the woods. What I take initially to be a pair of headlights following us, separates and passes one either side of the car. Two
cheap-looking motorcycles, smokey two-strokes, close in front
of us and slow down, slowing me at the same time.

'This is it. Look.' Marylka points over their helmets at the
corner of a building just becoming visible beyond the trees, yel-
lowed by a single lamp.

'Are they the Polish Hell's Angels?'

The motorcyclists stay ahead of us until we pull up beside
the building. It is completely dark outside and dimly lit from
within on the ground floor only. One of the bikes parks across
our bow and the other continues in a half circle round behind
us somewhere in the darkness.

'Shit, it's the police.'

'What do they want?'

One of them taps on my window with a gauntlet.

'Mark, you stay quiet; I will talk to them.' I roll the window down and Marylka starts straight away with, 'Good evening officer. Is this the Ujazdowski Palace?'

He isn't taken in by this; ignoring it, he recites a staccato list. She translates, 'Documents. Insurance. Licence.'

I hand them over, amazed that I have all these things with me.

'He says you turned round, and went the wrong way, in a one-way street.'

'Oh, no. Where?'

My documents must be incomprehensible to him, but he studies them anyway and hands them back one by one.

'Huh, angielski paszport.'

Passport. She keeps a constant dialogue going with him.

'He asks why you tried to run away from them down this track.'

'Oh, God. I didn't...'

'It's okay, Mark. I told him everything.'

He checks my likeness against the passport and produces a black notebook and pen from his breast pocket. A dangerous moment this. She throws herself across me to the window and inserts herself between pen and book, persuading him not to write my ticket. He hesitates, letting her argue, with the pen hovering over the book, but he cannot resist and slowly he lets it sink. Disarmed, he jabs past her in my direction with his pen, then back at her. I can feel her laughing against me; she knows she's won before he does. His eyes roll up into the darkness, he makes a parting shot at her and is gone, leaving my passport on the bonnet of the car.

'He says you are very unlucky.'

'Unlucky? Why?'

'To have such a bad navigator. I persuaded him it was my fault and he should charge me, but I have no driving licence.'

I wonder if all Polish police are so easily led astray, 'You are amazing, Marylka.'

'Yes, am I not?'

I let them go on to get a table while I move the car to the

front of the building where it will be safer, but before I go, I light their way across the broken ground with the headlights. Bronek offers her his arm and they walk on their own elongated shadows away from me. Something in the sight of them springs tears into my eyes: he is proud and flattered by the girl on his arm, his great affection for her is piqued by the old longing for a daughter. I know he can't sleep at night for coughing, that his hand shakes too much to comb his hair, that he's confused about the days of the week sometimes, but her company lifts his spirit and now none of that is evident in his gait. He is still an elegant walker.

In the penumbra of my headlamps his white head is bent politely towards her, her arm tight under his they turn the corner and pass out of the shadow into the floodlights of the façade.

I enter through tall French windows opening directly into a high drawing-room, and recognise the style immediately: bare plaster, metal furniture and a tiled floor. Waiters with black jeans, black hair and black eyes, distinguishable from the diners only by their speed, move balletically over the floor. Curved steel table legs, graphite lines drawn in space and erased white by long folds of cloth hanging over them. Papyrus, tall in big tubs. Opposite the entrance, under a broad gilt overmantle mirror on a long sofa with a wavy back and scrolled arms, reclines, with a cocktail, the starlet. The atmosphere is so dark and granular in here that patches of architecture fade from flood pools to total obscurity, a dusty theatrical black. It is opera, the opening scene of *La Traviata*. It is contrived, austere and exciting and everyone responds, walking more slowly, more self-consciously, holding their smiles longer, loving their imagined audiences. Their moments of intimacy heightened by a sense of voyeurism, couples revel in the semblances of romance. The air is heavy with love. And drama. The curtain is up.

Infected thoroughly by the atmosphere I choose a shadow with the vaguely discernible outline of a doorway within it, diagonally across the room. I square up my shoulders and make my entrance. This is a walk-on part. I have no dialogue but this one chance to shine. I'm a serious romantic. I know where I'm going, I've got the look. I smile with stage subtlety at a girl on the sofa as I pass on my walk into the black hole. Exit Mark, into a narrow-vaulted corridor that seems to lead nowhere. I can't go back, it's not in the score, so I venture on.

I found them eventually in a warren of rooms connected by a maze of corridors and short flights of steps that fill the ground floor. I adventured, and, with Escher-like repetition, emerged endlessly, by various different routes, into what always seemed to be the same chamber through the same doorway. In my disorientation, I imagined the palace as the illogical realisation of Musrum's castle, where all the rooms and halls were built on the outside, making the walls inaccessible and the castle therefore impregnable. I began to feel the rhythm of endless reprise, to assume the meaningless role of the the silent character who repeatedly enters and exits the scenes of a foreign film but has no bearing on the plot. I was lost, caught in a syndrome of recapitulation, a jumping record, until in that same room there were different people and, among them, Bronek and Marylka sit.

He is beaming, bathing in her attention.

'Now, Mark, where have you been? Were you lost?' Is that a hint of disappointment in his voice?

'I was lost. For ever, I thought.' I sit. 'What a place.'

'You like it?'

'I love it.'

'Good. I often bring foreign clients here; they say it has a typically Polish atmosphere.' Marylka works for an American company that invests in Polish industry.

'It must be the pasta.'

'Not the pasta.'

'Why is it typically Polish? I was thinking how easily this could be London or some other European city.'

'Well, that's a start. Warszawa is a European city.'

'But not a typical one.'

'Yes, why not? We have international banks, we have a housing problem, we have street violence, McDonald's, a high crime rate. It's a European city.'

'But its history makes it special, or different at least.'

'Its history defines it as Polish, identifies it as Warszawa.'

'And gives it a typically Polish atmosphere?'

'Yes, maybe. But I live here; it would be like asking me what Warszawa water tastes like, or Warszawa air smells like. They are normal. We are normal, we are European. Ask your father, Uncle Broniu, you are European, Polish, what?'

He pauses.

'European, in general of course. But Polish first.'

'What makes you say Polish first, Dad? You were born in America and you lived most of your life in Britain. In fact, you only lived in Poland for eighteen years.' He knows I'm winding him up.

'Only eighteen years?' He can't believe it.

'Most of that was in the Ukraine.'

'Ah no, this was Poland, Mark. You know that Poland has moved.'

'Only the frontiers have moved, Broniu. Some people would say it is where it always was.'

'His Holiness says so; he is Polish, he should know.' Sarcasm, uncharacteristic of Bronek.

'What? He should know better?'

'No, that is unfair. He came to Poland and said these things when the Russians were still here. In those times, what he said meant something different. You could say then that Poland was where it always was: it was nowhere. Except in our memories.'

'In our hearts, Broniu.'

He shrugs.

'What did he actually say?'

'I don't remember exactly now.'

'Were you there, Marylka?'

'Yes I was there. It was in the eighties at the time when Solidarność was the hope of all Poland. The park outside

Kraków was full of people who came to see him. It was an extraordinary day for Poland.'

'I read somewhere that he asked a child where Poland was, then he put his hand over her heart and said it was there, in the heart.'

'I didn't know he did that, but of course I know the story.'

'What story?'

'It's from Polish literature, a drama by Wyspiański called, *Wesele, The Wedding.* It's a romantic story set in 1900 in a village near Kraków. There was a fashion among the Kraków intelligentsia during the partitions of marrying peasant girls. At the wedding the bride recounts to a poet a dream that she was taken by the devil in a golden coach to look for Poland. She doesn't understand, she thinks they are already in Poland. The poet tells her that if you looked all over the whole world you will not find it, but, he says, "Put you hand below your breast, what do you feel there?"

"A pleat of my dress."

"No, your heart. Your heart is Poland." His holiness was paraphrasing Wyspiański. In the context of Solidarność, maybe he is saying the equivalent of: render unto Caesar that which is Caesar's, but keep Poland in your hearts. Appropriately biblical, revolutionary but pacifist.'

'Isn't that rather a sentimental view? I mean, you say the Russians were here and Poland was nowhere, as though there was a biblical enslavement; but wasn't Jaruzelski Polish? Weren't the people in government Poles? They weren't all Russians, surely?'

'They were the party men. And they are still here: many of the same officials still work in the government. The army still has the same generals as before "independence" and they were all Soviet trained. There was no real Polish officer training school here. But now the party itself has gone.'

Our soup arrives and we start.

Bronek grunts, 'Career politicians.'

'And the apparatchiks, the nomenclatura. The party gave them power and therefore money and influence. They will hang on to what they can. Now they are in business on their own account, saying they always hated the Russians.'

'Can't they be got rid of?'

'How? Who will do that? There has been enough "getting rid of". There has been a revolution here: we are no longer a client state of the Soviet Union. The old ideology which came from there has gone, even though some of the same people still have power.'

'And, apart from history and the old guard, who will design independent Poland?'

'There is no one view of what a country should be, or of where its frontiers should be drawn. In Britain you are lucky to have the sea on all your borders. In central Europe, identity is a different matter; it should come from the centre but unfortunately in our case the strongest influences have come from outside for a long time. That single fact is the most important in Polish identity and consciousness. Nationalism is strongest in repression, pushing our identity at these times into the realm of the spiritual. It is not a coincidence that our strongest personalities have been religious leaders and that Catholicism has become inseparable from the most general definition of Polishness.'

'Patriotism.' Bronek says into his bowl. 'Patriotism, not nationalism.'

'You are not a nationalist, Broniu?'

'No, I was a patriot. It's not a popular word today, old fashioned. Nationalism has taken over. It may be good to be a nationalist when there is no physical nation, then nationalism could include the patriot. But nationalism with the nation and an army is the most dangerous thing on earth. It is responsible for all war. Patriotism is generous in the extreme, nationalism the opposite. That is my humble opinion.'

'And therefore worthless, Dad.' That old chestnut.

'Exactly, Mark.'

'Is that why you can say you are Polish first? Because you are a patriot.'

'Everyone has a country; mine is Poland.'

Not everyone, I think, at least not so certainly, but this is a red herring. 'Even when you are not there.'

'That makes no difference.'

'Mark, your father is Polish because he was born a Pole and he feels himself a Pole: in his language, his religion, all that. It doesn't matter where he lived or that he was not here while something was happening. He is Polish. He could be a communist, a Roman Catholic, a Jew, even an atheist, though that's rare, and still be Polish.'

'Why are atheists so rare, Marylka? And what about you?'

'What about me? I have faith, yes. I believe in God.'

'Which God?'

'Oh, Mark. What are you saying? There is only one.'

'Sorry, silly of me. I mean, which religion?'

'Catholic, of course.'

'You don't feel yourself Jewish. Your father is Jewish, isn't he?'

'Yes, but I was brought up a Catholic and I go to Catholic church. Poland is mostly Catholic now. Broniu, you are Catholic, are you not?'

'Yes.'

'But lapsed, aren't you, Dad?'

'Lapsed? What is lapsed?' A religious state unknown in Poland.

'I am not lapsed.'

'You are lapsed: you don't attend Mass and make confession.'

'No, I don't, but I am not lapsed.'

'Mark, please. What is lapsed?'

'Lapsed is when someone stops going to church, when they no longer believe.'

'Do you believe, Broniu?'

He takes his time over this and finally is unable to commit himself, 'There is room for God.'

'You said that before, sometime. What do you mean?'

'Ah, I don't know, Mark. I have seen things which made me certain there can be no God, and what I have seen is nothing beside what has been seen, I know that. But, sometimes when there was nothing else to do, I felt there was room for God.' He shrugs again.

'You used to say, you didn't believe in anything.'

'No, I never said that.'

I hear an imaginary cock crowing.

'You did.'

'I don't think so.'

'Dad, you...doesn't matter.' But somehow it does matter. Not enough to hear the third crowing, but it does matter. I used to draw some strength from what I always thought was his atheism. I remember asking him what happened when you die, is there life after death? 'How can there be life after death? That makes no sense. You live until you die.' I was charmed by the simplicity of it. How obvious.

'And you, Mark. What do you believe?'

What do I believe?

'Well, I don't have any faith, but I think I recognise the existence, the importance of spirituality as one of the essential parts of life. I don't think there is a God as such but...'

'Mark, too complicated. What is that?'

'What?'

'That must be English religion. You must always be there, but not there. You must always be pulling out the threads to see how the carpet is woven.'

'Isn't Catholicism more complicated?'

'No, not complicated. You believe or you do not.'

'But how can you believe something and not want to understand it.'

'You have faith.'

'Well, I don't have faith, but I still want to understand. I am interested.'

'In the spirit only?'

'Isn't it possible to be spiritual, or at least to acknowledge its existence and not have faith?'

'In Scotland maybe. Here, not really. You are an old hippy.'

'Scotland is full of old hippies; it's their last redoubt.'

'The last doubt? What is that?'

'Mark will always pull your leg.'

'Pull my legs?'

Bronek explains in Polish and they continue, probably where they left off when I arrived, while I eat my pasta, cold. Bronek has already finished his. 'Eat while your food is hot, Mark. You can still talk when your belly is full.'

— 11 —
Fyodor

We did a lot of eating in Warszawa and many of my memories of the city are connected with food. Most afternoons would find us in the vicinity of the Stare Miasto, the old city, sitting outside a café or in a restaurant. Stare Miasto, meaning, the Old Town is a misnomer, for it is new. It is the reconstructed area around the medieval market square, it was the first part of the city to be rebuilt in the 1960s, the old centre of Warszawa and one of the centres of the uprising. When we came in 1970 only the square itself had been completed and one or two of the small streets around it. The Royal Palace, now completely restored, was then a heap of rubble behind a fence. These buildings, and those of the part known as the New Town, which was the baroque part, have been painstakingly reinstated using photographs, people's memory and even the paintings of Canaletto as reference. It's a remarkable feat of love and of remembering. Around the central part, which contains these rebuilt areas, is a concrete, Stalinist nightmare. Modern Warszawa.

One lunchtime, after a visit to the Royal Palace, we walk towards the Old Town looking for somewhere to have lunch. We are both exhausted by the visit and I am anxious that Bronek has overdone it. The palace is a magnificent reconstruction and he was keener than I to see everything, but now he looks grey in the face and makes obvious blowing noises as we walk. I suggest more or less the first place we come to, a very modest looking café at the entrance to an alley with tables set outside on the pavement in the mouth of the passage. He collapses on to a rickety garden chair that is surely a survivor of the destruction. He doesn't look well at all.

'Are you all right?' Silly question I know.

'Ah, Mark. You get me something to drink.'

'What?'

'Oh, a beer.' His voice is light and far away, saying the first thing he can think of just to get rid of me.

I find my way in through one of the identical glazed wooden panels doubling as a door that make up the corner of the building. Very French. I meet the waiter on his way out to us. It's not busy and he has seen us arrive and now follows me back outside to our table. Bronek has moved to a less unstable seat, one with arms that faces the sun, and is leaning back in it with his eyes closed. His old face is relaxed, his jaw slack and his mouth slightly open, hands flopped off the armrests, fingertips resting on his thighs. He doesn't move when I scrape a chair away from the table.

'Oh Jesu...' The alarm in the waiter's voice behind me alerts me to just how grey he looks in the sunlight, just how still he is. In the very instant the thought is crystallising in my mind, his great lids hinge open. In his eyes, once they bring us into focus, I can see he understands the shock he reads in our faces.

'Ah, I was dead asleep.'

The waiter, full of concern and relief, asks a barrage of questions, which Bronek answers as amiably and patiently as he can, then he hurries away.

'Where's he gone?' I couldn't follow any of their exchange, I wonder if he has gone for a doctor or even an ambulance.

'No no, Mark. Everything is quite all right. He recommends sweet tea, soup and then trout with almonds.'

'What?'

'Yes, and he says if I don't feel better after the tea he will call us a taxi.'

I pull my chair up beside his, 'How do you feel now?'

'What do you think? I am an old man, I am tired.'

'Not surprising, I'm tired too.' The colour is returning to his face; he lifts it back towards the sun.

'Marvellous palace though, Dad.'

'Marvellous palace, Mark.' He turns and smiles at me as

though at some private joke. Why shouldn't it be? I can't resist
putting my arm across his shoulders, patting the further one.
It's a reflex; this is how I embrace my own children, with patting. Now my sons are as tall as me and the embracing is
scarcer, but they pat me too. Our hugs are accompanied by
the sound of muffled flappings, gorilla noises. The more I pat
him, the more I miss my children. I look away through the passage to the cathedral of St John, across the street and opposite
the far end of it. Thank God, I think. Thank God. Another
reflex.

The tea arrives and the waiter chats to Dad making sure he's
feeling better, that the tea is all right and he's warm enough.
Somewhere in there Bronek orders me a beer and somewhere
else he introduces me as his son. I stand up and shake hands
with the waiter, Jan, but my attention has been caught by some
activity at the other end of the alley. A string quintet is setting
up, framed in the narrow opening against the sunlit wall of the
church behind them. Three women and two men, in their mid-
twenties as far as I can tell from this distance, with the excep-
tion of one of the cellists, a woman, whose hair is greying. She
has a folding stool, chrome and black plastic and they all have
music stands of the usual pattern.

'Ah, muzycy.' Musicians, 'Dobrze, dobrze.' Jan retires to
fetch our soup rubbing his hands with pleasure.

They start tuning up, rubbing rosin on their bows and exer-
cising, practising passages of runs and trills then stopping to
fine tune with pizzicato pluckings. The first violin is the last
to stop, octaves on A going down to the lowest, then a stroke
of the bow here and there until she is satisfied. They all stand
silent for a few moments then with exact synchronisation lift
their instruments. The leader bobs three, four...

'Ah, Schubert...' Bronek is full of surprises today.

The accoustics of the alleyway are astonishing, amplifying
the sound and carrying it to us with almost the same volume
and clarity as if we were sitting beside them. Bronek closes his
eyes bathing in the warmth of the afternoon; the music washes
over him. It is so clear, so sharp I can hear the naked woody

sound of the bows on the strings and occasionally a hoarse
intake of breath at the beginning of a phrase, as though it was
to be sung and not played.

Jan the waiter reappears on tiptoe with soup and bread, plac-
ing them so silently on the table Bronek is not aware of their
arrival until he has gone again. He could have been asleep and
only woken by his stomach responding to the smell of mushroom soup. We eat as quietly as we can. Half-way through the
soup, he says, 'Ah, there is "The Trout".'

'Where?' I look for Jan.

'Now, Mark. In the music. There is a reference to "The
Trout". You know, Schubert's Piano Quintet, "The Trout".'

'You're going to ask me what I learnt at school in a minute.'

'What?'

The music suddenly starts to come apart, the violins stop,
leaving the cello and finally the viola playing a few hesitant
notes on its own. Two policemen have become mixed up with
the players and I have the impression they are being physically
rough with them.

'Oh no, that's too bad.'

'The bastards!'

'Mark, moderate your language.'

There is a prolonged argument at the end of the alley, even
passers-by get involved, but authority in uniform has its way
and disbands the ensemble. As we are finishing our soup, the
two policemen make their way along the passage towards the
restaurant. One of them looks at his watch; I see them over
my soupspoon decide it must be their lunch break. Perhaps the
smell of mushroom soup, amplified by the narrowness of the
space, has worked on them too. They remove their hats as they
get to the tables and sit at one near ours. Jan, who has seen the
departure of the musicians disappears inside, turning his back
in an obviously impatient manner. A moment later he is back
with our fish.

'Schubert's Trout with Almonds,' I say.

Bronek translates this for the benefit of Jan and the officers.
The policemen call the waiter over. I see them pointing at

our lunch and Bronek's grunts supress a laugh at Jan's retort. The police put their caps back on and leave.

'What did he say?'

'He said there will be no more Schubert Trout. It's a shame to kill a harmless fish.'

'I thought I heard him say, szkoda.'

'You have learnt something today.'

Schubert's trout, even without accompaniment, is delicious. The last half hour of sunshine illuminates the mouth of the passage, just enough time for a cup of coffee.

The next morning I sense that Bronek has an agenda for the day already in mind. His conversation over breakfast in our room at the university hostel is not a series of questions accompanied by the folding and unfolding of city plans, finding routes to castles or museums, but about other things: worries about the condition of the car, trivia. It's not the usual question of what we shall do for the day. He already knows.

'Now, Mark, today we go to the National Gallery.' So we go.

At the gallery I follow him up to the first floor; he pokes his head into several rooms, taking in the paintings in a single sweep then moving on. The rooms are mostly full of portraits and of little interest to me, so I am content to follow him despite wondering a little at his technique. I hear an American accent in my head saying we'll have done the National Gallery before lunch. At about the third or fourth of these repetitions, he stops at the threshold, 'Aha, here it is.' He has found what he was looking for: *The Battle of Grunwald*, Jan Matejko's biggest painting.

It is a big painting, the biggest painting on canvas I have ever seen. It is done on the model of the great Italian battle paintings of the Renaissance, of cramming the whole canvas full of warriors and horses writhing in a forest of spears and lances. In the centre, buoyed up on a wave of straining pikemen, the victorious general in a golden breastplate wields a tremendous sword. I leave him for half an hour with a booklet about the painting. There is a line drawing of the painting on the front of it with a number on every head. Inside, a list goes on for pages.

Leaving the gallery Bronek says, 'What do you say we go to see Jan? I fancy another of his trouts.'
'Schubert's Trout. Will it be as good a second time?'
'We will never know unless we try it.'
'Maybe the musical accompaniment will be there too.'
'I hope so.'
But they are not when we arrive, and after enquiring of a different waiter if Jan is there, we are disappointed to discover that he will be working that evening and not on the lunchtime shift.
'Ah, never mind. How is the trout today?'
'Bardzo dobry.' Very good.
We sit ourselves outside again, with a beer. Though still sunny, today's sun has not the same strength as yesterday's.
'Are you warm enough Dad; it's not as warm today?'
'I am not so tired.' He does look much better.
'Marvellous painting, Dad.'
'Marvellous painting, Mark.' He pats my arm and smiles.
We sip our freezing beer.

Sometime during the onion soup I ask if he is up to continuing the story of the night he was released from prison. I think for a while he hasn't heard me, or that perhaps he would rather not but is too polite to refuse.
'You don't have to, it doesn't matter.'
There is still no response. In some discomfort I carry on with my soup. He finishes his first.
'Very good soup. Now Mark, when you finish yours, we go inside.'
Inside, the restaurant is layed out in half a dozen booths, highbacked benches stand out from the walls on either side of small tables. Any of them would be a squash for more than four people at a time. The corner opposite the door is taken up with a bar, behind which is the entrance to the kitchen.

At first it's dark inside, out of the sunlight but gradually the interior reveals itself. A nod has been made in the direction of old Polish hunting parties with pictures of bears and wolves but there is also a 1960s juke box and we have a plastic check tablecloth. The mixture is not unpleasant and the atmophere is homely, if your home is as untidy as mine.

We wedge ourselves into a booth to wait for the trout.

Without preamble, Bronek says,

'We slept in a cold store at the back of a Jewish shop. It was a tiny room and very cold. I told you, it was the winter, December 1939.'

'Who was the other man with you?'

'I don't know who he was; he told me his name but nothing more than that. He was very frightened that he would be re-arrested, he was sure he had made a mistake coming with me but what else could he do, he had nowhere else to go. He was frightened of the Jews. In this part, after the Russian invasion, many of the Jews became powerful people. Their situation in the Russian partition and after the First War persuaded many Jews to become communists. You have heard of the Bund? It was a Jewish communist movement which was one of the groups who later formed the Mensheviks, more moderate than the Bolsheviks. They believed, understandably, that in a socialist world things would be better for them, they would not be segregated, the pogroms would cease, they would be able to own property anywhere, and persecution would end. So when the Russians came, many secret groups of communists appeared, ready to take charge of local government and civilian organisations. Many of these groups had Jews in them or were all Jewish. Not only that, there were Jewish regiments in the Red Army too.

'So he thought he had jumped out of one hornets' nest into another. I don't know really anything about the man who rescued us. He maybe had nothing to do with the communists, not everyone did. In fact the arrival of the Bolsheviks in Poland split the Jewish community. The communists were of course atheistic, which was anathema to the orthodox Jews. There were as many shades of Judaism in Poland before the war as there was Christianity; it's a mistake to think they were just one thing, one group. There was everything from peasants to millionaires, from the orthodox conservatives to the international communists.

'In the morning we were let out sometime about six o'clock. I shook his hand, wished him luck and set off south towards Różniatów, my home. I had no money so I didn't know how I was going to get there. I didn't know how dangerous were the roads.

'When I got to Różniatów, I had to be extremely careful approaching the house. I had no idea what the situation would be when I got there, I wasn't sure there would be anyone there at all. For all I knew they may have already had to leave, or... well who knows. I left the main road half-way between Kałusz and Dolina and walked south through the fields to Różniatów. I knew the country perfectly, I could have found my way home in the dark. I spent my youth, hunting, fishing in the River Łomnica, wandering in the forests there. Beautiful country. It is flat until you get to the village, then some low wooded hills start to the west and south. I circled round to that side, the west, into these hills and approached the houses from the cover of the trees. The church and the priest's house were built side by side at the foot of the first of these hills on the western edge of the village. It had been flattened off maybe fifty feet above the level of the streets giving it an elevated view and prominent position, not very convenient for someone trying to be inconspicuous.'

'How did you get there from Tarnopol?' The question I wish I had asked him but never did. I have asked others since how people travelled then, what the roads or the trains were like. I don't know how he made the journey or how long it took.

I waited in the woods, watching the house to get an idea of what was happening. I knew I couldn't wait too long because it was so cold, certainly I couldn't stay out overnight without some shelter. If it looked too dangerous to come to the house I would have to be away from there before night time and before the temperature dropped too much. I would have to find a barn, somewhere warm to sleep. I knew a few places not too far away.

I sat in the cover of some bushes to the south of the church, it was not a good view of the house which was beyond it, but I couldn't risk being seen. If everything seemed all right I decided I would wait as long as possible into the evening before going to the door. Otherwise, if what I see means they have gone, I must be gone too, as soon as possible.

I am spying on my own home, playing the game I rehearsed a thousand times as a child. I picture the soup on the table in the kitchen that would have waited for me at the end of those games, and my stomach heaves. My mother was always cooking. Does she know I'm here, waiting? Is she making soup? There is blue woodsmoke in the chimney, but anyone can make a fire. I feel sick with nauseous hunger, I start to shiver. Time drags, but there is no movement from the house. Worse than bad news, there is no news. I need to move, it is getting dark and I am cold. I need to be going if I have to.

I creep back into the woods in a state of such melancholy, such unbearable dejection. My intimate knowledge of it, of each dip and hillock in the path I follow away from the village, fills me with resentment at its theft. I am stealing myself away, I the stolen. At the same time I know the wood is by nature neutral, and unmoved by those who lay claim to its possession. But it is secretive and complicated, and must conceal me. On a familiar path, one raced over by my younger feet, one lingered on with village girls, I fall into a trap of longing. Tumble into the black pit of morbid self-pity. I want to die rather than be torn away from here and I imagine myself dead in these woods, undiscovered, dissolving, decaying into the earth. Green shoots will push their way from my mouth and eyes in the spring, a sapling grows from my belly. I feel it there like a knot of hunger, a knot of emptiness, a concentration of the void. And I stop. I groan. I cannot go on. The light is dying in the afternoon, my breath comes in clouds, the bark of the beeches and the oaks is coal black. Crows caw grey and black.

Turning my face toward home, my fear wells up. I admit it, I welcome the beating wings flapping terror in my breast and like a ten-year-old in the dark, I start to run. I fly to the edge of the wood, breaking cover at full speed, tearing along the back fence of the church, water streams from my eyes, steam from my throat pumping to the back door. The catch in my hand, the door yielding, my body collapses into the passage.

'Mamo.' I see her upside down.

'Broniu?'

'Tak. Yes, it is me.'

'Oh, Broniu. Serwus kochanie. Thank God, thank God, Jesus, Maria.' Calling all the saints she smothers me, 'Thank God they let you go.'

She takes me to the kitchen, to the stove, to the heat. Thaw me, melt the ice in my limbs. I curl up on the tiled oven like a cat in the sun. I curl up...

'Now Broniu, you are so thin, look at you, so thin.' She admonishes my carelessness, 'You must eat something before you starve to death. You are hungry, Broniu?'

All well-being for her is to be found in food. She takes soup from the big pot on the stove, bread from the crock in the larder and some sausage, sets them on the table. 'Come Broniu, eat.' She watches me weep into my dish, 'Thank God they let you go.'

'Thank God.'

'Now we must hide you before anyone knows you are here.'

'Why?'

'Broniu. We have a Russian officer in the house.'

'What?'

'Yes, an army officer is staying here, a comrade lieutenant.'

'Why?'

'There is a small garrison in the village and the officers don't stay with the men. Some others have them too.'

'Christ! Is he here now?'

'No, no, but he will come soon, in an hour maybe.'

'Then I cannot stay here; it is too dangerous.'

'No, Broniu. You can stay, but we must hide you.'

'But where?'

'Tonight you stay in the house. Tomorrow we will look for somewhere less dangerous.'

'I will go out tonight, and come back again tomorrow.'

'No, Broniu. Stay here tonight; it will be more dangerous outside. There are patrols and a curfew. Really, you will be safer here. He will never know you are in the house.'

I look at my soup, onions, potato, mushrooms, herbs. Food I planted in the spring, or gathered from the woods in the autumn. I cannot go out again tonight.

'If you say so.'

'I say so, Broniu.'

'Where is Father Michał? And Hanusia?'

'Hanusia helps with the school; the teacher has been taken away. She will be home soon. Father Michał is here.' She points upstairs. 'Broniu, he is sick. You know he is not well anyway, now he is worse. The Bolsheviks hate the church, they have no faith, he will be sent away. Already he has been forbidden to say Mass in the church, but people come to the house to see him and he hears confession. It is only a matter of time until he has to leave.'

'What will you do?'

'I will go with him. What else can I do?'

'I don't know. Go back to Brzozowa?'

'No, Broniu. He needs me; I cannot leave him. You know that.'

Yes, I did know that.

'Come, you must see him and then I will make a bed for you in the roof next to my room.'

I sleep until the middle of the following day, and, lying with the roof timbers an arm's length above my face, I listen to the sounds of the house. The muffled indecipherable cadences of my mother's voice as she talks to Father Michał filter through the house like an old folk song. I don't want to understand the words or be complicated by them, only to be comforted by the rhythm.

Eventually, the perfect comfort of my repose begins to bother me. I cannot pretend that I can stay here indefinitely; there is a war. But I say to myself, just a few days, just a few days.

When I am sure there is no one in the house I creep downstairs. Replaying another childish game, of creeping to the door when I should be asleep, peering into a narrow vertical slice of their secret lives through the quarter-inch gap between door and jamb. There was very rarely anything to be seen, only the unchanging view of a section of the pine cupboard and half the stove. Occasionally someone would pass across my visible column, but conversation, that invaluable scource of information, revealed more than a wider perspective ever could have done. Some things I learned this way I wish I had not, but mostly the world I thought I knew was confirmed by what I heard.

'Did you find somewhere else for me yet?'

'No, Broniu. It is not easy. It is most difficult to ask this of the people you trust.'

'Because it is dangerous.'

'Yes, because it is dangerous.'

'Don't ask anyone, even asking is dangerous: it could give us away. I will have to go.'

'Where? What will you do?'

'I will have to fight.'

'How? There is no war here; it is over for us.'

'Mamo, it is not over, even for you. Less for me. I was not mobilised in Lwów, I don't know why, but maybe my unit is still there.'

'They will not be there, Broniu. Most people, young men, have been taken, as you were.'

'Then I will find another way. Maybe I will go to Romania.'

'It is not safe there, Broniu. Our government have all been put in prison. The Romanians are frightened of the-Bolsheviks.'

'Well, I don't know. I don't know what to do.'

'Broniu, I will ask in the village. I know that people are leaving. Polish people. I don't know how or where they go, but I notice that they disappear. I ask and no one will tell me, but I know.'

A new idea strikes her, 'There are partisans in the mountains.'

'They are Ukrainians, Mamo. They are fighting a different war. I am their enemy.'

'Ach so, I will ask Poles.'

'Be careful who you ask.'

'Broniu, I am an old woman whose son is supposed to be in prison. I will ask. What difference will it make to talk to me?'

'Not so old.'

'Old enough not to worry for myself. Old women are of little interest to the Bolsheviks; we are the only people they are not interested in. But you, Anna and Michał are.'

'I haven't seen Hanusia yet. Is she all right?'

'Broniu, I haven't told her you are here. She will never forgive me, but it will be easier for her if she doesn't know.'

I don't know what to say to this. She is right: knowledge incriminates, knowledge is dangerous. But it means that I can't see her, and I have one more person to hide from.

'Now Broniu, go and speak to Father Michał, I must cook and soon you will have to get back in the roof.'

As I am leaving the kitchen she says, 'Broniu, you do not have to fight. You can stay here; we will find a way to keep you.'

'They will not let any Poles stay here, you know that. No one wants to fight, but what else can I do? Lie down and go back to prison? No, I'd rather fight; there is more chance that way.'

I pass an hour with Father Michał in his study then repair to my mother's room. I lay down on her bed, unwilling to crawl through the low door into the loft space behind the wall along one side of the room. The winter sun in the afternoon intensified by the window panes, hot and soporific falling across her bed, folds me into a deep confusing sleep. I am still exhausted. I sink into sleep gratefully. It is still a place of comfort, still a refuge.

'Bronisław Zygadło.' Someone is shaking me, 'Bronisław Zygadło, wake up. Come, wake up.'

I am holding the reins of a horse, calling her name, 'Basia, Basia...,' looking up at her rearing head. Her eye, a blue film over the black pupil is rolled down, she looks at me unknowingly, in panic.

'Bronisław, get up.'

I must not let her go, her head far above me, the rein pulls over her head and I feel her hooves treading on my chest, 'Basia, be quiet,' but she rears higher. Someone is calling me from behind, but I can't turn to look, I mustn't let her go.

'Bronek, come on, wake up.'

She seems to be losing her strength, I pull her down by the rein. She turns her head in front of me and her right eye is close to my face, swivelling backwards, dark brown in the corner with fine black naked skin around it. But what is this? A white flash under the forelock. I don't understand; that shouldn't be there. That means it's not Basia, it's not her after all, 'It's not Basia, let her go...'

'What?'

'What?'

'Wake up now, Bronek.'

I roll trying to unravel myself. The sun is gone from the window, there is a lamp in the room. I have been asleep too long. Something is nagging me to think. Think of what?

'Bronisław,'

That voice.

'Who are you?' But I know who it is even before I see the uniform.

'I am Fyodor Andreyevich.'

How could I be so stupid. I am a complete failure, caught on the first day at home. Asleep.

'Ah, comrade Lieutenant.'

'Call me Fyodor, please.'

'Fyodor.'

'Good. Your mother tells me you play chess, Bronek. May I call you Bronek? Polish names are unnecessarily long, don't you think?'

'Yes, I play chess.' Why does he want to play chess? Is this some kind of a joke? I pull myself up into a sitting position, trying to arrange my confused thoughts. I have no idea where to begin.

'Please don't worry, we will play and decide what to do with you.'

'What do you mean?'

'Well, Bronek. You cannot stay here, but, equally, I cannot pass the opportunity of playing chess with someone who can play, not just move the pieces about, you understand. I am told you enjoy the game.'

'Yes, but...'

'Good, please come to my room when you are ready. I will set out the pieces.' And he leaves.

My first inclinaton was to jump out of the window and run away, in fact I cannot tell you why I didn't. I got up, I washed, went to the kitchen.

'Go, play chess with him. He is not a bad man.' She shoos me out. I kiss my sister, Hanusia. 'Go, I will talk to you later.'

On the table in what used to be my room is a chess board, a bottle of wódka and a lamp. He welcomes me politely and apologises for the inconvenience of his presence, generally in the country and particularly in the house. He tells me he is from Leningrad, a beautiful city, he says, a cultured place. Now he feels lonely and far from home, and is looking forward to some intelligent company. He has recently qualified as a lawyer. He snorts, 'A lawyer, imagine that, the law is in uniform. Well, while on duty at least.' He has removed his great coat and tunic and has on a Russian woollen high-necked shirt, the kind a peasant would wear.

He pours me a glass of wódka, 'Your health, Bronek.'

'Na zdrowie.'

'Now, Bronek, you be white. I cannot be white. I am Red, or black in this case.'

'Very well.'

He has an irresistible confidence about him and though he appears to be no more than my age, he has about him an air of greater maturity, a worldliness that allows him to be light hearted about our situation. Calculated, I suspect, to put me at my ease, it has the opposite effect. I am constantly anxious that this impossible scenario will disintegrate as soon as I begin to trust it, and that once I am used up as a new plaything, I will be disgarded.

He pours more wódka. 'Russians make bad wódka; the best is Polish. That is why the Russian is such a bad drunk. The quality of his inebriation is all baseness, animal. Polish drunkenness is a spiritual affair, a revelation.'

'Na zdrowie.'

'Na zdrowie comrade. Now, let us play the Royal, I beg your pardon, the People's Game.'

From the opening moves, he takes control of the board. He plays with mathematical vision but with an idiosyncratic elegance. I am taken in early in the game by a clever decoy, persuaded into throwing forward an attack and unwittingly exposing my Queen, which he removes.

'Fyodor, may I ask you something?'

'Certainly, Bronek, ask.'

'You have me at a disadvantage; I wish to know if we are playing something more serious than a game, if anything depends upon the outcome of it.'

'What could be more serious than chess?'

'You know what I mean.'

'You are too direct, comrade, you lost your Queen that way. Careless.'

'I am a little rusty; I haven't been able to play for a while.'

'You couldn't play in Tarnopol?'

How does he know that? I stare at the board unable to see my next move.

'Come, Bronek, you have lost your concentration, you started so well but for a momentary lapse.'

'I am a little preoccupied.'

'Of course, how silly of me. How can I expect you to play an intelligent game with the question of your fate hanging over you.'

'It is distracting.'

'Quite.' He leans back from the board, spreading his hands, 'but all life is here, there are no excuses.'

He pours another wódka and sighs at my silence. 'Very well. We are both pawns in this game, Bronek. I have nothing to gain by your re-arrest, and no desire to think up some reason for it. The truth is you are not a fugitive, nor are you wanted by the police at the moment. But you are Polish and soon all the Poles will be deported or resettled. There will be none left in the Ukraine. You should avoid being caught in that process and you are right to be circumspect. So, this would be a good time for you to leave, before anyone knows you have been here. You know what the police can be like. Tomorrow, will be soon enough. Things will only get more difficult here. Your family and the priest will be sent to Poland I expect. Your sister may be given the choice because she is young. You should advise her to go to Poland.'

'This is Poland.'

'Come, come, Bronek. Do we have to fight the war here too? I am not a sentimentalist like my comrades. I am a lawyer. Possession is what counts not their ridiculous dialectic. This was Poland for a while, now it is the Soviet Union.'

'What is so sentimental about the way your comrades behave?'

'The way they behave is irrelevant; they are animals. They have been persuaded to believe in an idea, to feel sure of it, and most important, to take comfort from it, when it is in fact a lie. A very transparent one. It doesn't matter to them that it is a lie so long as they feel sure, it must be felt. Sentimentality. If it was half true, you could call it romanticism. But this, this international brotherhood, comrade this and comrade that, all men equal. Where? I ask you? It is a blatant lie.' He pauses to pour another wódka for us both. Surely he has gone too far. 'The fascists are as bad: Aryanism, the Thousand Year Reich, the master race. A huge sentimental idea, disgustingly sentimental. Those great surging tunes of that Richard Wagner, he is a monster. Love in his operas is a heartless thing, all flames and swords. Ah, Bronek, I am sorry. The world is gone mad.'

Another wódka.

'I feel sorry for you Poles. You are the filling in a sandwich, as they call it in England: you know, two slices of bread with some sausage in the middle. You are the source of taste, the thing of interest suffocating between slabs of sentimental dough.'

'I know sandwiches. I was born in America.'

'America? How exotic. Good, then perhaps we should eat one together later?'

'I don't think so.'

'Ah, Bronek, you have every reason to be contemptuous. In theory I am your enemy, but in practice I assure you, I am not. Here, have another drink.'

'I don't know what to make of you, Fyodor.'

'That's better, Na zdrowie.'

'Na zdrowie.'

'What are you doing here? If you believe what you say, what are doing in the army?'

'I am a pawn, as you are. I am a Russian pawn. I love my country, as you love yours, I suppose, and we have little choice. History drives us on.'

'You are sentimental after all.'

'Oh no, to love one's country is natural, is it not?'

'To love Poland, or to love Russia?'

'What is the difference?'

'You have just described the difference to me. Bolshevik ideology is a lie, in fact.'

'Communism is not Russia. It is still natural for a Russian to love his country. Anyway, the Tsars were no better, you should know that.'

'You are lying down with dogs, Fyodor, when you get up you will have fleas.'

'You are typically sanctimonious. It is the privilege of the underdog I suppose, and a talent among Poles. But twenty years ago, when Poland was re-forming itself, you had no scruples about invading this very spot. Piłsudski was not bothered by his conscience on his march to Kiev or Wilno. Worse, if

Dmowski had succeeded, you would be another fascist state, of pure slavs, whoever they might be, all of whom would have loved their country.'

'These territories were Polish. They were being reclaimed.'

'They were Polish a hundred and fifty years ago. We have had Napoleon in Moscow since then.'

'I wish he had stayed. You wouldn't be here now.' I am becoming churlish.

'Bronek, no one wishes that. If he was in Moscow, he would also be in Warszawa. The wind blows from the east. It can take a strong wind one week to cross all of Russia, then only a day to blow from Moscow to Paris. You cannot conquer Russia by poking Moscow with a stick. We waited, and the wind just blew him away.'

How infuriating he is. I take the wódka bottle and pour another glass for myself, then, remembering myself, one for him too.

'Fyodor, you self-satisfied bastard. Na zdrowie.'

He raises the glass. 'Enough history, what's done is done.'

We are both feeling the effects of the wódka and something like a peace is arising between us. He looks at the chess board and appears to be returning his attention to the game, but then, still with his eyes on the board, I discover his concentration is elsewhere.

'Sometimes, when you bite a sandwich between your teeth, the sausage is squeezed out of the back and escapes the jaws. That is what you must do, Bronek. You must get out from between us. Get out of the sandwich.'

'I know.'

Fyodor studies the wódka in his glass, swirling it slowly.

'I am not only sorry for you, you know. I envy you too. We are in the same trap, you and I. It is only a matter of time for both of us. You cannot stay, and I cannot leave. You at least have a chance, I have none.'

'Why do you say that? You have just acquired half of central Europe, in a few months.'

'Bronek, is it not obvious? In Russia I am that detestable

thing, an intellectual. Soon I will be found out. I cannot escape my brains as easily as you can cross the frontier to Romania or Hungary.'

'Leave then.'

'Not possible. Where would I go? You Poles are loved and welcomed everywhere civilised. It is not so easy for us. No, my fate is in Russia, Mother Russia.'

'I don't understand. Here.' I pour him another wódka, 'To survival, Fyodor Andreyevich.'

'Survival, Bronek.'

'And, thank you. I never thought I would thank a Russian for anything.'

'Well, I will repay you that courtesy, with an apology in advance. I am sorry for what will happen here.'

'What will happen?'

'Things I will be ashamed of. You know Russian foreign policy. I am afraid we will have to demolish this house and the church, some other things too.'

'Why, how can you gain from that?'

'Stalin is painting with a big brush, painting everything red.'

'Will they be safe, my family and Father Michał?'

'I told you, they are insignificant. They can go; it makes no difference. This will be a new country of Russians. Stalin will even get rid of the Ukrainians if he can. You too are insignificant, unless you are noticed, then someone has to think of what to do with you.'

'Fyodor, I know it's unreasonable to ask, but as I am to leave, I have to ask. Will you make sure nothing unnecessary happens to them. Nothing excessive. Is that possible?'

'My friend, I have already done more than wisdom would advise.'

'I know. I'm sorry I asked. God knows why, but I want to trust you.'

'Bronek, we are pawns, we move forward one square at a time. Your trust would not alter that.'

'I understand. I will be gone in the morning, before you get out of bed.'

'Thank you, my friend, my conscience is heavy enough.' He gets up and offers me his hand, which I take.

'I apologise for the quality of the game, Fyodor.'

'Nonsense, you played magnificently.'

'Thank you, but I know enough to know that isn't true. And that you are a serious player.'

'I am a fanatic, Bronek.'

'Goodnight, Fyodor.'

'Goodnight, comrade.'

On Sunday morning Marylka takes us to Chopin's house at Żelazowa Wola, a village 20 miles from the city. Until he left Poland for France at the age of twenty-one, Chopin had lived with his parents in a very pretty little house surrounded by a large garden on the edge of this village. When we arrive, the grounds and the house are crowded with visitors waiting for a recital by a student from the conservatoire. Marylka says that these recitals are very popular with tourists, who come by the coach full from the Warszawa hotels every weekend to hear them. She tried to reserve tickets for us without success: it has been booked solid all summer. There are two classes of ticket. The first one admits you to the house, which is a museum of Chopinalia, and during the recital you form the audience in the music room where Chopin himself practised. The other kind of ticket admits you only to the gardens. During the performance, if the weather is fine, the French windows are opened and benches are arranged on the lawn to allow people outside to listen. We have the other kind of ticket, the garden kind.

Bronek cannot hide his disappointment: he loves Chopin and his hearing is not good enough to enjoy listening through the doors. Marylka watches him shrug and look away. She had tried her best through the usual channels.

'Come, uncle Broniu, we will try the other method.' She links his arm and they walk up to the doorman. There is a short conversation in Polish, Marylka very animated gesturing towards Bronek and then to me. The doorman considers us both for a moment, weighing up the plausibility of whatever she has told him, then reaches for his tickets and tears three off the strip. Bronek reaches for his wallet but he wags his finger, 'No, no, sir. Not necessary.'

Once inside I ask him how she did that, but he won't tell me; he closes his eyes smiling and shakes his head.

She says, 'You see, am I not fantastic?'

'Yes, are you not?' Marylka is.

After all, the performance is not wonderful, but not a disappointment either. We walk in the gardens afterwards and the gentle simplicity of the place makes up the meaning somewhat lacking in the playing. I try to remember a quotation I heard: good interpretation of Chopin requires the player to have the head of a man, the heart of a woman and the hands of something else. We speculate what it might be: a masseur, a bear, a regiment? Too complicated this for Marylka.

'Mark, you must be Polish only.'

I remind her that the pianist was Polish.

'Ah, but he was a bear.'

We agree that he was Polish but too young to have been in love, to have been transfigured.

When we get back to Warszawa Bronek is very tired and I persuade him that he needs a rest. He hasn't been sleeping well since we left England and the last few nights I have been aware of his coughing. I am surprised when he agrees readily to this and within a few minutes he is asleep.

Marylka and I go shopping for some supper and then in search of an exhibition she has read about. In the centre of town at a major road junction, a soldier steps out in front of the car and holds up all the traffic. Marylka explains what is going on, she realises that she has heard about it already on the radio. Today the government is unveiling a new monument to all the Poles 'lost in the east' during the war. We could be stuck in the car for hours while the the ceremony takes place, so we abandon it in the street and join the gathering crowd around the monument.

Things are a little disorganised; there are soldiers with dogs on patrol around it but people are not held back from the piece. Like dreamers, they come, as if unable to grasp immediately what it is or what is required of them, but elements of this image are indelibly written into Polish history and Polish memory. It is a very Polish monument. There are two miniature hills of black earth with a railway track running over them. The sleepers each have a name blackly burnt into them and are smeared and clawed by desperate hand prints, so fresh and wet I look up the track expecting to see those who have passed this way. Ragged ghosts who clung to each feature of the country clattering away from them, their attention grasping every handhold and leaving everywhere the smudged and dragged fingerprints of resistance, of fear, of farewell.

'These are the names of the camps in Ukraine,' she reads them out loud. 'These in White Russia.' We follow the tracks. 'This one you will know, Katyń. We have always known, families know who is missing, but only now can they mourn. The Russians have gone and finally the lists have been discovered.'

'Lists?'

'There are more than a million names.'

All is black and blacker still. On the second and higher of these two hills there is an open truck bristling with crude crosses, all black, all different, all covered with the same wet clay hand marks, and all leaning away from one back corner of the truck as if blasted by some violent wind. A macabre version of a summer breeze tracking across a cornfield. In front of the truck the lines stop, twisting up in the air. This track was never going anywhere.

As we step down from the monument a flower stall opens selling only red and white carnations. Poles know their flowers: every occasion has its appropriate floral accompaniment. Now, in a moment, people are calling out names and throwing flowers on to the black crosses until the truck is covered and the track is strewn. Red and white on black. Weeping fifty-year-old tears. Black loss. Red blood. White tears. When the flowers are exhausted we all stand back, stunned.

Marylka's mother, Krzysia, is one of Bronek's cousins. She

married Edmund Jakubowicz, a Jew from Kazimierz, the Jewish quarter of Kraków. When I phoned her to tell her Bronek had died, there was a long silence; I feel her step back, stunned. I hear her crying in Kraków and I can't stop myself. Finally she says, 'Mark, kiss your mother, I cannot speak now, I must tell Edmund. Please speak to Marylka.' But I can't and I haven't yet.

It is Marylka who suggests I go to Auschwitz. I am confused by my reaction to the monument, I can't speak for a while but she carries on bravely on her own till I offer her some chewing gum. She takes it very thoughtfully, carefully unwraps it, examines it. I am fascinated by this: what is she doing? She hesitates, 'Mark, I can't believe you did that.'

The gum goes in.

'What?'

'Give me gum to make me shut up.' And I can speak again.

She says, 'You go there; everyone must because you cannot imagine it. When you have seen it you will know, I cannot tell you. Also, go now because there is no more money to keep it open and soon it will not be as it was.'

In the evening the opening of the monument is shown on TV. We watch it together, three of us in silence. Lech Wałęsa makes a speech to the nation which I cannot follow, but I feel the air thicken. The same charge fills the room and there are no flowers here to let it go.

Suddenly Bronek is awake, 'Lost in the east, *Lost in the east?*' He beats the arms of his chair and shouts at the screen. 'What do you think happened? Did they wander too far from home and forget the way back? Was it too dark to see the way? Lost? They were *murdered*. When will those bastards say so?'

When I think of my childhood, when I remember my own youth I make certain my memories are happy, though I can recall times when I was not. Usually the question of happiness is only posed in hindsight, and now, whether it was or was not happy, the person my past has made me into freely applies a happy label to it. I look through my father tonight for the first time directly into his past and realise how infinitely distant from it I am. The momentary insight brings me closer to him as any confidence would, but what I glimpse through this outburst is impossible to really understand. I haven't the vocabulary. Standing on the monument in the afternoon with my fantastic cousin, I cried with a painful shock at the immense scale of the brutality and the loss. Sitting with my Dad I see clearly his loss, his bitter loss and my own distance from it. Did he never mention these things, never tell me the story of the Warszawa uprising, the deportations, or the personal details of his past because he also needed to have happy memories, or because there was no way to communicate them. Or maybe because the person he needed to be, essentially, would have to change if he carried these stories nearer the surface.

It's all speculation and, he would have said, pointless. He would have liked to deflect enquiry and say that the past is over and done with and of no interest to anyone. Yet history was his passion, particularly biography, though not his own.

'Mark, you are a nuisance. All you do is asking me questions, or pulling my leg. I didn't do anything much. It's nothing very interesting: I was just lucky.'

If you lie down with a dog, you get up with fleas. He never described the dog he had to lie down with, so I'm left with just the fleas as clues to where he lay.

— 12 —
Kraków

In Kraków, Bronek and I walk along Ulica Szewska towards the Rynek. I'm still worried about him. Since Warszawa his cough is noticeably worse. It keeps him awake at night. The lack of sleep makes him tired and that, in turn, aggravates the cough. Water accumulating in his lungs produces a dry, irritating bark, as though he is trying to bring fluid up through desert sand, and it is worse when lying down.

He had slept or dozed in the car most of the way from Warszawa, the upright position seemed to ease his breathing and he relaxed. In the last weeks before he died he had to spend his nights in a chair until his condition was so deteriorated that even sitting upright was an effort in itself. But now, here in Kraków, as we make our way slowly along Szewska, browsing in shop windows, the hacking cough racks his body. And to no effect, it doesn't bring anything up or get throaty, it just shakes him and he gets shorter and shorter of breath.

In a tiny, book-lined, upstairs room of an antiquarian booksellers he gets engrossed and I don't. I say, 'Will you be all right while I go to the post office? I'll be two minutes.'

'Yes, yes, of course.' He's not really paying attention, but I find myself ready to leave him. In the last few days he has become clingy, nervous of letting me go anywhere without him. Like today, I thought he'd rather stay with Antonina at the flat while I came out on my own, but just as I'm leaving, he's there, 'Maybe I'll come with you, Mark.'

'Why?'

'What do you mean, why?' What do I mean, why? I mean impatience.

So I say, 'Okay.'

Impatience, the corollary of responsibility. I was hoping for an afternoon off, but I can't say that. I didn't realise it then, I just felt impatient. And he's good company, Bronek. My dad. He doesn't talk much, yet he loves conversation, he cares about it.

'You don't have to be an alcoholic to love good wine,' he would say.

So I leave him in the bookshop and continue down Szewska and across the beautiful Rynek. I try to take my time, amble through the Sukiennice, the medieval arcaded cloth market, but I cannot and I give in to the urgency of my errand, and the nagging uncertainty of our last communication. After queuing too long at the post office, I dash back towards Szewska holding the image of the shop front ready to match against the real one, certain now that I shouldn't have left him on his own.

I tear in through the ground floor and up the narrow staircase to the room where I left him. He's not there. Jesus. Where is he? Losing him is worse than being lost, the same thing perhaps. I stare at the last place I left him reading his book, antimatter, a black hole. Why can't I see him? I'm not looking hard enough. But he's not there, or anywhere in the shop. Keep calm, I say to myself, keep calm. I step outside and very slowly scan the street. What does he look like? What the hell does he have on today? Christ, who am I looking for, will I even recognise him? I can feel my bladder go slack. I bounce from one foot to the other. God, stay still and just look. I will him to appear but he's a stubborn bugger, he won't. I think of babies left outside supermarkets, how could I be so stupid? Now I seriously need to pee. Where the hell are you? I think of the time Julian, Dad and I were going to London by train. At Swansea he decided to get off to buy a newspaper on the platform. Julian and I sat nervously in the compartment waiting for his return for what seemed like an age. Eventually the whistle sounded on the platform and the train started to move. It was a long steam train, the Fishguard to London express, and its first movement was hardly perceptible, I tried to convince myself that we weren't moving yet, but we were, accelerating all the time, pulling away from him. Julian and I stared at each other in horror and disbelief. I felt the same bladder panic I feel now, the same paralysis and the same tide of relief when he appears. On the train it was just as Julian was starting his nervous chuckling and I my chin wobbling, his smiling face confident at the compartment door. But now, in Ulica Szewska, Kraków, nearly forty years on, I see his back moving away towards the Rynek, hesitant, lost in his own city. I run through the mill of people and slip my arm through his from behind. 'I thought I'd lost you for a moment, Dad. Where have you been?'

'I found a book about Lwów. When I look up, you have gone.' We continue together in the direction of the Rynek once more and I keep my arm through his. Over coffee, later, in a pretentious café with atrocious service, he returns wistfully to the subject. 'I would like to see Lwów again: it's a beautiful city.'

'How far away is it?'

'From Kraków. I don't know, three hundred miles? Less maybe.'

'That's not so far, compared to the distance we have already come. If the roads are good we could get there in a day.'

'Yes, but I don't know. I don't feel so good, I am tired.'

'You're not sleeping too well, are you?'

'No, this cough is worse at night, my lungs are filling up.' What a horrible image. Drowning on land. Sitting comfortably in a cafe, warm, in dry clothes but drowning. I dip one corner of an off-white sugar cube into my rotating coffee, the black liquid capillaries up towards my finger and thumb, filling up the air spaces.

'I thought they had sorted all this out before we left. Isn't one of the things you take a diuretic.'

'Frusimide. Yes but…ach…' He looks away through the glazed arch next to us, out across the square.

'What?'

'What?' I hate the way he does this.

'The frusimide, what about the frusimide?'

'It's not so easy to take it.'

'But, it's just a pill isn't it?'

'Yes, but when we are travelling it's difficult.'

'Why?' I know I'm missing something, the something he doesn't want to have to explain.

'Ah, Mark,' finally he gives in angrily, 'because half an hour after I take it I have to piss, and half an hour later I need another. The water has to go somewhere.'

'But not to your lungs, Dad.' He shrugs. I realise that he is descibing a situation he has been avoiding rather than suffering. 'Are you saying you haven't been taking it at all?'

'Well, not on the days we have been going somewhere in the car.'

'Why the car?' That's nearly every day.

'I don't like to have to ask you to stop all the time for me.' Only that.

'You have to start taking them again, Dad. I will stop the car as often as you like.'

'I know, I know. But, that frusimide, it makes me feel sick too. I hate to take medicines.'

'Well, we can go to a doctor. Antonina must have a doctor, she's always complaining about her health. Perhaps there's an alternative that doesn't make you feel sick.' This idea seems to brighten him a bit.

'Maybe Edmund will know something.' Edmund, Marylka's father.

That afternoon he and Bronek get down to the subject of his condition and treatment like true amateurs, discussing the merits of one drug over another and recounting anecdotes about their life-saving or fatal effects. He makes an appointment at the hospital for Bronek to have tests and a re-evaluation of all his medication. I am a little sceptical about this. The tests he has been subjected to over the last year have been exhaustive; it always seems to take months to reach any conclusion about his condition and then the balancing of his medicines and suppression of the side effects takes even longer. I can't imagine going through this process all over again while in Kraków for a week.

'Don't worry, Mark, it is different here.'

I watch these two old friends disappear into the hospital chatting enthusiastically as if they were going to watch a football game. I wait in the car park for an hour. They emerge again, continuing the same conversation.

'What did they say?'

'He said I should keep taking the frusimide.' He looks disappointed. He has always been independent about medicine, varying recommended doses, or even refusing to take some things, now I realise where this comes from.

A typical Polish medical scenario. Bronek is feeling unwell so his friends and family gather round and come up with their diagnosis. Bronek goes to the doctor or the hospital to confirm this and see what treatment they recommend. He goes to the pharmacist to argue about the relative merits of the medication he has been prescribed and what he thinks he should have. He takes home drugs according to who won this dispute and what is available for sale without prescription. At home the family gather round again to have a look at what he has and between them decide on the best course of treatment. Poor Bronek, for the last fifty years he has had to do this all on his own. We all thought you just did what the doctor said. How boring we are.

We agree that he should take it easy for a few days, restart the frusimide, and recover some of his strength. I spend a bit of time being a tourist in Kraków, surely one of the most beautiful cities of Europe, not only for the Rynek. I have a cynic's worry that before long economic forces will transform this charming place into a replica of all other European commercial cities, with identical high streets. I am told that it is likely Poland will be in the European single currency before Britain. They could be right if the atmosphere in Kraków is a barometer of Poland's improving prosperity.

We also go to a travel agent to discover how easy or difficult it is to get to Lwów. It would be possible, but we are advised against it. Looking back I cannot convince myself that we were right not to have gone. Taking the car would have been impossible in the time we had available. New insurance would be needed and probably difficult to get in the light of the Ukrainian reputation for car theft, a real risk in itself for us. Obtaining visas for the Ukraine is also a lengthy process, and Bronek was not keen on the uncertainties of using public transport. But the thing I feel almost ashamed of is that we paid attention to the dangerous reputation of the place. In Poland there is a general feeling that the Ukraine is the wild west, or east, and that all Ukrainians are villainous cut-throats. The long and complicated history of the relationship between these neighbours has fostered this feeling particularly in Bronek's generation.

When I was planning my trip to Lwów two years later, Antonina wrote to me saying that she could not understand why I should ever want to go to such a place, full, as it was, of murdering treacherous dogs, 'who stole in by night and betrayed us to the Nazis'. She filled me with misgivings and fear about taking the trip, but I had made up my mind, I would go.

When, while we were so close, we had allowed ourselves to be put off by these the terrible tales of the mafia and the old Soviet-style bureaucracy, seeing Bronek's disappointment made me decide that when I could, I would go.

His decision, in spite of the difficulties, was really made by his cough.

In the back of my mind is the conversation I had with Marylka in Warszawa about Auschwitz and I had been trying to find a way to ask Antonina where it was. I looked on the map, I know it is somewhere near Kraków, but I also know that the name was Germanised. So I'm looking for something similar sounding or the symbol for a historical monument, some clue. What might the symbol be for death camp I wonder. Finally, having no success in this avenue, reluctantly ask Bronek if he will ask Antonina for me. I'm nervous about it, I'm not sure what her reaction might be. I had hoped that if I found out where it was I could have gone there alone one day while Bronek arranged something else for himself. I was convinced he would not be interested and even disapproving in some way.

As it was I need not have been nervous, she told us in detail about her visits to Treblinka and Buchenwald. We are sitting in her narrow kitchen at breakfast time and I watch her demonstrate something about hair. Bronek is incredulous, 'She says there is a room full of hair.' I don't understand this, yet.

'Yes, yes, you should go there.'

Bronek now changes his mind and decides to come with me.

'Are you sure you wouldn't rather stay here for the day and rest?'

'Sitting in the car is resting.' So we go, and he knew where it was all along.

On the drive out of Kraków towards Katowice, Bronek tells me the story of Antonina's family. Before the war it had been a big family; her father was a butcher and farmer in the village of Nowy Targ. After the German invasion in 1939 the control of animals for slaughter was taken over by the occupying forces and very strictly controlled, food being one of the main problems for a conquering army and a very effective form of control and intimidation of the vanquished population. At some time, probably in early 1940, the Gestapo discovered the buried remains of a pig's carcass, slaughtered illegally by Antonina's father, who had distributed the meat to various villagers. The men from each of these households were arrested, some twenty in all, shot in the village square, and buried in a pit. All in the space of an hour. This included Antonina's father and three of her brothers. The youngest boy of the family was not at home the day the rest of them were taken. Antonina found him that night and warned him not to come home, which he did not do until 1945. He spent the rest of the war hiding in the woods and foothills of the Tatra. The Gestapo knew about the youngest son and interrogated Antonina and her mother regularly, possibly violently to begin with. Later the soft technique nearly worked. They managed to convince her mother that they meant no harm to the boy, they only wanted to talk to him and let him come home.

Didn't she want to see her son again at home? Just tell him he can come home and we'll talk to him there.

The two women maintained they had no idea where he was,

but Antonina could see that her mother was weakening, she did want her son at home again. That day Antonina made her brother move on to a new hiding place and from then on she refused even to tell her mother where he was. He survived.

There is a darker side to this tale, if such a thing can be imagined. Bronek thought the information which led to the discovery of the pig's remains and the arrests was supplied to the police by one of their own neighbours. Someone who wished to be a butcher perhaps.

Two years later, on my way back from Lwów, I sit with Antonina in her kitchen again, but alone this time. She shows me her old photographs. They are not in an album but loose in a shoebox. She digs her hand down one side and lifts out a slab of them. Black and white, old, dog-eared pictures, all of people, mostly posed groups of family or friends, but some taken spontaneously on days out or of some unusual event.

A picture of three young women in a street walking side by side towards the camera, Antonina is on the left nearest the kerb. She grips the picture hard, bending it in her old hand and taps it with a fingernail. 'This Lwów. I...here,' she strokes her own face with her index finger: it is a fine almond shape with a high forehead, her hair scraped back under a beret right on the back of her head. She is the smallest of the group but has a jaunty confident style that draws my eye to her first.

'Hania, you...father...sister.' Hanusia's round face smiling shyly. 'This...' the third girl, 'I don't remember. Dead.'

Antonina's voice is deep almost like a man's and her accent is from the east, the Ukraine, she rolls her r's and her l's are Russian, though she would hate to hear me say so.

'Lwów, beautiful city. We were students there, your father, my cousin Michał and I. Your father and Michał, vet...er... in...aria. I...pharmacia.'

'What about Hanusia?'

'Ah, Hania, I say to her many times, why don't you study something? But no. She stays at home with her mother, she likes to have a new dress, she doesn't to want to do nothing.'

She makes flouncy movements with her hands and puts her nose in the air. 'Yes, she always has new dress. In the war I had to be nurse, I had to learn it German way,' her mouth makes an upside down U shape. 'Hania, because she can't do nothing, they send her to Germany to concentration camp and then she has to work.' This seems to give her some pleasure. 'But somehow, I don't know, she was given to German family to look after baby.' She laughs a single-syllable laugh. 'Ha!'

She studies a picture of herself floating in a canoe, the paddle laying across her knees. 'Ninety thoorrty six, Różniatów.' A little deeper in the picture standing up to his ankles in the river is Bronek, a slim light-boned youth, smiling at the girl in the canoe he has just pushed off. A tiny bow wave spreads out beside her.

'Your father.' She hands me the photo. It was taken from quite a distance. The figures are small in the expanse of water but sharp against the white rocky background of the opposite bank. She is tiny in the boat, caught at the moment of gathering her wet hair at the nape of her neck, one elbow raised and from her other hand hangs a ribbon. Her laughter ripples out half a century past the camera into the kitchen.

'You are beautiful, Antonina.'

She winks at me, 'I was.' She takes back the picture, massages his tummy, 'And your father was.'

She flushes, a wide irrepressible smile spreads across her face, then she does the Polish shrug and digs into the box again.

'Again, Lwów.' Bronek, Michał and two other friends in front of the Opera. Without warning Antonina holds up a V sign in front of my face, 'Dead,' she shouts and she taps their heads. 'Two. Dead, dead.' She does her inverted mouth thing, 'Everybody dead in Lwów. So many beautiful yunk mens dead.'

She starts to cry openly, takes back the picture,'Tak, tak beautiful mens. And look at Lwów, was beautiful.'

Her memory is a wounded animal.

And she slaps the photograph angrily with the backs of

her fingers. 'Polish is Lwów. Polish. Why you go there? To Lviv, to Lview, ooh…Lview.' and suddenly she is laughing, 'Ooh…oooh Lview.' The new Ukranian pronunciation. The funny sound of it scoops her out of despair into the giggling girl in the canoe.

But in the next instant she is grim again, growling at me for going there. 'They are only murderers there,' she slits her throat with her index finger, chin thrust forward and her mouth stretched right across her jaw.

'No, Antonina, Lwów is beautiful, still beautiful, and it's not full of murderers. I had a wonderful time there.' It sounds limp in my mouth as I say it.

'Yagh,' she turns away, 'you were not there.'

From the box on top of the next handful is a picture of a group standing in a crescent behind what appear to be two or three bundles of rags laid on the ground. Taking it from her something warns me, she is quiet. The bundles reveal themselves to be two exhumed corpses wrapped in the rotting remains of the clothes they were buried in.

'It iss picture of my father and my brother. Nowy Targ, Ninety Foorrty Six.'

'Bronek told me the story last time I was here.'

'He tried to find the people responsible but what can he do from Scotland? He was not here,' there is reproach in her tone. 'He tried to persuade us that they must be found by the police but we were tired, and the Russians don't care. They were buried again by the church. That's all.'

In the picture I recognise her little pointed chin in the shadow of a shawl; she looks even tinier, childlike next to a bigger, older woman. The shapes of the shawls covering their heads and shoulders are inclined slightly towards each other, their wrapped up bodies pressing against each other, one amorphous shape staring at the earth.

Later in the day I stop at a florist on my way back to her flat. I ask what flowers are right for an aunt. When I give them to her she laughs and links my arm in the hallway, 'Nobody gives me flowers for foorty years.' She holds up four fingers, 'Foorty?'

'Yes.'

'Foorty years. Too long time.'

'That can't be true; someone must have brought you flowers in forty years.'

She shrugs and winks at me, 'Yes, of course.'

There were many camps at or near Oświęcim. The oldest of these was originally a Polish army barracks just outside the village. It was considered ideal for the purpose of a concentration camp, not only because of the buildings and design but more importantly because Oświęcim was a major railway junction. Later, rail links were specially built to connect the camps directly to the main railway network. KL Auschwitz I, as this camp became, received its first prisoners in June 1940: 728 Polish political prisoners from Tarnów. It was expanded until it peaked in 1942 with a total of 20,000 prisoners. By this time other camps had been constructed. In the neighbouring village of Brzezinka work started in 1941 on KL Auschwitz II – Birkenau, the largest of them all, with a maximum transient population of 100,000 in 1944. In 1942 at Monowice another, KL Auschwitz III – Monowitz, which was built to provide slave labour for a chemical works, and many other subsidiary camps connected to specific industries. Of these only Auschwitz I and II remain today as monuments.

KL Auschwitz I. I realise immediately that I'm in a familiar place. We walk under the famous, jaunty art-deco sign, 'Arbeit Macht Frei', into the spaces between the brickbuilt barrack blocks. In how many jerky black and white newsreels have we followed this path already? For an instant I see the ragged figures in striped pyjamas shuffling along the paths, the waxy emaciated corpses loaded naked on to carts. I hear the scratchy sound track goosestepping in the background. There are certainly ghosts here, but not these flickering images of light and machinery. Though true, they were unbelievable. Film, even this macabre footage, was a Hollywood kind of haunting, rendered neutral, sanitised by its objectivity.

Life in the camps, portrayed in commando comic style.

Drawings of laughing SS men putting the boot in. The doomed are beaten, kicked, experimented on, flayed for lampshades, gassed, starved, enslaved, used up, discarded. Killed. A photograph of an ordinary-looking man, schoolmasterish. The Angel of Death.

Looking back on it, I'm embarrassed at my indifference to this exhibition. We passed politely through that chamber of horrors with inane whispering thoughts, 'How awful, how dreadful.' The kitschness of it. Could I have been that cheeky SS chappy then? Could Bronek? Some poor bastard was. Or the victim? The naked cowering wretch with a boot on his throat.

It's possible this is a clever piece of design; we need to be softened up a little. It's not quite Son et Lumière, but it's comfortable, we know where we are with it, who's side we're on. It is thin ice though, and it gets thinner.

Behind a glass wall across the middle of a large room are piled the shoes of the men, women and children who passed this way. They are not paired, they are not organised, they are heaped behind the partition until they reach to the ceiling. Inside a brown toecapped gentleman's shoe, the flanks thumbed apart and the laces slackened, the maker's name and the size have been obscured by a sole-shaped black sweat-mark. The leather of the upper has taken the shape of, and still describes a foot. A foot for every shoe in this place. I hear them marching, barefoot.

And behind another wall is their hair, behind another their prosthetic limbs, their spectacles, shaving brushes, their suitcases for God's sake.

My friend is staying at his grandfather's house. The old man is dying, it is the end of a farmer's life full of the strange tales and incomprehensible sayings. He'd say, 'A'm jist shoowin the cat's erse tae the sun.' No idea what that means. 'Dunnie poisin yer cuddy wi' shavins.'

The old man dies peacefully in his bed in the afternoon of a fine day. The young man, his grandson, takes from the dead

man's hand his pipe, now cold. He sits by the bed for a while
looking at the pipe, turning it over. Held by the pipe. What
would the old man say? He knocks out the ash, fills it, lights it
up and takes a last pipe with his Grandpa.

Ordinary neutral objects these, still with the wear and dirt of
use on them, the detritus of their lives.

In the Polish section there is a list of names. I have always
hated lists because my name begins with Z. Usually I'm last
and whatever treat I'm waiting for runs out with Williams.
Like the time I was going to fire a field gun on a range. I was
a good shot as a school boy, a .22 and 303 marksman, and,
as a result, had the chance to go to some army range near Stir-
ling and shoot real guns off at the side of a hill. You didn't
need to be much of a shot to hit a hill, I remember thinking
at the back of the queue, they should have brought the guys
that could never hit the targets. We start with Atkinson, who
fires the field gun. He pulls a cord, a huge flame squirts out
towards us from the back of the gun. We all throw ourselves
to the ground. Down at our end of the line, from say Morgan
to Zygadło, this is a bit of fun, we are playing soldiers after
all in our Second World War battledress and big boots, but
Brian Bamford thought he'd been shot. The real soldiers are
all falling about laughing; this is their weekly joke. They work
their way through the armoury, not in alphabetical order surprisingly, but in a descending order of size and power of the
weapons. Morgan firing a mortar, Thompson, a Tommy gun,
Howard a howitzer would have been more appropriate. What
would I have got? Which ever way they do it, they have run
out of ammunition by the time they get to Z. I could cry with
disappointment. I am dying to send curving tracers a mile
through space, syringing into the ground opposite. Can gravity act on something so fast? How can we even see it? A com-
passionate gunnery officer, if such a thing is possible, takes
pity on me and hands me a flare pistol, I fire it high over the
glen, a white flare to signal that we come in peace now, we
have nothing left to shoot. A great sloping arc in the sky, a

silver star with a parachute rocking its way gently on to the hillside across the valley, taking the longest route to the same target.

Lists. I saw once in a Philip Roth short story the only reference to my own name I have ever seen in print. In the story the recruits at some American army base are being lined up for something, from Aaron to Zygadło. I found this shocking. I'm used to being unusual and anonymous at the same time, and I have the sense that my name just refers to me, particular and exclusive. I have grown up with the feeling of being a stranger, or at least the son of a stranger, and part of this is because I was not a Williams or a Jones or even a Rees. And my name is always the last in the phone book.

On this list in Auschwitz, there are no Welsh names but there are whole tribes of Aaron, Aaronowicz, Aaronowitz, on through the alphabet. They range around the sides of a dormitory on screens which have to fold out from the walls to accommodate them all. All these names. Now the boot is on my throat. Zygadło is not the last name on this list, there are many from it to the end, all unusual, all anonymous now.

Bronek and I take a coffee in the Auschwitz café. I collect some information and buy shares: 20,000 złotys' worth of Auschwitz belongs to me and my number is 2217, not a very high number. He looks grey with fatigue and he won't speak. We have been standing side by side looking at the mechanics of what? Ethnic cleansing, holocaust, annihilation: the language of murder; mass murder. Killing people.

What's going on in Bronek's head? Wiggly fingers clutch his coffee cup and it shakes as he puts it to his lips, but no more than usual. Usually he would say, Now Mark, shall we go home now? Nothing.

I say, 'How do you feel Dad?' He does his okay shrug, half closing his eyes, mouth down at the corners, eyebrows and shoulders together lifting just a fraction. He nods to some inner beat, but he says nothing. I eat a whole packet of chocolate biscuits.

'Shall we go to Birkenau?'

'Brzezinka,' he emphasises. Then, 'Yes, we can go there but I stay in the car. I am tired and I have seen enough.'

It is true: of course he has seen enough.

What does he feel to see his name in print on this list. He would never say and perhaps, without saying, he can never really know. There are so few times when he declared himself to me that the feeling of shock and privilege at these rare confidences has stayed with me. Once he told me, he loved the spring more than any other season. We were walking in the shed-field on the top of the farm inspecting the grass or the fences. He stops and takes in a sweep of the view, blue Preselis east and north, west over Farthings Hook towards the Gwaun valley, dark green the wooded folds, south-west into the wind and sun, fresh all fresh. Screwing his face up into it he sniffs loudly, 'That is the best time of the year, everything is new again.' Now, the spring is my favourite season too, and I tell my children it's the best time because everything is new again.

In my daughter Hannah's first spring, before she can talk, I carry her, a hot little bundle in the crook of my arm, up the lane from our house under the huge beech avenue. The new leaves of the beech are so fresh and clean, like gems with the sunlight passing through them. I tell her seriously that this is the spring and it is my own and her grandfather's favourite season. I pull a pendant branch towards her face: pale-blue eyes take a long cool look at this new form of life. Something is happening, something new this spring. She cannot understand what I say and I don't know how to speak to her, our first child, but I understand in that moment that I love the spring and love saying so in part because it evokes that day in the shed-field. I hear him sniff, I see the blue hills and feel the freshness of that day, and now I am saying those same words. I wonder who said them to him and who will say them after me.

Birkenau: the city of the dead after fifty years.

I return from the dead with mud on my shoes. There are footprints in the mud in the few remaining huts. There are footprints in the mud of the ash pits. Mine are among them now and I have ashes on my feet. Grey ash creeps through my shoes into my soul.

How the dead overwhelm the living. They always have.

To be a witness at this remove of time is not possible, but, not every time, I step through the back door of my home and see the rows of my family's shoes, with worn-down heels and turned-up toes and I think of the ghosts of their feet inside. Not every time, but, sometimes, I remember what I saw.

— 13 —
Lwów/Lviv

In 1998, after Bronek had died, I made the trip to Lviv. In the interim I had started to collect material for this story, but it was a haphazard collection of his memories and some of my own. Just a pile of stuff. In the back of my mind the whole time was an insistent reminder of the decision I made in Kraków. I didn't promise anyone else and I hadn't actually promised Bronek, but I did decide that I would go to Lwów and I began to find that I needed to. It was his disappointment when we realised we couldn't go there from Kraków, his resignation, understanding that it was out of his reach and too late. These added weight to the decision and made it an imperative. Like a promise.

All other things could have been overcome with difficulty, but his health was obstinate. The visit with Edmund to the hospital and the new regime of taking his drugs instead of not taking them arrested the deterioration in his condition, but it was no instant cure. He did slowly start to get better sleep and his cough ameliorated, but we still had a long way to go with the trip we had planned: over the Tatra to Slovakia to visit his sister and her family in Poprad, on to Prague, then home via Pete in Paris.

So, another departure. On my own this time. At nine o'clock on a Sunday evening I waited for a bus at Victoria bus station in London. A bus with Kiev written on the front of it. I stood in a crowd at the lobby door with fifty or more Ukrainians. My heart sank at the prospect of being on a bus for thirty-two hours with this many people: it would be hell but I had to go. I worked my way to the front of the crowd with my eighty pounds cash ready.

'Lviv, please. Single.'

'Ah, it's you.' He takes my money.

'Yes, it's me. What?' I had spoken to someone on the phone trying to book a ticket. 'Just bring eighty pounds and you can go to Lviv.' So here I am.

'You are the passenger, the only passenger.' He's already looking past me at the next person.

'What?'

'You are the only one, these are just freight.' I'm surrounded by woven polypropelene bags of clothes, car dashboards and wings, bedding, all sorts.

'Don't I get a ticket?'

'What for?'

So I get on the bus, with three drivers and fifty empty seats, and they take me to the edge, the Ukraine.

The journey takes two whole nights and the day between them. I slept and read my way across Europe, trying to distract my own attention from the unknown country before me, and my usual uncertainty about my reasons for the trip. To the casual observer looking into my mind, I was unsure why I was travelling to a country I didn't want to think about.

But really, I was keeping my powder dry, for me there was an irresistible attraction in coming to this place. Bronek's story was consuming me and somehow his accounts were incomplete until I could come to stand where he stood, and see for myself. This situation extended also into metaphor: travelling across frontiers to discover the past and so on. Over the edge.

Tired and nervous I descend from the empty bus into the rain holding my bag in front of me. It is my identity: I am to be met by a friend of a friend who will recognise me by my son's Adidas bag. It is seven o'clock in the morning in a rainswept Stalinist housing estate on the edge of Lviv. The sky, the buildings, the people, all look unremittingly grey. I am looking for a tall, dark guy with longish hair, moustaches. 'You know, like a musician,' he said. He finds me without difficulty as I am the only passenger.

We make our way though the city to Melnechuka, the street where he lives. His family have managed to occupy this house continuously since his grandfather's time at the turn of the century. They would have been living there while Bronek was at the veterinary academy, there when the Nazis invaded and when they gave the city over to the Bolsheviks. There when they re-invaded again in 1941, through the communist years and finally to independence in 1990. During this time both Roman's parents have served prison sentences in Siberia. His father served ten years after the war for being a member of a Ukrainian partisan group who refused to surrender to the communists. In the 1960s his mother was imprisoned for ten years, though she was freed and pardonned after seven in a period of relative liberalism. Her name was given to the KGB by an asthmatic who, under the torture of having his medication withheld during attacks, gave any names he could think of, irrespective of their political inclinations. I share the middle floor of the house with her. She is a tiny, gracious lady who is constantly amused at my attempts at Ukrainian and exhibits no obvious scars of her ordeal.

Melnechuka, like much of the city, shows the signs of neglect and decay. Outside the road is rougher than a Galloway farm track, chewed up by the construction traffic of a Coca-Cola plant one block away. The plant is in operation now and the roads around it are new. But this street, on the rainy morning I arrive, is a district of brown lakes with narrow ribs of land connecting the pavements. Ladas and Volgas, navigating by memory, weave from side to side, keeping to the shallows and the pavements as much as possible. Bow waves wash along the foundations and into the basements of these crumbling nineteenth-century houses. But in a few hours, when the water has drained away leaving only the deepest puddles, it gets hot and steamy in the sun and Melnechuka is charming. The spaces between the houses are dark with fruit trees; walnut, cherry and apple trees overhang the pavements and shade the network of gardens and garages. Petals of white apple-blossom float on the puddles.

I don't mind the rusty iron roofs and guttering, the broken patchiness of the repaired stucco and missing mouldings. My eye is a natural restorer; it sees what these pretty houses were and what they could be, but I prefer them the way they are. The wing of an old Moskvich riveted to a broken gutter or windowsill and fifty-year-old palm prints left in the mortar jammed into rotten stonework, have an elegance of their own. These little houses, locked in a maze of streets and gardens, have an Austrian formality about their flat fronts and regular framed openings, but also an irresistible Slavic flare for rustic decoration and detail. The effect is of the country come to town, earthy, intelligent and energetic.

It's easy to imagine this city in the late 1930s, at the time when Bronek was a student here, as in the centre there has not been much change; it would have been emerging from another depression then. The last period of prosperity and new building would have been before 1914 when it was nominally an Austrian city. I think of him walking these streets to college every day or strolling by the Opera with his dog.

The veterinary academy is the most likely place to pick up Bronek's trail, so the day after I arrive we make it our first visit. With Roman as my guide and interpreter we search through records in the college archive, through lists of graduates of the 1930s, group photographs of students with diplomas but without success. Bronek's studies were interrupted, and no records were kept of students who did not complete their courses. I begin to despair: there is no trace of him and none of the buildings fit his descriptions, or rather, none of them fit my image of his descriptions. We are directed from the archive to another office in another part of what has become a large campus, from under 500 students in the 1930s, the college has grown to over 3,700. In the general office I repeat my story to an administrator who has done some research into the history of the college, and he in turn directs us over the hill to the 'old academy'.

The old buildings are a haphazard collection of extensions and additions to a grand town house and stables. They are arranged along two sides of a large open rectangle of grass which slopes up from the street on a third side. Inside we met ancient professors who listened again to the story but no one knew anyone who had been there at the time, 'They were all Polish, then they were Russian.' It's along time ago.

Coming out again into the sunlight I have a flash of recognition, remembering a description of his return to the college after leaving Różniatów at the suggestion of the Russian chess-playing officer. He described these buildings and the open grassy space, the stable-like clinic and surgery running behind the main building and along part of the top edge of the lawn. This is the first independent link I have made between his story and history. Inevitably there are many dead ends, and threads which have been lost in time. Not many of his contemporaries are still alive even if they survived the upheaval of the war years. With the problems of language and the difficulty until recently of visiting the Ukraine, it seemed sometimes as though I would never flesh out his memories. There is also always the suspicion that his reticence was deliberate, that there was something in his past he wished to keep in his past. I never seriously believed this but it is impossible, unwise even, to ignore the possibility, if venturing into someone's past, that you may discover they are not what or who they say they are.

At the corner of this building we fall in with two jovial lecturers in white lab-coats and chefs' hats. By now Roman has got my story off by heart and he launches into it with only an occasional nod in my direction. I stand there, rather like the subject of a veterinary demonstration, grunting when prodded and exhibiting my symptoms, those of a fortunate westerner in search of his roots.

'Yes, many people come here looking for their roots. Are you Canadian?'

'No. I am from Scotland.' I have learnt not to confuse others with the confusion of my pedigree.

'Scotland. Ah, *Braveheart*. Freedom.' They raise their fists in the air.

'Yes.' I have also learnt not to admit to never having watched this film. In central and eastern Europe this film is taken very seriously; it is an icon, portraying the elemental struggle of the subjugated against the tyrant. Saying you are from Scotland immediately identifies you as one of another oppressed people who fought heroically against insuperable odds, gaining glory for a moment before defeat and martyrdom or re-enslavement. On another level, it is the honourable 'barbarian' against civilised but unprincipled politics, the edge versus the centre.

Beyond them under a cherry tree, a convalescent horse is grazing a wide circle into the grass at the end of a radius of rope and a second link to Bronek's story falls heavily into place.

It takes me a while to get from Różniatów back to Lwów. It is mid-morning when I arrive at the station, a clear cold December day. I walk to the college across the centre of the city, past the opera. Everywhere there is evidence of the new regime. Not least when I get to the college. Pieces of military equipment have been parked around the perimeter of the grass and a handful of bored Russian soldiers are going through the motions of patrolling the grounds. I enter by the gate, without arousing the slightest interest in them and start across the lawn towards the student rooms.

I had been too preoccupied by the presence of the soldiers at first to notice the carcass of a horse lying on the lawn under the branches of an old cherry tree which stands in front of the the building I am making for. Behind it, a mound of fresh earth is being enlarged slowly and with great difficulty by a figure bent over a spade. In the time it takes me to reach him, the solitary excavator adds with painful effort only one spadeful of earth to the heap. As he straightens himself slowly, I see his silver hair and the pallour of exhaustion on his old face. A face I know.

'Professor. What is happening, what are you doing?' It is Michalski, the professor of anatomy. He looks up at me without a flicker of recognition. Steam rises from his shoulders and he is trembling from the unaccustomed effort.

'Burying this animal, er, comrade.'

'Professor, don't you know me? Zygadło. Veterinary student.'

'I know no one.'

'Where is everyone? What is happening?'

'God knows what is happening. The students have all gone, new ones will be coming, new professors, new commissars.' After a moment, he adds, 'Comrade.'

I stand on the rim of the pit looking down at the old man. The professor of anatomy, a grumpy old academic who none of the students much liked, a hard marker without much sense of humour.

'Why are you digging this pit, Professor?'

'He is burying a horse.' The voice from behind me makes me start. I turn quickly to face a short stocky man in a big padded coat. 'I am in charge here now, comrade. What do you want?'

'I am a student here.'

'No longer, comrade. The college is temporarily closed. We are dealing with the wounded animals the Red Army brings us.'

'What has happened to the Director, Professor Szczud-łowski?'

'Gone. There is a new Director. Comrade Professor Ivan Chynchenko, a Ukrainian, but he is not here yet and until he arrives I am the commissar.' He struts around the pit inspecting the professor's work as if to demonstrate his authority. The old man cowers away from him and starts to scrape his spade in the floor of the hole to very little effect.

'You lazy fool, that carcass will have been eaten by crows by the time you have finished this pit.' And he places his boot on the old man's back and shoves him against the mound of earth.

'Hey, what are you doing?'

'Getting my own back on this old bastard.'

'What has he done to you?'

'You say you are a student here?'

'Yes.'

'And you don't remember me?'

'No.' But I do remember him. Yurii, the general caretaker.

'No, you damned Poles don't notice who you tread on. I was

the caretaker of this academy for years and every day I had
the same thing from these bastards. They treated the animals
here better than me. Didn't you?' He kicks out at the professor
again. 'Didn't you, you old bastard.'

'Yurii!'

'Eh?'

'He is an old man; you will kill him like this.'

He comes and puts his face near mine. He stinks of alcohol.
'Yes, I remember you too. Polish. Zygadłowicz or something.
The poor kid trying to keep up with the big boys. What happened, did they leave you behind? Yes, I know you all right.
Marching up and down with your bloody dog. What a sight.
Ha! You Poles, you thought you had it made here. Well, the
boot is on the other foot now and we'll see how much you like
it.' He calls to one of the soldiers, who, as though roused from
a dream, comes slowly to the centre of the lawn. 'We have a
new volunteer for digging graves for the animals. He is going
to help the comrade professor with his work. Keep an eye on
them.' He gestures to me with a tilt of his head, 'In the pit with
you, comrade, give the professor a rest.'

'But, I have to...'

'Dig, comrade. Or I'll lock you up and fetch the militia.'

I jump into the pit and take the spade from the old man. He
clambers out and stands on the edge, his old back locked in a
digging position, and stares down at me unable to understand
what is happening.

'Put your coat on, sir, you will catch pneumonia in this cold.'
The old man follows my advice and then sits with his coat
around his shoulders on the lawn.

'I have buried two horses already this week. A horse requires
a big grave you know. It's a lot of digging to bury a horse.' He
points out two patches of bare earth in the grass of the lawn.

I work my way around the pit in a spiral getting deeper. The
ground is soft and easily shifted below the frozen crust, there
is a kind of pleasure in the work, a satifaction in the increasing
depth and the rising pile of spoil.

'How deep must we go, sir?'

'They say, two metres, but if there is a metre of soil on top of the animal that should be sufficient.'

'This pit is the wrong shape, long enough but not very wide.'

'No, it will be all right.'

'The horse will not fit; its legs will not go in.'

'I will sever the tendons at the knees and the hocks to overcome the rigor mortis. The legs will fold up. Believe me, Zygadłowicz, I am an expert in the interment of horses.'

'Zygadło, sir.'

He takes a long look at me, the gears of his memory slowly engaging, 'Zygadło, yes maybe.'

'Do you remember me now, Professor?'

'Maybe. So many things have happened here. Yes, maybe.'

'How did Yurii come to be commissar of the college?'

'He told me that for the last ten years he has been a member of a secret communist cell here in Lwów. When the Russians came, these worms crawled out of the ground and made themselves our leaders; the Red Army was our saviour and liberator. Our jailers more like. He is a thug, like the rest of them. "All men are equal now, comrade." Huh, equally miserable.' He continues the catalogue of the woes he has had to endure now that he is no longer the master of men like Yurii. 'Wait till the Russians have been here for a while, he'll change his mind.'

I continued digging, not really listening. Yurii is an oaf, but he is right about the treatment he received from the staff. Now, he is no longer at the bottom of the pile, he is kicking and punching everyone below him, exorcizing the pain and humiliation of his years of oppression, emulating in his own way the treatment he has been liberated from. It is a form of justice: revenge. But the professor is right too. History here is a layer cake of oppression. Before the present rearrangement Ukrainians were at the bottom, sat on by the Poles, who in turn have been sat on by the Austrians and by the Russians in their different guises: first the Tsars and now the Bolsheviks, each with their own characteristic forms of cruelty. And within these layers there are others like the Jews and the Armenians. The

Polish yolk has been broken from Yurii's back and he is enjoying the weightless feeling for a few moments while the new one is being prepared and one layer, the Polish one, is removed from the cake.

I know that it was a risk coming back to Lwów, but at such short notice it was difficult to see any other alternative, I had nowhere else to go. I had left without going to bed that night, and still with all that wódka sloshing about in my head, and caught an early train from Dolina. All the way to Lwów I ask myself: why was I let out of prison? Was it sport for the Russians or, if not, what? My mother said she came several times to bring things, food and blankets, for me, but I never saw her and never knew she had been to the prison. I didn't have time to find out what she knew about it.

My work has fallen into a rhythm, an automatic pace which I am sorry to interrupt when the professor tells me I have gone deep enough. He helps me out of the hole and we call another soldier to help us drag the horse to the edge of it. A dark-grey bloodstain is revealed in the flattened grass, an imprint of the horse's head. From its mouth, a smear trails after the lifeless hulk fading to pink across a white crescent, the negative shadow of frost left in the grass where the dead animal's distended abdomen masked the low winter sun. Four of us struggle against the inertia of its dead weight to position the animal next to the pit.

Professor Michalski removes a scalpel from an instrument roll and swiftly carries out the procedure he described. Without ceremony we roll the animal over and it falls the distance into the pit untidily, on to its legs. I hear the crack of a breaking bone under the heavy thump of its body landing. It is lying upright, huge, and barely below ground level, the head stiffly extended and legs tucked under, as if alive and resting in a field on a warm afternoon. I let myself down beside it to rearrange the limbs. It takes all my strength, wedging myself between it and the wall of the pit, to finally roll it on to its side. I stand panting next to it and waiting to recover my breath. I notice it's a mare, a beautiful bay, with the bulges of an udder sagging now in the soft dun area between her back legs, 'She was in foal.'

'Yes, it had died in her and she was septic. She was being used as a draft horse. Shame.'

'Two horses buried here, then. I thought she was heavy.' From the floor of the grave I look up against the ice-blue sky at the silhouettes on the ground. The two Russians bend together to share a match, exhaling swirling silver clouds like haloes around their heads, muttering to each other. Sunlight slants across the lawn, igniting the professor's white hair and incising deeper the lines of his face. He looks haggard with exhaustion. He turns slowly, stooping over his instrument roll and totters unsteadily away from the edge.

'Please,' I hold my hand out towards the soldiers, 'help me out of here.' They look down on me from the lawn, indifference and contempt in their lowered eyes, not even bending their necks to look at me. I feel the weight of the earth walls around me, the cold air congealing in the new shape pressing against my chest and immobilising my limbs. I am squinting up at them, my eyes uncomfortably level with their boots, my raised arm frozen. I am very very frightened.

They mutter again to each other, smiling.

'Heil Hitler!' They raise their arms like mine, snapping their clunky heals together and crack up with laughter, slapping their thighs and pointing at me. I laugh too, realising how pathetic I must have looked, but feeling anything but amused. One of them, still laughing, bends and offers me a hand. I have to take it even though I do not trust it; we have to play this game. As I anticipated, half way up the side of the grave he lets go of my hand. I let myself fall, sprawling backwards cartoon-like onto the dead mare.

'Stupid Polak.' I am badly winded, but I know I still have to be amused. This game could go in any direction. More laughter, it's not over yet.

'Hey, what are you doing?' The professor appears over the horizon.

'Burying a donkey, comrade.' More thigh-slapping laughter.

'Do you want to dig the next pit?' They do not. They wander off laughing about Hitler and donkeys.

'Thank you, sir.'

'Get out of there, Zygadło. A grave is no place for the living.'

I stand unsteadily on the horse's pregnant belly feeling the skin slip under my boots, 'Sorry old girl,' and haul myself out.

'They are jackals.'

Together we fill in the grave quickly, anxious not to leave a gaping invitation.

We bury another horse that afternoon, a thin wasted animal half the size of the last one but just as dangerous. I lead him out of the hospital stalls on to the lawn. He is dying of anaemia, the professor says, caused by infestation of parasitic worms and is so far gone that he cannot be saved. Yurii, standing with the professor on the lawn, beckons me to a point he indicates at his feet. 'This is a good spot, the ground will be soft here.'

Our progress towards them is painful and slow; the animal is almost dead. The sole purpose of bringing him out alive is to avoid dragging the dead carcass all the way from the clinic.

'Come on, I am getting cold waiting here,' Yurii removes the glove from his right hand and produces an automatic pistol from his coat pocket, 'and you have a hole to dig before it gets dark.'

The horse, beyond my help, cannot make it. I feel the shaking of his knees transmitted through the halter and he stops ten metres short of our destination. As though in embarrassment he puts his nose to the earth and blows on the grass, his head swaying from side to side. Yurii and the professor come to us.

'Hold his head up, comrade, this will have to do here.' Yurii is excited and impatient to kill something. I pull his head up. As he raises the gun and points it at the animal's head, I realise that he has no idea what he is doing. There is elation and terror in his screwed-up eyes and the barrel waves uncertainly in the general direction of the horse which could easily include me.

'Jesu…' I release the rope and duck out of the line of fire.

My exclamation is drowned by the professor, 'Wait, imbecile!'

'Eh?' In surprise Yurii jerks the trigger. We all recoil at nothing, at earsplitting silence. The horse groans and a distant laugh comes from the two thigh-slapping soldiers on the wall.

'Eh?' Yurii puzzles at the gun in his hand, pulling the trigger again with it pointing across the lawn towards the house.

'Yurii, for God's sake, stop that!' The professor resumes his former role, intimidating, authoritarian. 'Give me that pistol, before you kill someone!'

I realise immediately the danger in this and intervene, 'Excuse me, professor. I think Yurii should keep the gun. I will show him what to do. Have you used one of these before? Did you shoot the horse this morning?'

'Well....there was a lieutenant here...and, er, not one like this.'

'No. All right, is there ammunition in the magazine?' I show him how to remove it and replace it in the handle, slide the top back to put a round in the chamber and cock it. Then I point to the safety catch, a little lever on the side of the casing, 'When you are ready to fire, push that forward and squeeze the trigger.'

'I know how to fire a gun, comrade.' And he immediately raises the weapon.

'Wait!' The professor again, 'Yurii, please! Let's kill the animal with the first shot. The horse is a big animal with a small brain, *comme toi*,' he's back in the lecture hall. 'He's easy to hit but not so easy to kill with that little thing.' He puts his index finger on a spot in the middle of the horse's forehead. 'Here, Yurii.' With his other index finger, held like a gunbarrel behind it, he demonstrates the way Yurii should hold the weapon. Yurii nods.

We stand in a row. I hold the rope and with my right hand I cup the horse's bristly chin to steady his head. Yurii, next to me, raises the pistol to the spot the professor is still indicating, adjusts the angle and when the professor nods, he shoots the horse.

'Roman, do they know there are horses buried under this grass?'

'Buried where?'

I tell him the story of the day Bronek spent burying horses, which he relates to the others. They nod and we all look at the horse on the lawn.

'They say, "Could be." but they were not here, they don't know.'

The report of the shot echoes a double beat back to us from the surrounding architecture and the animal drops on to its belly, its life put out of it, it rolls to one side, dead.

In the evening I return to my old lodgings, exhausted, hungry and unsure of what to expect.

And he finds his sister waiting for him.

— 14 —
Ternopil

In Roman's car we rumble out of Lviv towards Ternopil. After a short climb out of the town on the eastern side we emerge into the beautiful Galician country. Undulating, lush, well tended and fertile. This country is rich and desirable. From here to the Black Sea, thousands of miles of the best wheat growing soil in Europe, the black earth of the steppe. Even the Greeks knew it, and from the sixth century BC established trading colonies along the Black Sea coast. Wheat from the Steppes has fed Europe since Hellenic times.

Recent history has also left its relics. Every few miles there are the neglected hulks of the Kolkhozes, the collective farms of the communist era. Some of these are still in use and some of the land is still run collectively, or cooperatively farmed, but these concrete hangers are most often crumbling away. I think of the accounts I have read of young school children learning by heart the heroic tonnages of wheat harvested or beetroots dug in their collective, or daft songs about the number of combine harvesters produced in Irkutsk. Look at this beautiful place: shivering poplars line the roads, the land sloping away to the north is an ocean of fecundity. There are storks nesting on the telegraph poles and cottage rooftops. Primavera, Persephone has returned to the world.

Near the villages of prettily painted wooden houses strung out along the roadside, the surrounding land is divided into small strips, a hangover from peasant times. Whole families stripped to the waist hack at the soil with mattocks and forks. It is an essential way of feeding themselves when the salaries are not paid for months on end. Surplus produce will be taken to Lviv and sold in the illegal street markets that spontaneously appear, and disappear again at the approach of a police car.

In this beautiful spring it's difficult to concentrate on the reasons for this trip. We are bowling along towards Ternopil with
a large box of chocolates and a bottle of champagne on the
back seat. They are for Svetlana, an assistant at the Museum
of Ternopil we met yesterday, who will take us to the headquarters of the security police and make a formal request to search
for my father's documents. We had come unprepared the day
before, without my passport, which could have been a little
awkward, but this oversight on my part led indirectly to finding Svetlana.

We had started our researches by looking for Bronek's
prison, the Ternopil town hall, only to find it had been demolished. At the new offices no one seemed to know the story
about it being used as a prison and we were directed to the city
archive. There it was confirmed that it had been a prison but
there were no records with the civil archive. The prisons were
run by the NKVD, the forerunner of the KGB, and any records
that had survived the Nazi invasion of 1941 would be held by
the security service, the new secret police. So not wanting to
visit them without my passport, we wandered into the museum
thinking there would be general information there about the
town during the war. And we met Svetlana.

We were working our way through the history of the
Ukraine, and specifically of Galicia. We got as far as the twentieth century and entered a new gallery. The Russian invasion.
The Russian invasion portrayed as the liberation of the poor
Ukrainians. Roman began muttering fairly early, then about
half way round the room there was a poster from the the
1920s, showing the different stages of Ukrainian history told
through the eyes of a very simple-looking peasant in a white
tunic. It was called 'Ukrainian Misfortunes', a sort of comic
strip with captions. In each frame there was a different tyrant,
the Tsar, Hetman, Skoropadski, Marshall Piłsudski, Petlyura,
all against a background depicting the special nature of the
misfortune visited upon the poor Ukrainians by each of these
regimes. The peasant looks into each of the pictures, bewil-
dered, scratching his head, offering his backside to Skoropad-

ski and ducking out of the way of Piłsudski. In the central
image he sits in the sunshine in a landscape of plenty with the
arm of a Bolshevik soldier around his shoulders.

'Look at this shit.'

'What shit?'

'Look at this patronising shit.' And he reads the caption,
'"Ukrainians find peace and plenty under Bolshevism." Shit.
Shit. Shit!'

I do look, and next to the smiling seated pair I notice an
anvil with a hammer laid on it.

His outburst attracts the attention of the assistant in that
room.

'Can't you change this exhibit, who wants to look at this?
It's a lie, it's a shit lie.' She follows him from one display to
another, all showing the poor Ukrainians being helped and liberated, given new tractors, forging ahead with their Russian
brothers into glowing red sunsets. She weathers his rantings
without betraying any emotion, her broad Slavic brow and
Asian eyes impassive under the onslaught. When Roman calms
down a little she says simply, 'There is no money to change
anything. It is a dreadful insult.'

Once she cracks, like most Ukrainians she is open, humor-
ous and generous. She offers to ask her father, who works at
the police headquarters, if he will help us find Bronek's prison
records but we will have to come back tomorrow. Roman
makes the arrangements with her and asks her how we can
repay her for her trouble.

'She just asks one cup of coffee.' He tells me later.

'Just a cup of coffee?'

'Yes, but a cup of coffee means something else. For her, a
young girl living at home with her parents, it means a bottle
of champagne and some chocolate. Ukrainian champagne, not
French. We can buy it in Lviv tomorrow. It's okay?'

'Of course. Are you sure that's enough?'

'Sure, I'm sure.'

That's the way everything works here: salaries are so small
and unreliable that everyone does something on the side. This

simple transaction seems to me to be very straight forward and honest, we all gain and we are, I hope, all pleased by the outcome. No one is threatened or exploited by it. At the other end of the scale, corruption is probably the biggest single problem that affects everyone in this country.

At the Coca-Cola factory near Roman's house, a menial job could cost about $250, the equivalent of more than three months' salary. A good job, one where you are in a position to take bribes, costs thousands of dollars. A career in this country is not a matter of professional progress but of working your way up a ladder of corruption, the more you take the higher you can go. And politics is the tallest of these ladders.

On the road again between Lviv and Ternopil I keep looking out for something I might recognise from Bronek's account of his cycle ride, but as with everything he told me, my imagination has been there first, reshaping the landscape, making it hard now to fit his memory to mine. It might have been simpler not to have come, to have relied on the images his stories conjured up in my imagination and left it at that. But something I cannot resist draws me to the edge, to see for myself, to stand where he stood in that turbulent time.

I saw in my imagination a long sweeping curve to the right, the crowded road raised above the fields. On the banking the grass is long and dry, late summer grass with poppies and oxeye daisies, and a lone figure furiously pedals along a rough track at the foot of it. It is a clear September afternoon, warm, and he sweats in his overcoat. But there is nowhere on this road like that. Mostly the banking is on the other side, the left, and it's low and only there to keep the surface level on a slope or through depressions in the undulating land. And it looks too new. I am struggling to put together a picture puzzle with too few pieces of the past and too many of the present. The spring, the storks, people hacking at the ground are not special to his story; they are always here, but too present now to ignore. I feel myself stretched between this beautiful vernal landscape and the other: the other landscape, the well of memory and history.

In the Ukrainian landscape of my imagination there is one towering figure: Koskowicki. Every weathered face of Slavic lines carries his likeness. His cropped grey hair, the fan of creases beside each eye. The dry yellowness of his face comes back to me on a long thread and transports me to Wales in the 1950s and 1960s.

We had two lives, Welsh and Polish. Everyday Welsh and holiday Polish. Weekday Welsh, Sunday Polish. Sometimes, I would arrive home from school, English school, south of the Lanscer line (but that's another story, another edge), and be met by my friend David on the bank. David went to a Welsh school, north of the line.

'Hey, Mark, that preacher is at your house, Father Potok... ks...sk...sksy. You got Polish lessons when you go home.'

A summer afternoon, we'd sit on the mounting stone outside the blacksmith's shop listening to the ringing anvil. Mr Thomas the blacksmith, said he was made of iron that leached blue-black out through his skin into the blurred pattern of navy tattoos. He said.

Sixpence to hold the horse, Mr Thomos? Sixpence to pump the bellows, Mr Thomos? There was no light in his shop save the orange glow of the fire and shower of sparks and scale splashing off the anvil. There were dark recesses behind the forge which I never saw into and a stone quenching trough which we always looked into, full of a black liquid, like oil.

'Don't fall in the trough, boys bach, it's deep.' I'd believe it, but not David.

'How deep would you say it is then, Mr Thomos?'

'Diw, it's deep, boy. It's connected to the sea.' David and I bend over the trough in the near darkness, our faces inches from the surface.

'He's right, man. I can see a ship in there!'

Suddenly, he's upsidedown, held over the water in the blacksmith's iron grip, 'I can't swim, I can't swim!'

We creep down the road to Mot Isaf, our house, keeping out of sight along the hedge. At the end of the wall in front of the house, over the milk stand, I see the priest's car. David is right, and the prospect of an hour with mothbally old Father Potoczny on this fine afternoon awakens my fugitive spirit. We creep back along the wall, dash across the steps and up the road again. As I pass the old stone gateposts I fling my satchel in the hedge and we race through the village to David's house, Mot Uchaf.

'Ooh, Mark, Father Potoksy will be disappointed.' David had already attended sarcasm lessons.

'Never mind, Julian's his favourite anyway.' I'm learning too.

There was a small but strong Polish community of Second World War exiles in the three counties of Dyfed, maybe one hundred families in all. Some were mixed, like ours, and others were entirely Polish, complete in some cases with grandparents. Mostly, they were involved in farming in one way or another, but not all. The man of the family was invariably Polish because of the military nature of his exile and he would have been the first to arrive, alone, during or just after the war. He then either brought his family from Poland as soon as he could or married a native British girl and started a mixed family. There are such Polish and half-Polish families all over Britain, but many were drawn to the edges, Scotland and Wales, where land was cheap after the war and there was the usual shortage of men after large-scale conflict. Later, in the 1960s and 1970s many of these families migrated to the cities when the price of farmland had risen and the older generation started to think about retirement. This precipitated the end of many of the rural Polish communities such as the one I grew up in. Bronek's generation are dying out and my generation are part of the mobile group who benefited from the short period of free higher education and the easy prosperous times. We have dispersed and become assimilated, indistinguishable by our accents or culture from middle-class British. The diaspora's diaspora. Names are an obvious clue, and in some cases, though not as obvious, is the feeling of otherness, of a connecton with somewhere else. And the desire to go to the edge.

Dr Zaleski, Madame Torczyńska, Karmen and Gabby

Sierosławska, Koskowicki, Gutowski, Cierniewski, De Kulik
de Walciak, Lorenz, Father Potoczny and the Polish lessons,
Hetman, Slisczyński, Bojankiewicz, Major Tomaszewski and
his army colt, Dr Jawec, Big Michael, Micharowski and the
wild girls. A list in no special order of the names I can remember from
my childhood. My dad's friends and compatriots. These were
strange and exotic people; everything about them was different: their smells, their voices and language. The thing which
bound them together, their exile, their common roots, was
stronger than personal feeling. They were like a family in the
sense that they were held together despite themselves, bound
to each other by only one bond, nationality in exile, and often
with nothing else in common. But as with families, sometimes
the fascination and attraction is heightened by the relationship,
by the bond of blood.

As a boy, this family of exiles was a matter of fascination.
The women were colourful as exotic birds, like Alice Micha-
rowska with her huge gold teeth and bright-red lipstick. At ten
years old the first newspaper I ever read was to her husband,
Toni, and my dad, Bronek. It was the story of Harold Mac-
millan's resignation. We sat in their freezing kitchen, all of us
struggling with the language.

Madame Torczyńska, an ancient lady, whom everyone
treated like royalty and we called Torchy.

'Hwat iss diss sonk you are sinkink?' It was Torchy, Torchy
the battery boy, 'From Karmen, no?' She had huge amber
beads like hen's eggs forcing her chicken's neck towards her
sternum. She loved bridge and opera. Or a matter of embarrassment, like Potoczny and the Polish lessons. They were different, hard to understand, unpredictable and excitable, and
there were the casualties, for whom the circumstances of their
uprooting was impossible to get beyond and they became, like
Zaleski, trapped and broken by the experience.

Dr Zaleski, God rest his unhappy soul, was a highly educated, cultured gentleman who lived in a filthy, moss-covered
caravan in the corner of a farmyard, alone and reclusive. He

lived from day to day by washing milk bottles in the dairy
when he could bring himself to leave the security of the van.
Bronek sometimes succeeded in persuading him to spend Chist-
mas Eve with us. He was as many older Poles can be: a mixture
of formal archaic charm and personal neglect. He would kiss
my mother's hand, call her Madame, and treat her with such
deference we all felt like oafs, but as he bent over we could see
his grey neck and greasy collar. For us kids this was great material for imitation. Julian and I would be grabbing each other's
hands, bowing over to kiss them, 'Dear lady, would you be so
kind as to feed the calves?'

'A pleasure my dear, after you.'

'No, no, I insist, after you.'

'Too kind, too kind.'

Poor Zaleski, now I wonder what his story was, what his
doctorate was, who he had been and why he became such
a shadow.

Koskowicki was different. He was a fantastical figure. He
claimed to be a count from the Ukraine, but who knows? I
only doubt this because he was so extraordinary as a plain
man that he could have been anything. A count seems unnecessarily modest. Though they were about the same age and
equally poor, he was the antithesis of Zaleski, physically so
powerful and so present, he was irresistible. They lived in the
same village: Zaleski alone in his caravan, Kosko a mile up a
track on a smallholding, never alone.

A visit. Bronek and I bump up the track in a black Morris. I
have never been to Kosko's before but I know him. He always
comes to help with haymaking and the harvest, the jobs that
require lots of people. For this sort of work he is invaluable,
his physical strength and capacity for work are legendary in
the village but it's not just for this. Although he will only work
on his own, he brings to everything he does a kind of positive
energy and purpose that infects everyone near him, and work
gets done.

I am struggling with a bale of straw, light as air to him.

'Look, boy, you take two bales, not one. This way.' He puts

the twine through each of my hands and steps back. 'Now you are yoke with two buckets. It's balance. It's better.' His favourite words, 'It's better.' His voice sounds far back in his throat, the t's and r's clear hard beach pebbles folding under a wave. His face is yellow, leathery, almost Mongolian and always smiling, showing off the gap between his front teeth. He has a corresponding gap between the index and ring fingers of his right hand, the pinkest visible skin anywhere on Koskowicki covers the D-shaped section through the very base of his ex-middle finger.

We turn into his stoney yard. A court of crumbling tiny steadings and the house makes three sides of a rectangle open to the south with the view over Maenclochog, on a clear day to Milford Haven. He and Bronek meet, shaking hands and smiling at each other. They look like brothers with their gappy teeth and Slavic heads. Koskowicki is the model for all that ghastly heroic sculpture of communist town halls. Tree-like limbs, collarless shirts open to the waist, wide leather belts, hands clamping tool handles too tightly. Total rubbish. The noble image, what utter bollocks. Life imitating art, especially bad art, is always a disaster. As you queue for bread before dawn knowing there's unlikely to be any left by the time you get to the head of the line, does it help to be standing under one of these heroes of the wheatfield. And where are they? Buried beneath it, or flown with the wheatears to Wales maybe, like Koskowicki. Now I know about the famines of the 1930s in the Soviet eastern Ukraine, the deliberate murderous starvation of the peasant farmers by Stalin's government, forced requisition and export of all crops. Bread stolen from the bread basket. Now I know that, when I think of Koskowicki, I see him simultaneously walking in the corn stubble on our top fields in Pembrokeshire at the end of a harvest day. A colossus, with the blue Preseli hills behind. And I see him standing in the corn stubble of the endless steppe, a stone statue in a heroic pose. Behind him here, the view of a pastoral idyll gives way to devastation, burning villages and sun-bleached bones.

But I knew none of this then, the day of our visit. We were

going to see Kosko, the strongest man in the world. I don't remember it warm or cold, wet or dry. Bronek and Koskowicki talk and laugh about something I don't understand; they turn and look at me, question and answer looking at me, nodding, shrugging, laughing. Dad puts his hand on the top of my head, stroking my hair then he pinches the back of my neck shaking my head from side to side. This is such a frequent feature of my childhood, one of the few ways he showed affection but I never gave up hating it. To break this horse-show routine I do the equivalent of lifting my tail and farting at the judge while he inspects my hind-quarters, I say, 'Kosko?...' as if about to ask a sensible question. I know I don't need to have thought of one.

Suddenly, he's not grinning any more, he shouts, 'I am *Koskowicki*, no Kosko. You call me Koskowicki, it's better.' He looks at me hard. He means it.

Bronek says, 'What's the matter with you, Mark?' and lets go of my neck.

'Sorry, I forgot.' They look at each other shrug and carry on about something else. What do I know, I'm just a kid.

In the house there are some dogs, some hens and a woman. Kosko's irresistibility meant that he had a succession of partners who came to stay with him. One of these was his undoing but not this one. This one provided them with some wódka and me with some milk, fresh, thank God.

Poles used to savour the taste of sour milk, maybe they still do. When my grandmother, Gabriela, lived with us (for the second time) in the mid-1960s, she used to stand jugs of milk in the back kitchen on the huge slate salting slabs, in a daily series. After a few days, when one had reached its putrid prime, she or Dad would go through a ghastly routine of decanting the lumpy gobbits of curdled slime into a glass and drinking it. They could never believe that we didn't find it attractive. I must have been about twelve when I was first offered this delicacy and being always eager, I did try very hard to drink some.

Smiling after forcing the first mouthful down my rising gorge. 'Yes, it's very nice.' I tried to hand the glass back to Dad.

'No, no, Mark, you finish it; it will make you grow.' Granny says something in Polish and she and Dad laugh, 'Tak, tak,' watching me struggle to bring the glass back to my lips. Can't they tell I was only trying to please them? Now I'm stuck with the sour milk and I have to drink it.

My own children in the same situation a generation later would just say, 'Get lost, Dad, it smells like shite.'

When we leave the house to go back to the car we find it occupied by a goat. A door has been left open and Kosko's goat is standing in the front seats eating the contents of the glove compartment: log book, handbook, maps, that sort of thing. Bronek is furious and drags the bleating animal out by the tail shouting and cursing the goat and Koskowicki. Kosko and I are on the same side now: we think it's hilarious and he tries to placate Bronek with a long story in Polish. Bronek stays furious, unmoved by Kosko's efforts, until we are half-way home. I ask him what the story was.

'You boys must learn to speak Polish. I will look for a teacher.'

I ask him again and he translates.

'He said one day the goat got into the garden and ate all his pants off the washing line.'

'What, only his pants?'

'That's what he said. Anyway, he was philosophical about this, "She can eat my pants, it is less washing. If she eats anything else, I can always eat her. I could fatten my stock on a diet of my underwear and your literature. Underwear, who cares? But books, it's a shame to eat books. It's better to burn them, eh Bronek?"'

Years later, I heard this story. The woman he lived with, the last woman in the succession to have found him irresistible, began to tire of competing with poultry and goats in the kitchen. The rough and ready lifestyle which suited Koskowicki did not include comfort. Perhaps, when she had fallen in love with him, she had dreamt of civilising the Cossak, hoping that he could be tamed. She was much younger than

him, say in her late thirties, and he must have been getting on
for seventy.

I imagine their situation. Koskowicki lived as he always had,
in a kind of rustic chaos, unimpressed by the changing lifestyle of everyone around him. I imagine his passion dwindling
but his temper worsening and his attitudes hardening. In short
her lot may not have been very different from the poultry or
the goat.

At some time her brother came to live with them and they
conspired to do away with Kosko. Why they didn't just leave is
a mystery, for he had no fabulous wealth to tempt them.

This was their plan: one night they will start an argument
which is calculated to enrage Kosko to the state where he beats
his wife or starts a fight with her brother, then as though in
self-defence, they will stab him seventeen times with the handy
bread knife, then they will race down to the village in a terrible
flap to the police station wringing their hands.

'There's been a terrible fight! It was self-defence. He would
have killed her. I didn't mean it!'

All this goes to plan, but Koskowicki won't lie down properly after the seventeen stabs. They are not quite enough for
him, though too many for her and the brother. They make a
run for it, all their scheming forgotten in panic and fear. Why
won't he die?

We all knew he was made of something harder than the rest
of us, something more determined, less doubting. He makes
it, crawling, staggering somehow, down his rocky track, a
mile to his nearest neighbour, his life almost leaked away.
And lives.

Roman and I roll on through the long villages. All of them
watched the Red Army front pass over them from the east. All
of them saw the stream of refugees from the west. Some have
a ruined church that could have concealed a sniper, but many
have new churches.

There is a rash of new church building in the Ukraine, raw
and rough-looking red brickwork on the outside with shiny

new galvanised steel onion roofs in the orthodox style. They are squarish in plan, tall solid buildings with arcading in relief around the small windows, but it is the roofs which are most surprising. The steel is used in the same way we use lead on English church roofs, in flat sheets folded over each other, but on these eastern shapes the effect is wonderful. From a distance over the flat landscape, these roofs shine out like solid silver against green baize, like jewelry in a presentation case, their facets breaking off and throwing back carat chunks of sunlight. History repeats the same story of the poverty surrounding these churches as in medieval France or modern Latin America. I don't know who paid for these buildings either. I notice them gleaming 10 miles away and I think of the road from Dreux to Chartres. The twin spires of the cathedral, the index and ring fingers of Koskowicki's disfigured hand growing out of the wheat.

By the third passage along this road, on our way to meet Svetlana, I give up thinking I'm going to spot the village I'm looking for. And I give up wondering what I'm doing here. I'm not a serious researcher: some stones can remain unturned.

We arrive at the guarded car park by the railway station in Ternopil and meet with Svetlana. Our rendezvous is in the little kiosk where the attendant takes money for car parking. Svetlana, in her best clothes quite at ease, sits on the attendant's stool in the scruffy wooden box. We are late but she is not at all anxious or impatient, she would have been happy to wait all day.

As soon as she is in the car, from her slim document case she produces a photocopy of a large photograph in a flimsy plastic envelope and passes it back to me.

'This is the town hall, where your father was in prison.' A large two-storey building sited on a corner. In the foreground next to the town hall is a monument, a statue raised on a stepped base and square pedestal. It stands at the front of a small garden between an avenue of young trees. The facade of the building facing the square has a neo-classical pediment over three arched windows on the first floor and the ground floor has rusticated stonework, but the side facing the the gardens has a plain stucco wall with flat pilasters running up to the roofline between every window. I look at the grainy image of these windows and imagine Bronek looking out on to the gardens and the statue in the winter of 1939.

'But this building is gone. It has been demolished.'

'Where was it?'

'In the main square somewhere, I am not sure.'

Nothing very terrifying happened at the security police headquarters. We met the archivist and Svetlana earned her cup of coffee writing out a long official request to see my father's records, if they still exist. I had felt as nervous of asking about that period as if raking up dangerous unexploded bombs. But there is no hangover here at least from that time. The archivist explains that so many people lost during the war are still unaccounted for, NKVD and KGB files are usually meticulously kept and therefore a good way to trace people. So many people were lost during the war, so many people have been lost since then too. Her frankness makes me realise the prejudices and the tragic sense of Polishness I have inherited from my father. Here at the edge many tides have washed in and out since then, by turns taking away and depositing millions of stories like his.

Roman and I sit outside a café in the square with the photograph Svetlana gave me, trying to match it to a location. From the photo it's impossible to be sure where the prison stood, not enough of the adjacent buildings is shown. I think that the trees are the clue, the monument has gone or been moved but the trees haven't offended anyone, offering the same shade to all. Collaborating. Arborating.

On the way home we take a picnic into the woods. Roman, on impulse, turns off the road on to a track running next to a railway embankment. After a hundred yards it ducks underneath it through a narrow tunnel and we emerge on the edge of a wood. As we are decanting the picnic, a black and white police Lada appears through the mouth of the tunnel.

'Mark, you say nothing. Act like a Ukrainian.'

With a Ukrainian accent, I carry the bag of food to the grassy slope at the margin of the trees. 'Djakyooyoo, I come from Lview.' My Ukrainian mantra. I walk back to the car, still in a Ukrainian accent, and generally fuss about until they have gone.

'Very good, Mark, you are just like a real Ukrainian.'

'Djakyooyoo.'

—15 —
Różniatów

Różniatów church seems to hover weightlessly two feet above the ground. I feel I could push one corner of it and the whole structure would slowly turn on its axis like a merry-go-round or one of those rotating summerhouses. This is a huge building with a tower and an open porch the full width of the west end; it would be heavy, resistant, inert as a ship floating at the quayside very slowly yielding to my insistent pressure. It is constructed on a raft of massive beams whose support, if there really is any, is not visible but lost in the shadows on which the vessel rests. It is all bare wood, a naked golden body in the sunlight of the warmest day we've had, warm to the touch, the body of the kirk.

Something's wrong though. At the end of the narrow path we follow to find the priest's house this feeling becomes stronger. In the garden, between the old fruit trees, the house looks wrong. I study the clapper boards and the doorframing only half listening to Roman and the priest. Dark, even-grained planks surround the door and ripple away the length of the building. There is a dog chained to a kennel and muscovy ducks have their own path through the fence to a neighbouring field.

'What was the priest's name?'

'Michał Szczęk.'

But he shakes his head, 'No, there was no priest here with that name.'

'Are you sure? It was before the war.'

'Yes, I have all the records.' And he repeats some names and dates. Roman asks me if I am sure of the name, and then if I'm sure it was Różniatów. We are all embarrassed. I knew it, this is not the place.

'And your father was here?'

'Yes. Well, he said so.'

'What was his name?'

'Bronisław Zygadło.'

He shakes his head again; it rings no bells in there. We are starting to withdraw, to thank him for his trouble and apologise for the inconvenience.

'Ah, wait.' A last-minute inspiration, 'Szczęk, Zygadło. Polish names, of course. They were Roman Catholic, yes?'

'Yes.' Roman strikes his forehead, 'Of course. This is the Ukrainian priest, not the Catholic one.'

'There are no Catholics here any more,' he says. 'But, come with me, please, there are still two Polish women who live in the village. They will know.' He reappears at the door after a moment's absence in a strange flat cap with ventilated sides and leads us back along the paths to a white house near the church.

Olga listens to Roman tell my story. Not understanding the words but knowing the meaning they convey, I watch her face closely to gauge the outcome. At first she is confused by the torrent of information and the physical presence of two men on her doorstep who appear to want something. But, as the story takes over, she starts to nod, to understand what we want and with a series of appraising looks, to accept who I am.

She leads us to a small plateau just west of the village centre, pressed into the flank of a wooded hill. Raised up on a steep bank on the village side, it is a big circular platform about two hundred yards in diameter grassed over and golden with dandelions. On the village side is the inevitable poet's monument; Shevchenko this time, I think, but I could be wrong. Ivan Franko perhaps. At the back of the circle a track follows the rising ground into the woods.

Olga stands at the centre, arms spread, 'Here was the church, and here', she walks to the northern side, 'was the house, under the trees. There is nothing here now.' Only dandelions. The church I construct in my imagination is modelled on the one we have just walked by, made of wood and hovering like a spaceship above the dandelions. Moveable, removeable. I imagine Bronek, Gabriela, Hanusia and Michał Szczęk hovering in the air in the spaces where their lives were temporarily housed. I am looking for the vacancy left by these buildings, a negative church, a negative of the house, for their wooden absence.

Bronek showed me once a photograph of his mother and sister in a garden. There are neat rows of vegetables behind them, an air of organisation, comfort and pride. But there is no house, no church over the picket fencing behind them, no clue. Hanusia is in her early teens, she is happy, sitting in an old chair in a summer frock, in not-best clothes, looking at her mother. It is homely, it could have been taken here. Now, I place these trees in the background of the photograph and I include the unstructured pattern of the village roofs below the slope. Almost anything can be added but the image remains unanchored, I am stuck with the idea of floating churches. Of castles in the air.

When Bronek left the village, early that morning in December 1939 on his way to Lwów, he never returned. His memory of the village was always dominated by the church and the manse. Mine will be equally, but by their absence.

Hanusia was waiting for him outside his lodgings in Lwów, freezing in the coming night. She had not been inside the house but had watched from across the road the many strangers who had come and gone from there.

'Hanusia, what are you doing here? What has happened?'

'I have come to fetch you back, we must go straight away.'

'Why?'

'There is a group of men leaving from the village, going to Hungary.'

'How do you know this?'

'Pan Lubaczewski, the judge, told mother and she has made him promise to take you with him.'

'But, Hanusia, I cannot go back to Różniatów, I was already told I had to leave.'

'It is all arranged, Father Michał will meet us near Krechowicz with a pony and trap and take you to meet the others.'

'Where?'

'I don't know where.'

'Who else is going?'

'I don't know any more than I told you, I just came to fetch you. Now we must go or we will never get there. Where have you been all day?'

'At the college, burying Bolshevik horses.'

'Can a horse be a Bolshevik?'

'Probably not. Why were you not inside, you must be freezing out here?'

'I watched for a while, there is no one there we know any more. People came and went all afternoon, strangers and soldiers, no one I recognise.'

'We should enquire about the family.'

'What for, Bronek? We are leaving now; it is too risky.'

'But I was in prison with a friend of theirs.'

'Bronek, we must leave. It's too dangerous to ask.'

We walk back to the station, Hanusia has brought me some bread and sausage, which I eat while we walk. On the train she tells me that all Poles are to be deported back to German-occupied Poland, the so-called General Government, or to Russia. Mother and Father Michał have to go but she would have the choice, she could stay in the Soviet Union if she wanted to. What should she do?

'Hanusia, don't stay here, you know what will happen. The Russians are worse than animals and the Ukrainians hate the Poles. Fyodor Andreyev, the lieutenant, told me this would happen. He also said you should not stay here, you should go to the General Government.'

'But will it be any different in Germany?'

'I don't know, but I think so. They will probably try to make you a German, but better that than being made into a Russian.'

The prospects for everyone are appalling, and we sit for most of the journey in mute silence. Rumours have come from the General Government part of Poland since the invasion, but I find it difficult to imagine what it will be like for her there.

Once again Poland does not exist. The question is, in this new arrangement, where will it be easiest to survive? For Hanusia alone there appears to be a choice, but the most apparent truth is that all Poles will be removed from the Ukraine, which is effectively where we now are. Fyodor Andreyev's advice was to get out before you are removed in some other way.

I recall my impression of the Red Army rolling into that village on the road between Lwów and Tarnopol. A primitive and rough rabble mounted on poor-looking horses or side-saddle on the open backs of lorries. Horses drawing pieces of antiquated field artillery, the same pieces they used against the sniper, and the odd motorcycle. They looked old fashioned and ill equipped. However, what they lacked in modern machinery they made up in reputation. News of their barbarous occupation and the brutal treatment of the population of the Soviet eastern Ukraine had gone before them. Information about the horrors of imposed famine and deportations had leaked through the military cordon and prepared us for the arrival of this beast. Even those who didn't believe it at the time would reflect at length during their internal exiles or sentences in the gulags. But that all came later.

When atrocities are taking place, people around them don't understand or believe what they are seeing. It is easier to believe that such things are not possible in a modern world when the truth is staring them in the face; nothing changes, people have been slaughtering each other since Cain killed his brother. Mietek's grandfather, the old man who was beaten up for hiding the rifle, was right. He had fought them before. He said, there was nothing to be gained from surrender to them, they would kill you anyway, sooner or later. We are all leaving, while we can.

What cannot be killed is hope. What was never irradicated in Poles through the years of the partitions or now in this new crisis is hope. As we sit in silence on the train to Kałusz, the solid world dissolves into darkness and the night comes. Hanusia stares into one possible future and I into another, our reflections staring back out of the darkness of the train windows. The last night we spent together for twenty years.

Out of this emptiness, between regular interruptions to check our travel certificates, which Hanusia miraculously produced without explanation, and out of this unassailable hope congeals during the night a nascent patriotism. The focus of my hope and hopelessness sharpens itself on this journey into something like resolve and purpose. It seems possible now to refuse, to avoid the jaws closing on the sandwich, not just to escape being crushed myself, but also to fight back.

My patriotism is self-conscious and fragile; it won't even stand my own scrutiny. I can't explain to myself why it should be right to fight for Poland and not, as Fyodor said, for Russia or Germany. It is no less a lie. I have seen in Lwów the effects of nationalism, the feuding between Ukrainians and Poles, Poles and Jews. Assasinations, riots and demonstrations. What is the country I feel connected to? A repressive occupying force in this part of Galicia. A double-crossing tyrant that promised autonomy for the Ukrainians when it needed their help against the Bolsheviks twenty years ago, and never gave it. Yet, I feel it. I feel it with almost religious fervour. I believe it, hearing at the same time Fyodor's voice, sneering at the sentimentality of it, quoting to me the opening stanza of Mickiewicz's *Pan Tadeusz*.

Oh Lithuania, my country, thou art like good health;
I never knew till now how precious, till I lost thee.
Now I see thy beauty whole,
Because I yearn for thee.

It says it all. Our national bard, a Lithuanian Pole, mourning the loss of his country to the Russians in the eighteenth century. Lithuanian but his country was Poland, the Polish Commonwealth. Lithuania, like Galicia, in the minds of Poles like me and Mickiewicz who lived there, was a part of Poland. To the Lithuanians and Ukrainians it is, of course, another matter, but I yearn just the same. I smart at having been invaded in a week and not even mobilised to fight, but now for the first time I see that it has not started yet: we are down but not out.

By the time we are nearing Kałusz the night is nearly over. Hanusia has slept for much of the way, I have not. I have been aware of a rising excitement, a sense of the coming adventure and it has stolen sleep from me. Like love, the same fascinating image circulates in my mind, alluring, glorious and exciting, the beginning of a real journey.

In the early morning Hanusia and I walk out of the village of Krechowicz in the direction of Różniatów. Not far out of the village we are met by Father Michał in a pony and trap. I conceal myself under a blanket behind the seat while she rides beside him. Just short of Różniatów, at the river, Hanusia descends and continues home on foot. She says the briefest farewell to me, patting the blanket.

'Serwus, Broniu.'

'I'll be back soon, Hanka. I'll see you in a free Poland.'

Michał and I trot in the direction of Nadworna, skirting Różniatów to the east then heading south again towards the mountains and the Hungarian frontier.

'Where are we going, Father?'

'You will see.'

'Won't you tell me?'

'Rather not, Bronek. If we are caught, the less you know the better.'

'But I already know that there is a group led by Lubaczewski, going to Hungary.'

'By the time they found out where from, Lubaczewski would be in Hungary.'

I am surprised at his thoroughly cold grasp of the situation and it chills me. The closer we get to our point of departure, the smaller the number of possible places it could be. In the end we will commit ourselves to one of the dead-end tracks leading to a village in a valley and no further. Our hope is that we will not be noticed.

'Thank you, Father.'

'Do not thank me yet, wait until you get to Hungary, then you can thank me.'

'By then you will be in the General Government.'

'God willing.'

'Where will you go?'

'To my family in Nowy Targ. Antonina and Michał will be there too I hope. And you Bronek, you could take that chance, you could ask to be deported to the German side.'

'You know it's too risky, Father. I would be made to join the forces or put in a prison again. Anyway, the Russians might not let me go. They will fight the Nazis one day, they don't want to send them troops now.'

'You are right.'

Thinking of what Fyodor had said I say, 'At the moment no one knows or is interested in where I am, so this is a good time to leave. People say there is a Polish army forming the other side of the mountains, preparing to fight its way back. I don't know how that could be, but I will find it if it exists. Otherwise, I will get to France and join the Allies.'

'I wish it could be an easy journey for you, Bronek, but I fear it will not be.'

The fine morning wears on. It is cold and clear; the remains of a light snowfall is still on the ground, like fine dust accumulating at the edges of the track and in the ditches. The frozen earth is light grey and hard as stone.

'It's a beautiful day, Bronek.'

There is no visible sky from my viewpoint: just the priest's legs and boots, the horse's back and bouncing black mane, the steam from her nostrils like a bow wave each side of her.

'Father, may I ask you something?'

'Certainly, Bronek.'

'Do you know why I was let out of prison?'

'You should have asked your mother when you had the chance, now it is too late. But yes I do know something about it.'

'Why, then?'

'You probably know that she made several visits to the militia and the NKVD to try to persuade them to release you. You were accused of being a counter-revolutionary, a nationalist and a Polish officer disguised as a civilian. Eventually your mother managed to get your release by bribing someone to give

a good opinion of you and testify that you were none of the
things you were accused of. You were officially released from
lack of evidence against you.'

'Who?'

'Whom did she pay? I don't know, she never told me.'

I doubt this, but even when I press him further he refuses
to divulge anything more. We continue at a leisurely pace, not
to draw attention to ourselves. When we approach a house or
hamlet I hide myself, drawing the blanket over me, until Father
Michał gives me the all-clear again. This journey is as dangerous for him as for me, but, besides the danger, I saw from his
face as we met him on the road near Krechowicz that he is
still not well, he was pale, almost yellow in the early morning
chill. Yet he had decided that he would deliver me to the rendezvous himself, thinking that a priest would be of less interest
to the police than a young man travelling alone. I know these
roads, of course, and as the day goes on I guess we are heading
for Osmoloda.

Olga invites us to go with her to visit her aunt, who lives in
the road just at the bottom of the mound on which the church
had stood. Walking back across the grassy plateau, she nudges
me with her elbow and confides something in Ukrainian. I
look at Roman, on the other side of her. He looks away, a
little embarrassed.

'What's she saying, Roman?'

'She says she knew your father, you know, very well.' Olga
nods enthusiastically and keeps nudging me. I look at her, wondering how old she could be. It's difficult to tell: she has a dark,
weathered face which makes her look older than her years. I'm
sure she would have been too young, maybe too young to have
known him at all. But I don't want to offend her.

'Oh, yes.'

Roman waves his finger in warning, 'She probably wants
something.'

Olga still jabbering on and cackling, nudges me again and
winks. Roman exhales his cigarette smoke noisily, groaning in

obvious disbelief and Olga moderates her suggestions. When we get to her aunt's she forgets them altogether, but I'm flattered in a way however ridiculous the story was.

Jadwiga Wołosynowicz, a gentle and refined lady of nearly a generation older than Olga, is embarrassed at being caught in her nylon housecoat. She admonishes Olga for not warning her that she was bringing visitors to her door. Olga in exactly the same housecoat feels no awkwardness, she just shrugs, 'They haven't come to visit your overalls.'

She makes us tea, then produces a photograph taken in front of a porch of a group of children clustered round a seated priest. From the size of his head, which is almost the only part of him visible among the children, he looks like a big man, in his fifties perhaps.

'Father Shchenk. In Polish, Szczęk.' The Polish pronunciation of his name involves one of the most difficult sounds for a non-Polish speaker. The e has an accent below it indicating something like an 'euwng' sound. Under an a, the only other letter it affects, it changes it to 'ong'. I practise this sound to everyone's amusement; it sounds fine to me and hilarious to everyone else.

Jadwiga says, 'He was not well then, I remember. He had been in bed for some time and this was soon after he recovered enough to get out of doors. He had tuberculosis.'

'Are you in this picture?'

'Yes.' She points to skinny kid sitting on the ground in front of the priest's chair, then she names those of the other children she can remember: Janina Frenczuk, Janina, Elenora and Kazimierz from Krehowicz, Helena Rataj.

The other adult in the picture is Bronek's sister, Hanusia, who stands side on, looking over her right shoulder at the camera. I guess that she is about eighteen.

'Anna, she was so beautiful.' Jadwiga says, 'Everyone loved her, all the children. She used to help with the Scouts and with all the very young children who came to the church. She was good with children.'

'Do you remember my father, Bronisław?'

'Yes, I remember him, but, you know, I was much younger and he was not here very often. He was at the gymnasium in Stanisławów, then, I don't know, a student somewhere. Kraków perhaps.'

'Lwów.'

'Ah, Lwów.' She looks at me for a while, 'Do you look like your father?'

'Some people say so.'

'Yes, you look familiar.'

'Do you remember Antonina and Michał Szczęk, the priest's nephew and niece. They must have stayed here sometimes.'

'Antonina, I remember well, but Michał, no.'

'He was Bronek's age, they were good friends. He is dead now, but Antonina lives in Kraków. I will be staying with her on my way home.' I tell her about Antonina's family and promise take her address. 'You did not leave with the other Poles in 1939?'

'My parents wanted to stay; I was a young girl then. This is our home. Later, after the war, I married a Ukrainian, I have a family here. But I remember everyone leaving, they took all the Poles to the border at Przemyśl and left them. The Germans took them from there. They had to leave everything behind. The priest, your grandmother and Anna left together and a few days later they destroyed the church and the house. The Bolsheviks hated the church.'

'What happened, did they burn it down?'

'No, they blew it up. They were so incompetent, they had to do it twice. The first time they did not put enough explosive in it. When they set it off, there was a bang but nothing happened. The windows were broken, that's all. So they set the charges a second time. This time, making sure they would destroy the building, they put too much. When they set it off they broke all the windows in the village and pieces of the church crashed into the houses all around, falling through the roofs. It was terrible. People were deaf for days.'

'Do you remember a group of men leaving from the village in December 1939?'

'There were many groups that left here that winter, some to Hungary, some to Romania. The borders were different in those days; Hungary was nearer. The Nazis in Czechoslovakia gave Ruthenia to Hungary because there were Hungarians living there. There were Ukrainians too. Well, anyway, now it is Ukraine.'

'Do you remember a group led by someone called Lubaczewski?'

'Lubaczewski, yes. They were caught. I remember, they were brought back to the village by a patrol.'

'No, it can't be. My father left with them and he got to Hungary.'

'With Lubaczewski, the doctor?'

'Wasn't he a judge or lawyer?'

'Ah, no. Yes, you are right. Lubaczewski was a judge, he was a great friend of Father Michał and your grandmother. It was another group I was thinking of that went with the doctor, but they didn't get out.'

'What happened to them?'

She shrugs. I should understand. 'Who knows?'

There was something in her reference to Father Michał and Gabriela, the way their names ran together in her sentence. 'Did you know my grandmother, do you remember her at all?'

'Oh yes, we spent a lot of time in that house. Anna looked after lots of children. There were always children there. Father Michał, he loved children. He was a very generous man, he helped everyone.'

'And my grandmother?'

'Your grandmother was a brave woman.'

'What do you mean?'

She hesitates.

'Please, tell me.'

'Well, there was great poverty here then and there had been fighting after the Great War between the Poles, the Russians and the Ukrainian partisans. It was not an easy time. Your grandmother was on her own with two orphans to feed. People said this; I was too young then to know about these things, they said she "looked after" the priest, you understand? Well, it's not uncommon. People disapproved, but in the end she found a way to live, to keep her family, and now I think she was a brave person. She was a good person. Later, people said that she was the one who got your father from prison but I don't know. They left, when, in early 1940? You are the first time I have heard any news of them since then.' She stops, looking back through a half century, 'She was a good cook too, she used to make beautiful biscuits for us children.'

When it's time to leave, I ask her if she would mind if I took a photograph of her. She says she'd be delighted but disappears from the room. After a long time she comes back wearing a black lace gown, she has done her hair and her make-up and she looks wonderful. She stands very straight and still on the back steps of the house with her hands clasped at her waist. She looks straight at the camera, holding her smile after I have taken the shot. When Roman tells her it's all over, she looks so disappointed that I say, 'No, no. Please stay there: I want to take another.' I spend a long time peering through the lens, ask her to move a little this way and that, take some of her with Olga, who isn't interested at all in having her picture taken, until I have almost finished the film. I take a couple of shots of her photograph of all the children with the priest and a last one of Jadwiga and Olga at the front of the house as we are leaving.

'Now, Mark. I take you to Sheshory and we swim.'

The river runs through a gorge near the village, cascading from one pool to another between huge rocks worn flat and smooth by the winter torrents. We take some beer and some sausage and stretch out on their warm tops in the sun.

'Everybody comes here in the summer: it's the best place on this river. I bet your father came here to swim. Sometimes there isn't room to sit down, there are so many people. Like the beach in Spain.'

'Have you been in Spain, Roman?'

'No, but I watch the English travel programmes on the TV.'

'How do you do that? Have you got a satellite dish.'

'No, but we have "Private Enterprise Cable TV" in our street.' He stands to attention, saluting the technological age. 'You know my friend Fred across the street? He is very clever with electronics. He made a dish and a decoder and he has linked the whole street to his system. We all have to watch the same programme at the same time but you can make requests. Sometimes when there is nothing interesting he plays a video movie for everyone.' The street is a good community. Independently communist you might say. There is a money exchange at one back door with better rates than the bank, there is a petrol station at another selling unadulterated fuel in twenty-litre cans cheaper than the regular stations and now I discover they have their own TV cable network.

'But we are poor: our government are all bandits. This country is controlled by thieves.'

At the top of the rocks behind us someone starts calling out warnings. Roman says there is a guy up there who is going to jump into the pool below. I get my camera and we join a few people waiting at the river's edge for the leap.

Against the sky on the top of the cliff among the trees and bushes a tanned young man is shouting for everyone to clear the pool, and to pay attention. Even after everyone has left the water he seems to hesitate, coming to the edge and then backing off again, talking to someone out of sight to us. Is he frightened or is this part of the build-up? A way of focusing our attention on the one second it will take him to fall to the water. He comes back to the edge, stands quite still looking down into the pool. We are all quiet down below, I am watching him through the lens, zoomed in. He is frightened but elated. He will jump. He breaks the spell, taking a step backwards and half turning away, then as though bouncing off something behind him, he springs over the edge into the air.

I catch him near the top of the drop, with his legs drawn up towards his chest, his arms paddling the air against his forward trajectory and then against descent, and with a terrified expression on his face. But he is out there, in the air, over the edge. Later he appears on our rock still dripping and asks me, through Roman, if I will give him the photograph when it is printed.

In Guilin in southern China, in the terminally eroded limestone landscape of the Li river, I paid an old lady in a sampan to ferry me and my bicycle across to a place to swim. Half-way over the wide expanse we divert to an enormous rock, a limestone stack jutting out into mid-stream, attracted by the sound of children playing in the water. She deposits me at the base of the rock to find my own way. On the top I find a school party of nine and ten-year-olds flinging themselves off the edge in the most fantastic attitudes of flight. They go head first, feet first, side ways, backwards, holding hands, without a thought about who may be below. As soon as they see me, I know I am lost. A hundred yellow hands take my bag, force me into my trunks and push me to the edge. There is no way back. I look down from an impossible height at the tiny frog figures swimming in the khaki water below. A child beside me leaps into space, turning as he does to watch me watching him. A thousand tiny finger-pressures on my back. I leap.

When it's time for them to go back to school we leave off our leaping and their teacher puts into my hands an English textbook, a reader. We settle on the top of the rock, fifty Chinese children in white shirts and red neckerchiefs cross-legged around me and I read to them in my best English voice the first chapter of their book: *The Life of Karl Marx.*

In the evening Roman takes me to the ballet in the Lviv Opera. A friend of his in the band owes him a favour and gives us box tickets for a performance in this superb building. A copy of the Vienna Opera house built in the period of their occupation. In the first interval we go to the artists' bar and drink wódka with the bedraggled players. I watch the Russian prima-ballerina sink a half-litre of beer, smoke a Sobranie and stroke her son's head. She is known here as the Fat One, but she is good on stage, she has great presence. She is so named only in contrast to the Thin One, a fifteen-year-old stick-person who is also very good. They all smoke to keep their weight down, because they all drink. We stagger back to our box to find it has been invaded by badged-up delegates from a conference in town.

After another bout in the bar between the second and third acts we also migrate. For a small fee to the attendant, the orchestra box is ours for the third act. Through an alcoholic haze I look down on the players in the pit below our box. The narcotic effect of the intervals are taking a deleterious toll on the accuracy of their playing. The flautist wanders through his solos unable to keep his disorderly quavers from sliding around before his eyes on the staves. He continues to stare at his score in disbelief for some time after the conclusion of his solo.

After the performance we walk in Svoboda Prospect, the beautiful long square in front of the Opera house. By day, under the shade of young horse-chestnuts, this area is crowded with gamblers who play chess or dominoes on the benches set between the trees. Teenage chess-heroes in black leather play bearded aesthetes in brown suits, a slow-motion prize-fight. Their games are cocooned by small audiences frozen in impossible attitudes, craning over each other to watch the match. It's illegal, but almost everything is here.

At night the wide pavements are lined with makeshift bars of beer crates and portable fridges staked out with the ubiquitous plastic tables and chairs. Folksy rock bands play in the no-man's-land between them. Power cables are drawn from a public building, the windows conveniently left open for a small fee. It's illegal too. But so is the drinking in the street, and the dancing, but hundreds of people do a bouncy-on-the-spot sort of polka, chest to chest and kicking their legs out to the side on the hop. They laugh, drink. Children and dogs run into the shrubbery to relieve themselves, ignoring the rather self-conscious-looking gangsters in Armani suits. It's all illegal and dangerous, but all alive and exciting: dancing at the edge.

On my way to the shrubbery I hear the only American

voices of the whole trip. Four young men sprawling at a table trying to blend. They have beautiful long hair, expensive spectacles and bulgingly unobtrusive bum-bags. And they all talk loudly in Russian, like Arnie in *Red Heat*.

'Wow – you're Scotch.' And I'm asked why I haven't got a skirt on.

Scotland is another country on the hemline of Europe, semi-independent and famous only for its spirits and skirts, it seems.

— 16 —
Brzozowa

It was 17 December. Father Michał and I trotted towards the hills, south towards Hungary and my escape. We followed a meandering route through the country tracks and byways which avoided villages on the major roads. The journey took all day and when we arrived at our destination, near Osmoloda, it was already evening.

In a clearing just at the edge of the forest, where our track deteriorates into a path and we can go no further with the trap, Lubaczewski emerges from the cover of the trees. He and Father Michał speak softly to each other as I extricate myself, stiff and bruised on one side after the bumpy ride, from my hiding place behind the seat. Others also reveal themselves gradually from the surrounding woods and gather around the leader and the priest. I know some of the men by sight from the village, and some I do not recognise. Together we make a small group of nine, including Lubaczewski.

In an atmosphere of jittery anticipation, we all check our knapsacks or retie our boots, nervously preparing ourselves, making unnecessary adjustments for the walk ahead. Father Michał produces a bag for me with some food: bread, cheese and sausage; a few items of extra clothing that mother had assembled, some personal papers and a knife. A meagre collection of belongings to be setting out with.

Some of the party are older men, in their thirties or forties like Lubaczewski. Leaving for them includes abandoning their families to the uncertainties of the occupation, it heightens their sense of urgency and anxiety. For them the exile must be short; they must do what has to be done quickly and return home as soon as possible. We stand, stamping our feet on the frozen earth, some of us hesitating, some fidgeting to be off.

We smoke, we wait. Cigarette smoke mingles with our condens-
ing breathe; impatience and reluctance mixed in clouds hangs,
adrift like us, in the still air.

Two brothers from the village are arguing; the younger has
a pregnant wife in Różniatów.

'I don't want to miss the birth of my child. How will she
manage without me?' It is their first perhaps. He is a youth, no
more than twenty.

'How many months is she gone?'

'Five months already.'

'In another three months we will be back, don't worry. It
won't take long to get the Ruskis out. You've seen them: they
are a hopeless lot.'

'Yes, but I hate to leave her; we've only been married since
Easter.'

'Listen, little brother. We all have families; everyone is leaving their loved ones behind. Look at these men, they are fathers
and husbands. Now we have to be soldiers too.'

'I know, I know.' Tears like stars glint under his eyes.

'Come, be strong, brother. By next Easter, you will be at
home in a free Poland, bouncing a new baby on your knees.
Ask Pan Lubaczewski.'

I am told I met Lubaczewski when I was a child but I can't
remember him. I know about him the single fact that he carried Bronek some of the way across these mountains. Reading
these words shames me. I know that his son's family used to
live in Wiltshire.

Since writing these words, I have found his number through
directory enquiries and spoken to the son, Ryszard Lubaczewski. I have arranged to meet him.

'My father was the chief justice for the area, the criminal
judge. He was the youngest judge ever appointed in Poland, at
only thirty-two. By the beginning of the war he would have
been about thirty-six or thirty-seven. Since you called me I
have been phoning relations and friends all over the place to
find out as much as I can about it, because I know less than

you. He never talked about those days unless he met some of his old friends, and we were not that interested in it anyway when we were children. I always thought they left in September but when you told me it was December I started to think about what else I didn't know. And, you are right, they left in late December and arrived in Budapest on Christmas Eve.'

'That's the last time anyone could go because the borders were closed finally on 26 December.' Leonard Konikiewicz, Ryszard's cousin from Tennessee, an authority on the period, is staying with him when I visit.

'The next day the Russians came to the village and removed 622 people by train to Khazakstan and then to Siberia. My mother and I among them.'

'How old were you then?'

'I was two so I don't remember it. I do remember later in Siberia, I went blind from malnutrition.'

'Did they give you onions?'

'How did you know about the onions?'

'I read it or heard it on the radio, blindness from malnutrition could be cured by eating onions.'

'I still eat raw onions, I love them.' He produces the evidence from the fridge.

'Your father had a narrow escape if the Russians came the next day to take them away.' Leonard is piecing together his family history, too. For this short walk our family histories ran beside each other.

'He knew they were coming, he was tipped off.'

'Who tipped him off?'

'The strange thing is, it was prisoners that my father had sent to jail.'

'Wait a second.' Leonard's heavily accented disbelief. 'You mean the people your father sent to jail were so grateful they wanted to help him later? Come on, Ryszard.'

'It's true. After they came in, the Russians opened the prisons and were releasing criminals; maybe they needed the space or something for all the new people they were arresting. Some of these prisoners, the criminals, came to him and told him

that they knew the deportation from Różniatów was going to be the next day and he was on the list, he better leave quickly. And they offered to guide them over the mountains.'
'That's fantastic. Why should they do that for the judge?'
'Maybe they needed a leader. They knew he was a fair man. He was famous in the area for being the judge you could not bribe. He was rich enough already. Anyway, think about it. They arrive in Hungary on their own, what are they? They are just a band of convicts. They arrive in Hungary with a group led by the famous judge, they are heroes.'
'Maybe.'
Remembering the name Hanusia mentioned on her tape, 'Was there someone also called Haszczewski?'
'Jacek Haszczewski, yes there was. He came to London with my father in 1946. They were together for the whole war, Tobruk, in Monte Cassino. I knew him well.'
'Is he still alive?'
'No, he is buried next to my parents. We were at his grave yesterday, with Leonard.' He picks him out in the photograph album.
'So far we have your father Kazik Lubaczewski, Haszczewski, my father Bronek Zygadło, and some ex-convicts. How many of them were there?'
'I don't know, only that it was a small group. Not as much as a dozen.'
'Have you heard anything about a pair of brothers who went?'
'Brothers? No. That's all I know.'
'What happened to you and your mother, Ryszard?'
'As soon as they knew that my father had to go, they sent my brother to visit my grandmother in Buczacz; he was nine. The next day they came with a list and took all the people from the village. Your father's name would have been on it too. Six hundred and twenty-two people. Twenty of us came back in 1941.'
'Why did they send your brother to Buczacz?'
'The families did that. They knew that the chances of sur-

vival were slim anyway, so they tried to spread the risk as thinly as possible and increase the chances of at least someone surviving. With two children to feed, maybe none of us would have lasted. They knew because there was nothing new in the way the Russians treated their prisoners, even under the Tsar. As the trains passed through the neighbouring villages, people were throwing notes out to those left behind, saying who was taken. That's how my grandmother got the news that they had gone: a note thrown from the train.

'When the Russians changed sides in 1941, they let us go and we travelled for months, mostly walking to get to the Middle East.'

'You walked from Siberia to the Middle East?'

'To Persia I think, I was only four or five. We were taken by the British to Lebanon, where we stayed until the end of the war and then we came to England.'

'And your father?'

'There is a blank spot, between 1940, when he was in Hungary, and 1942. I will have to find his war record from the same place you got your father's.'

'Did he go to France?'

'No. I don't know what happened to him. But you have started something now.'

'Everybody leaves it too late,' Leonard growls, 'that's why I have written my own memoir. For my daughter.'

'Yes, we will be back by Easter if we leave by Christmas. Come, bless us, Father; it is time.'

Father Michał improvises a short blessing on our journey and shakes hands with everyone. Some of the men give him letters or messages to carry back to their families and finally he comes to stand in front of me.

'I wish I could be going with you, Bronek. God bless you and keep you safe.'

'And you too, Father'

He takes my hand but then embraces me. 'Be careful, my boy.'

'Thank you. Kiss my mother and Hanusia.'

'You will be back. In the spring perhaps. Goodbye, Broniu.'

'Goodbye, Father.'

At Lubaczewski's signal, we set off in silence; every man alone with his thoughts. I have less to worry me than many of my companions. I know what will happen to my family, or think I do, and I have no wife and children to leave exposed and unprotected. Fyodor, I felt sure, would do what he could to help them, as he had done for me.

Fyodor the chess fanatic. Why do I think of him as a friend? Why should I think I could trust him? A Russian. I imagine the end of our chess game, a school-boy war of attrition, down to the last few pieces. A pawn reaches the far side of the almost empty board and becomes the queen. In the wódka haze of that evening, a synod meets in my head to debate whether the pawn is transfigured or the dead queen is resurrected. An alchemist screeches that every base pawn is a queen in waiting. Madame Bławacka joins the argument with a chain of being, pawns reincarnated as Aryan queens before I shut it off. We are still in the opening gambit, doing what we can one square at a time. Almost all the pieces are still in play.

On the first ridge we make our first stop for a few moments' rest. We stand in a line looking back over the trees at Poland. We have been walking through the forest for two hours, maybe more, with hardly a word of our thoughts spoken. It is so clear and cold up here that my breath crystallizes in front of me into minute glittering flakes. The full moon over the mountains is surrounded by a halo of ice in the upper atmosphere rimmed with the faintest spectral rainbow, luminous in the freezing air over the plain stretching to the north. Villages and farms below us glowing smoky yellow in this beautiful night. The most beautiful night I can imagine.

From up here everything looks so tranquil I can't help wondering why we are doing this. From here the war, the invasion seems like an illusion, like a bad dream we are climbing out of. I am left with a sense of the disturbance but with only a vague notion of the actual horrors of a few days ago. From here I can't see the Russians in the villages or on the streets of Lwów, I can't see inside the prisons, on to the trains or into the pits. I am no longer in the nightmare. I look down over the sleeping, dreaming body of my country, apparently so peaceful, and feel guilt at stealing away in the night.

This is the moment of my farewell, we turn and descend behind the hill. There may be other backward views of Poland further on, but they will be successively smaller; we will see no villages only the backs of these hills. This is the picture I will keep, the one I will think of and describe when I am asked by my children. This moment.

On the descent I chide myself about my boots as I skid about on the snow. I have the habit of wearing ski boots in the winter because they are perfectly waterproof and short journeys are often taken on skis. They are good boots but they have little or no grip, the soles are made to fit the skis and are smooth. The higher we climb into the snow the harder my progress becomes. I had no opportunity to change them before we left, even if I had wanted to, from now on these are my only boots.

Antonina, Bronek and I leave Kraków heading south towards the Slovakian frontier as far as Nowy Targ, then east into the hills. We are not going to cross the border today, we are going to Debno, a village in the foothills of the Tatra on the Dunajec river where Michał Szczęk had his last parish and where he is buried. The wooden Parish church has recently made Debno into a tourist attraction, not because it is new, it is not, but because tourism is.

It is a charming spot, the tiny village in a broad valley. The church is made entirely of wood, from the shingles to the foundation, but most remarkable is the interior. There is hardly a square inch that is not in some way decorated with carved statues, icons, miniature shrines in boxes on the walls. It is not high ecclesiastical art, like the golden interior of the Mariacki Cathedral in Kraków; it is bare wood, a lot of it, quite rough but powerful and real.

Around the churchyard is a circular wall, also made of

wood, with its own little roof running along the top of it. Inside this and clustered around the church itself are the graves of the parishioners, and their priest. I am unsure of whether Bronek knew this village, if there was any connection with it before he left in 1939. He stands at a gate across the track from the churchyard, staring for a long time at the priest's house as though there was some memory stored inside it, but he says nothing and I don't ask today. He and Antonina are preoccupied. Maybe he visited him here in 1962, on his first trip back to Poland.

They stand together in the graveyard at the foot of his grave. He is laid next to the wooden perimeter at the east end of the church. I look out over the wall to the river and the valley, and into the face of a cold katabatic wind funnelling down the Dunajec from the mountains, from Slovakia. It's a late afternoon wind; the cloud breaks up and the cold air trapped above it rushes downward, bending the tall pines standing around the building and upsetting their plan. Bronek and Antonina have produced from their pockets: a nightlight candle, a glass jar and some matches. In an appropriately respectful manner, wishing to remember their dead friend and uncle, they are trying to ignite the candle, to keep a light on his grave, at least for a while. The grave is serious in Poland; Bronek is slipping back to Polishness. They turn their backs to the wind and open their coats to prevent it from whipping the flame from the matchend. Some way through the box they manage to transfer fire to the candle and the candle to the jar. Their moment of contemplation is marred by the guttering flame. I try shifting this way and that to mask it from the wind. I wish it would just blow out but instead it teases us, threatening to extinguish but never quite dying. In the sun the flame looks weak and eggy, a nightlight in daylight, difficult to see by.

When we enter the church it is already occupied, almost to capacity, by a coach load of architecture students who are listening to their self-important teacher deliver a lecture about the building. She is very put out by our entry; her energetic flow interrupted by the slow and elderly seems to exasperate her. Antonina is not at all bothered being the object of her glares and huffings. She does a comical mime of the pompous woman in my direction, her eyebrows raised to her hairline, eyes closed and her jaw going up and down automatically. We are being told to sit down on the only vacant seats, a couple of school forms set out almost in front of her. Within spitting distance.

We manoeuvre around each other, Bronek and Antonina colliding over the same seat; they finally come to rest in front of different forms. Antonina sits tidily facing the lecturer, folding her hands in her lap and deliberately giving her the fullest attention. This she communicates by her wide grin and a gracious nod in her direction, you may continue now. In the meantime Bronek can't decide between sitting down where he is or taking up more valuable lecture seconds by coming back and sitting next to Antonina. He feels the red hot-blade of this woman's impatience, and, muttering an apology, stays where he is.

But he is sitting on the very end of the bench, on the overhang beyond the leg. With his eyes on hers he lowers his weight on to the seat, initially unaware that as he does so the other end is rising like a seesaw. He reaches the point of no return before the point of realisation. The bench rears up on end, six feet in the air. Bronek wails and slides off the other end and, once his weight is removed, the erect form crashes back to the floor.

There is a moment of pure silence before the congregation breaks into rapturous applause. Antonina and I gather Bronek up from the church floor: she is shaking with laughter as we haul him up; he is not. He was very embarrassed.

We are pointedly ignored by the teacher afterwards; our antics were beneath her contempt, but on our way out of the building a few of the students speak to Bronek. Later he told me that they asked him if he was unhurt and apologised for laughing at him but it was the funniest thing, the best lecture they'd had: they might even remember some of it just because of him.

A few days later we leave Poland for Slovakia. We take the same route as we took the day we went to Debno but at Nowy Targ we continue south to Zakopane. Zakopane is at the beginning of the high Tatra, a cluster of high peaks in the Carpathian range on the frontier between Poland and Slovakia. With its northern Baltic coast this is Poland's other natural boundary.

We've been in Kraków longer than we planned to be, what with visits to the hospital with Edmund and calling on friends that came to mind now that we are here, time has overtaken our schedule again. There's Kazik, another ex-veterinary student from Lwów, with his wife, children, grandchildren, now living an apparently comfortable life in retirement. In Poland it couldn't have always been like this, but released from the Soviet fetters, things are booming here. This was even more noticeable on my second trip, two years later. The baby Fiat Polski which swarmed the streets are now in the minority. Students are not desperate to come to Britain any more. Suddenly, this is an exciting place to be. It was Antonina's grandson, a student at the Jagiellonian University in Kraków who told me he thought Poland would be in the single currency before Britain is.

We spent one day out at Brzozowa, the village where the Zygadłos and the Małczyńskis came from. And we also lost a whole day in a police station. Not all of Poland is shaking off its communist legacy. Coming back from visiting Brzozowa, my wallet is lost or stolen, probably lost at a petrol station. To claim insurance for it I have to get a certificate from the police to the effect that I have reported it. A simple matter. Not here. The police seem to be the last bastion of the old regime.

Bronek and I peer through a hatch into the reception office at a room full of smoking, lounging thugs. I explain, through Bronek, what has happened and that I wish to report it only for insurance purposes.

'Okay, you've reported it.'

I wait, thinking he will make some record of this. Maybe, out of sight, someone is making out a certificate, so we wait.

'And...?'

'Well, don't I get a piece of paper? Something to say I reported this?'

'No.'

There's a chuckle from the heavies in the background. My heart sinks.

'Why not?'

'We don't do certificates.'

'But, I have to have some official record that I reported this to the police. It's for insurance.'

'Yes, I know what it's for. You give the certificate to the insurance and they give you the value.'

'Yes. Can you do that.'

'No, we used to, but we don't do it any more.' The thuggees can't believe anyone could be so stupid.

'Look, I don't want you to do anything, I don't want you to investigate the possible crime and I know I'll never see my wallet again. I just want a note to say I was here telling you I lost it.'

'I told you, we do not issue certificates.'

I look at this greasy guy, what am I doing wrong? Have I missed something? Maybe he gets hundreds of arrogant bastards in here every day saying they lost this or that and he's fed up with it. Maybe he's not appreciated, been passed over for promotion. Maybe, maybe, maybe. This should be a five-minute job and we've been here too long already.

'Can I use your telephone, please?'

'What for?' The mob has gone quiet.

'I want to call the Embassy.' He wants to call the Embassy! They're laughing out loud now and my bravado turns to embarrassment.

'No, we don't let people use our telephones.' Simultaneous translation, I say it in English underneath the Polish version.

'Dad, ask him once more, please can we have a certificate.'

'I told you already, we don't do certificates.'

On the way back to Antonina's flat I consider letting the thing drop. There was not much cash in the wallet, I have cancelled the cards, but there is a problem about my driving licence. I could be in trouble with no licence and no record of having had it stolen, so we have to follow this through.

Back at the police station half an hour later, the same officer opens the hatch to us, and we get the same kind of reception from the smokers and sitters. They're back.

'I have telephoned the Embassy: here is the name and number of the officer I spoke to. It is my right to have this certificate. If you do not agree, please call this number and speak to this officer.' I hand over the piece of paper.

He retires to his desk, the boys are now busy minding their own business, puzzling over the crimes at their desks. Our man makes a call, a short one over which he does a lot of nodding, cradles the receiver and comes back to the hatch.

'Did you speak to the Embassy?'

'No. I spoke to my superior officer. Follow me, please.' He presses something under the counter and a door opens to a loud buzzing sound. He leads us to a completely bare and windowless room. But for a metal-framed table and chairs the room is a uniform dull cement grey. A corner of my brain is panicking, have I compounded a hopeless situation into an illegal one? I try not to think of Kafka, or of my dad. I don't even want to look at him.

'Back in the cells, eh, Dad?' I try black humour.

'What? What are you talking about?' It doesn't work.

'Nothing.'

We are put through the most pointless and idiotic interrogation, and what started as threatening descends into farce. We find ourselves taking part in a living museum display. All the elements of my worst nightmare are there but none of the power. This policeman is an anachronism, a parody of the old days. The irony of it is that in the days of the Iron Curtain this is what intimidated people, this is one of the ways the huge files were assembled on nearly every one of the population. Now that everyone has moved on and isn't intimidated any more, the police are still taking the same pains to record the minutiae of our lives, they don't know how to stop. Perhaps they think it still works. No one goes to them unless there is no alternative; you know that you'll lose the whole day filling out a report. Like us.

They ask who my grandmother was, where she was born, where she is buried. They ask where Bronek was born and I see it coming, 'Chicago, eh?' followed by lots of note scribbling. Very significant in the loss of this capitalist wallet. They ask us a million irrelevant questions. The report is written out in long hand, then we have to go to the typing department, another grey room but with windows, where the same officer sits at an old black typewriter and types out three pages using carbon paper. He is literally a one-finger typist, his left hand is occupied with a cigarette, so this part of the process takes about an hour. I dread him making spelling mistakes. When he's finished this, there is still no certificate.

For this we have to go to another room. He searches the stationary cupboards for the right form, which of course does not exist now that they are not doing certificates any more. That has to be why they ran out of forms. His own impatience with this monstrous bureaucratic game is more than he can hide any more. He kicks the tin cupboard door shut and returns to the typewriter with a form for the loss of relatives in police stations, adjusts it to wallets in petrol stations and we are eventually allowed to leave.

At Brzozowa, where this tale started, we spent the day in a village of Zygadłos. Or that's the way it seemed to me. Things had changed there since Gabriela brought her two children back here from America, some things but not many. Since Bronek's last visit with Pete, a bridge has been built across the river which must be crossed on the way up to the settlement, but the roads are still tracks and the way of life has a rustic timelessness to it. People are self-sufficient in the same way as ever. The scattered smallholdings all have a variety of animals, poultry and crops. Any new building seems to be done slowly by the occupant as and when they can afford it. And, as always, the men go to other countries to earn enough money to support their way of life.

After crossing the river by the new bridge and following a track steadily uphill for a mile, we arrive first at a farmyard of ancient wooden buildings. They make an L shape implying a square at whose other corner stands a new house. It seems deserted but for the geese in the yard, which have paddled the ground to a fine grease, their spined, kite-shaped footprints concentrating on the edge of a tiny pond and by a low doorway into the barn.

This barn, the long leg of the L, is an advent calender of windows and doors cut at random into the side facing the yard. Bronek goes to one of these, a sizeable one, and bangs on it. Only by scrutiny do I discern that it is in fact a door, so like the surrounding wall is the surface of it. Almost immediately a shutter opens higher up, and an old woman pokes her head out.

'Marysia?' Bronek calls to her.

'Tak. Kto to jest?' Who is it?

He says it's me, Bronek. Marysia cries out, 'Aah!' and slams the shutter. A moment later she appears at the door Bronek clattered on and falls on him, hugging him, patting him with her big knobbly hands and starts a continuous chatter that doesn't stop till we drive away at the end of the afternoon.

We walk with her to the next farm up the hill, passing on the way a building site with a half-completed house on it. Bronek explains to me who will live there, but it's much too complicated for me: they are all family and they are mostly called Zygadło. We arrive at the spot where their house used to be when they came back from Chicago. Gabriela, Bronek and Hanusia. He stands on the spot, looks down the hill into the valley, towards the village.

'I remember well this house. A small house, all wood, with cherry trees around it.' There is nothing of it left now, not the slightest trace, not even a cherry tree. Next to the site it used to occupy there is now a new house built by a carpenter cousin who is away in Austria working on building sites for the summer.

We continue on, further up the track between the shoulder-high maize crops towards another farm.

Mietek, the patriarch, is an elderly gent, living with his extended family in a kind of paradise, a cherry orchard kind of paradise on the top of a hill in Galicia. The house stands among the trees and the whole is fenced around with a high, industrial-looking metal mesh, like tennis-court fencing. This is the only concession to the twentieth century I see while we are there, otherwise the place is as Bronek remembers it. It is a farm, yet there is none of the machinery of farming in evidence; it must be somewhere else, beyond the orchard, outside of paradise. This is the place where Pete spent the day in the trees helping harvest the fruit, this is the place where Bronek was a child for a few years.

The views all round from up here are of small-scale farming. It's a dry version of the landscape of south Wales: the smooth, old, round-topped hills stitched into the wooded valleys remind me of home. Geographically the reverse works for him, his memories started here and, I see now, it's obvious that Wales reminded him of this happy place.

Indoors Mietek offers us sausage. I don't like to refuse food and in Poland it's insulting to reject hospitality, but in every house today I have eaten a sausage. I look at Dad imploringly, clutching my distended abdomen. Mietek understands, he picks up a bottle of wódka, slaps me on the back and leads us into the front room. He and I sit on the tiled stove, Bronek and Marysia on armchairs, his wife in various places but for never more than a minute at a time. It seems to me that there were others too, so complete is their hospitality.

Mietek slips his hand under my arm and urges me to my feet, 'Come, come.' Waving his glass of wódka in front of him, he leads me across the hallway to the room opposite. As he opens the door, the hot sweet-smelling air from the interior flows out over us. He puts a finger to his lips and tiptoes in. A large girl is dozing on the bed, she tries to get up as we enter but Mietek waves her down again. She smiles a dreamy, heavy-lidded smile at us and waves. I wonder what Mietek is up to but he beckons me towards the bed, indicating a little box next to it. Two steps nearer and I see over the rim that it contains a tiny newborn baby. 'My granddaughter,' he says and there are tears in his eyes. I am allowed a moment to marvel at her perfect newness and Mietek herds me out again. I wave to the girl and she waves back. In the sitting room after he too has been taken for a visit, Bronek tells me that she was born two days ago. 'Mietek says if we had been here on time we would have witnessed the birth.'

He produces an ancient framed photograph of his grandfather and hands it to me.

'You look like him. Bronek, he looks like your great uncle don't you think?' The picture is of a young man, who could indeed be me or my brother but he is in fact my great great uncle. His generous Piłsudski-like moustaches hide much of his chin as well as his entire mouth, but I have his eyes, or some very like them. How strange to come to such a distant place and find my eyes looking back at me from three generations ago. The room is darkened against the afternoon sun. The eyes glinting from the picture are like my father's eyes in a photograph of him at the same age, and like my son's eyes. My son's eyes that may never see these people. My eyes blur and I take a shot of the hard stuff to cover my tenderness. The eyes in the room, Polish eyes.

Bronek blends, receding into the soft embrace of his folk, more here than anywhere else. In a landscape that shaped him, nurtured his softness with these lush hills and defined his pressed-down firmness, his hard darkness with its shadowy valleys, he becomes real and wholly embedded. Watching his silhouette in the darkness or standing with him later in the cherry orchard, it seems to me he has shed the atmosphere of foreigner in his own land, he relaxes. He doesn't seem retired, awkward in smart clothes, or displaced as he sometimes does. I see that his displacement was from here and that he minimised it, unconsciously perhaps, by choosing something similar in Wales. We have not come to the edge to find an extreme connection, we have come from the edge, and, for Bronek at least, we have come home.

He and Marysia walk behind us, in step, their old heads bent together, next to the maize field on the way back down the hill. She is chattering to him, her knuckly hands dancing before them in a complicated description of something. Dad nods, he shrugs and sometimes closes his eyes and throws his head back in laughter, but nothing stops her flow. I walk ahead with a six-year-old cousin, she holds my hand and twitters away in Polish. She drops to the ground at the edge of the maize and catches a cricket and shows me for a moment before it pings away into the corn again. I nod, I laugh at her imitation of cricket noises. Nothing stops her flow.

— 17 —
Zakopane

I feel a younger, weaker version of the way he feels as we head up into the mountains from Zakopane to the frontier. The road twists and turns upwards through the trees deliberately delaying its arrival at the border, wishing like us to stay longer in Poland. But Bronek is practised in acceptance. In the face of an overwhelming argument against something he wants, he will shrug, turn his mouth down at the corners and humph a capitulation. Letting it go apparently with ease. Sometimes.

Out of the blue, he says how pleased he was to have spent some time with Krzysia and Edmund, Marylka's parents.

'I was hoping she and Pete might, you know, stay together.' For a while Marylka and Pete conducted a long-distance relationship which had started on one of the earlier visits. Pete had come to Poland for a Christmas skiing holiday with her and for another, at Easter perhaps.

'Were you?' I had missed all of this, I was at college or in London, in my not very interested in the family years. In self-imposed exile and my memory of it is vague. 'Why?'

He flaps his hands, 'Ah, I don't know. You boys never do what I expected.'

That is true but in this case the truth is that he loves his family, he wishes that they could be closer. This connection wouldn't change the distance of miles between us all but it would bind us tighter, going some way to replacing the ties that will disappear with him. I have had the sense on this trip that he is handing me the mantle of responsibility for this. It's not exclusive or obligatory, but it is there. It is also there because I wish it to be. After all, perhaps I am doing what he expects.

'How did Edmund survive the war?' I have a list of questions like this I meant to ask but never did.

'Ah, Mark. That is another story.' He would have said. 'Not many Jews did. Ask him next time you come here.' He is priming me.

We continue our weaving course. There are road signs to let you know how many bends there are in the next series, how many denials, how many attempted refusals. Unsentimental tall pines point like arrowheads straight at the sky.

'When I think of how many Jews there were in Poland before the war I can't believe there are so few now. They were such a big part of life here. The Ukrainians used to say that the Poles owned the streets but the Jews owned all the houses, and they resented both.'

'Did you resent them too, you Poles?'

'Ach, Mark. It's a long time ago; things were different then.'

I have always been easily infuriated by my father; he has such a dismissive way of deflecting questions he doesn't want to answer, at the same time making me feel a fool for asking. He knows what I think about his anti-Semitism, we have fought about it before, but I still don't understand what appear to be contradictions in his life. His life in Poland was shaped by his contact with Jews, saved by it you could say. Edmund is a Jew, someone he loves and respects, yet he is unself-consciously anti-Semitic, as are many of his contemporaries. Not in the skinhead style we saw in the university, but something deeper than that, something cultural. I know that the subject cannot be hit head on with him; it wouldn't work anyway, and I won't risk destroying the ease with which he now talks to me by offending him. He takes days to recover from a personal slight, so I drive on trying to think of an indirect approach but he beats me to it.

'I will never forget the sight of that column of people walking out of Lwów. Knowing what I know now, knowing what happened to 90 per cent of them I am ashamed of what I thought then, what was the normal attitude. But at the time we had no such insights. We resented them. We resented their success, their wealth and, a cynic might say, we resented them because they were even more tragic than the Poles themselves.

'There was a growing atmosphere of nationalism in the new smaller Poland after the first war which everyone felt, an excitement, a chauvinism among the Poles. Jews were not included in that; all the history and culture of central Europe was excluding them. Poland was not special in that way, Poland was different because more Jews lived here than anywhere else.

'Like everywhere else, they kept themselves apart. When I was at the gymnasium in Stanisławów, for instance, a big school, there were Poles here,' he indicates a chunk between his hands, 'Jews here, and Ukrainians next to them.' Chunk, chunk, chunk. 'We lived side by side with each other. Not mixed, but together.'

'Who did the Jews resent?'

'Good question, I don't know. Maybe they resented everyone else in Stanisławów, because it was mostly Jewish, that town.'

'Mostly Jewish?'

'Yes, before the war more than half the population, up to 60 per cent, were Jews. Stanisławów was a Jewish town until the Nazis came. Then after the war it was Russian. Now it's Ukrainian; Ivano Frankivsk after the poet.'

I find this hard to imagine, never having thought of it as anything but a Polish town in his descriptions of those years. His vehement assertions that Galicia was Poland seems to cover aspects of nationhood I hadn't considered. Did Polishness include Jewishness to the same degree as Poland included Jews, in a way that has disappeared now? I get the sense that the cataclysm of the Holocaust was so complete that what is left somehow misrepresents the past. I have heard the stories of Jewish headstones in Stanisławów being used as paving slabs and foundations for monuments since the war, and after fifty years of being trodden on, they are being lifted and the cemetaries reinstated.

'It's hard to imagine what it was like.'

'Yes, Poles were the minority there.'

I struggle with visions of shifting borders and disappearing populations.

'So, what do you think now?'

'What about?'

'Oh, Dad. About your attitude then.'

After some thought he goes back to the beginning, 'No, I will never forget the sight of the columns of people walking out of Lwów. They were mostly Jews. At the time, I thought it was simply fear, like chickens running away from the fox. Terrified, mindless because the fox strikes at random and kills beyond its needs. You know, you have seen it. Now, I have a picture that's coloured by what I know comes later, for them and for me. When I think of them walking out of Lwów, I also think of the night I walked out of Poland. When I think of the beautiful clear days of that September, the harvest in the sunny fields below the road and the dust in the air, I also remember that clear night in December with the sky full of stars, looking back over the treetops at the country sleeping in the moonlight and my breath sparkling in front of my face. I see the endless stream of them, black like a column of ants in the hot afternoon, and I see our group that night, like a file of sheep following a path through the snow. At Oświęcim, I remembered the prison at Tarnopol and the trains.'

'That's what came later for you; what about what came later for them?'

'When we stood in that death camp in Oświęcim, I thought of them pouring from the city like a haemorrhage, a stream of consciousness dissolving into the land, becoming the ash and the mud we stood on.

'What I saw was not the real thing for them: it was a rehearsal. They were safe for a while, they went back to Lwów behind the Red Army, and, in fact, as I told you, they became even more powerful until the fox came again in 1941 and they were murdered. But Mark, in 1939 it was the real thing for us, it was the Poles first and Jews later in that part.'

'The Russians?'

'The Russians. They had their own ideas about who to exterminate first. Now we know that Stalin's crimes were as great as Hitler's, just as horrific and he had longer to carry them out, but we didn't know it then. At the same time as he was starving the Ukraine to death, it was fashionable to join the Communist Party in Britain. While I was swanning around the bridge parties and musical soirées of Lwów, people were dying of starvation even on the streets of Kiev, just across the border. You remember in my study at home, there is a photograph of all the staff from the gymnasium in Stanisławów?'

'Yes.'

'They killed every one of them, for the same reason I was arrested. Counter-revolutionaries. They were bloody school teachers. You think of the hundreds of Poles you have met in other countries: they are the lucky ones, the few. And there would have been even less if the Nazis had not invaded Russia. All the Poles from Ukraine, Belarus and Lithuania were released from the camps in the east to find their own way back, or join with the Reds. Those still alive. These were the blackest days.'

Then he says, matter of factly, 'We are wise after the fact. It is impossible to think now what we thought then. All we can do is judge it and think what we think now.'

'And that is?'

'That I was lucky.'

'What?'

'That it was only chance.'

'That you survived?'

'Well, that too, but I thought we were talking about something else.'

'I thought we were talking about anti-Semitism.'

'People will discuss for centuries this question and the answer will change as we do. It will even change in the light of what happens in the Middle East. No, all I know is that I was nothing special, I had no particular insight that made me the way I was. Insignificant incidents make you choose one thing or another, say one thing and not another, despite yourself. Now we are safe, relatively speaking, and the consequences of these insignificant things are not so extreme. Then, the consequences of the insignificant were often final.'

'What's that got to do with anti-Semitism?'

'Mark, I'm trying to tell you: prejudice is not a decision. The opposite usually. Looking back, probably I owe my survival to luck and to Jews. At the time I didn't think that much of either.'

'Are you talking about that incident at your college, with the Jewish student?'

'I defended him by accident, because I didn't like the way I was being patronised. It was chance.'

'And he saved you somehow?'

'No no, we are talking about anti-Semitism. I'm saying the incident changed my ideas about Poles, the type of Poles who had those prejudices, and I stopped wanting to be like them. It is possible that the consequence of that accident of listings got me out of prison, with my mother's help. It's possible, but also it's possible that they are not connected at all...'

An unusual out-pouring for him.

'Did it make you think twice about going back to Poland after the war?'

'What do you mean?'

'You've made it sound as though you were disillusioned or disappointed by some of your compatriots. I thought perhaps...'

'No, we didn't come back because the bloody Russians were here.'

'You would have, otherwise?'

He shrugs his Polish shrug. 'Who knows.'

'What about that night then, the night you left?'

'Ah, Mark. Not now, I tell you later.'

I came into Poland travelling the opposite way along this same road two years later on my way back from the Ukraine. I left Lviv by bus for Slovakia, caught a train at Kosice and arrived in Poprad, where I broke the journey for a few days with Hanusia, Bronek's sister.

I recorded her voice on a machine answering my questions through Adrian, her grandson. I still have the tape, still have her voice on my dictaphone saying things to me that I can't follow in a half-Czech, half-Polish hybrid language.

'Babbi,' Adrian and Henryk call her Babbi, short for Babunia or Babka, grandmother. 'Babbi, Mark wants to know where Uncle Bronek was in prison.'

'Prison?'

She is totally blind now. When I was here with Bronek two years before, I took a picture of them together. The flash, straight in her eyes, produced only a slight frown, 'Is that lightning?' she asked. 'Is there a storm?'

A splinter of light broke into her imagination, perhaps flashing across the picture of her older brother the last time she saw him. How does she see those with whom she is in constant contact, but hasn't seen for many years? Perhaps she sees Bronek as he was the day they parted in December 1939: his head poking out from under a blanket behind the seat of a pony trap, saying goodbye. Or perhaps the way he looked the next time she saw him, in 1960, a middle-aged man from the west. Or during the series of visits he made over the next twenty years as her eyesight failed, a progressively dimmer picture. I start this story saying that when I think of him, now that I no longer see him either, he is the sum of all the different ways I have known him look. He has simultaneously the attributes of a young man and an old one. But Hanusia has longer gaps and shorter moments to refresh her memory. A few days every few years after a gap of twenty. Their relationship seems to have gaps too. They are not close as I expect brother and sister to be. Perhaps they never were, he rarely spoke of her and never with affection. The war interrupts lives.

'I was four or five when we came from America, to Siemiechów.'

'Siemiechów, where is that?' Adrian asks, 'Near Różniatów?'

'Nie, I can't remember where it is exactly,' she waves towards the mountains, 'over there, near Tarnów somewhere. I think Mark has been there, or Peter has.'

I listen to the tape picking up the sense by the odd words I understand. A description of their life in America: a house with a veranda, Uncle Franek had a car, Bronek went to school there. They left when she was four or five.

I take her back to her childhood in Brzozowa, to the beautiful house on the hill with a garden and cherry trees around it,
where Bronek had stood two years ago remembering his vanished life, and she tells me the story of the chocolate causing
trouble with her grandmother.

Listening to her voice on the tape now takes me back to
her apartment in Poprad with the stupendous views of the
high Tatra through the glass wall. I sit on the pull-out bed
Bronek and I slept on. She talks for about half an hour into the
recorder. I let her go on, thinking I will translate it later with
Adrian and his friend Sylvana.

'Did you ever go to Lwów, Babbi.'

'I was there, at the veterinaria. Michał was there; Antonina
was.'

'Were you there at the time of the invasion?'

'Nie, at that time I was...where was I? I was...Ach, I don't
remember where I was.'

I say to Adrian that Bronek told me that she came to Lwów
to find him after he was let out of prison, to tell him that
people from Różniatów were leaving to go to Hungary. Here,
the first side of the cassette runs out in the middle of my question, she starts to answer while I am still turning it over. Now
I have half a sentence to fill a whole gap '...nothing about that.
Prison in Tarnopol? I remember nothing about that. He was
never in prison.'

I wanted to protest that he was, but she moved on and I
didn't want to break her flow. I could find out later.

'I was taken to the river at Przemyśl by the Russians, to the
bridge. On this side of the river was Russia and on the other
side Germany. We were left there, to choose. I went across the
bridge, that was the end of it. We didn't hear anything from
Bronek or Lubaczewski until after the war. We had a letter in
1945. He wrote to us in Nowy Targ.'

'When was the last time you saw Uncle Bronek? When he left
with Lubaczewski?'

'Yes, I gave him my hat; it was very cold.'

'Do you remember anyone else who went with them, Babbi?'

'I don't remember who else, only Jacek. Jacek Haszczewski. Maybe he went with them.'

Adrian and I wait in the windy doorway of Sylvana's block of flats. The snow-topped Tatra just visible across the town but the rest of the view is of the windswept, unrelentingly bleak housing estate. The names are bleak. Yuh, Vah, they sound like the buffets of wind that constantly roll in from the mountains, breaking against these megaliths like waves.

Sylvana appears with a bag of shopping from behind a flat-roofed single-storey pub. It's an ex-pub, boarded up. She produces a bottle of wine from her shopping and we settle down to translate the tape. It's cold in her flat, spartan, and I find it difficult to concentrate on the recording. The others are not especially interested either and gradually conversation and the wine take over. We decide, after wading through it a second time and finishing the bottle, that we should adjourn to the local night spot.

Adrian and Henryk, my cousin's sons, show me off to their friends with a kind of pride that flatters me. A big group gradually gathers at our table in the bar and I begin to forget I'm the same generation as their parents. I forget what I'm doing here, I forget myself appropriately in the house of forgetting. Now when I think of driving over the Tatra to Poprad listening to Bronek's description of his walk over the Carpathians and the flight from Lwów, the loose and magical atmosphere of forgetting is also present. Strobe-lit dancing and shouted conversations with Sylvana's Irish boyfriend about Flan O'Brien swim into my memory. It comes as an undercurrent this feeling, a charge of friendly heat with a thread that connects it to every abandoned insignificant moment. To every time I laugh. Like a short circuit, like a short cut.

From Poprad I had crossed by bus to Kraków, to Antonina. In our correspondence since Bronek's death, Antonina and I have come to a misunderstanding about two things. The first and most difficult was the question left to us over what to

do with Bronek's remains. He had specifically asked to be cre-
mated but seemed uninterested in the subsequent disposal of
his ashes. When asked about it on his deathbed, he seemed to
have regained his erstwhile matter of factness, refusing to be
bothered with it as though it was of no interest to him. 'How
could it be? I will be dead.'

We had thought it would be appropriate to take his ashes to
Poland and have them buried or scatter them there, and Brzozowa seemed to us to be the obvious place. This idea was met
by his family and friends there with disapproval to say the least.
Cremation hardly exists there, perhaps the industrial cremato-
ria of the war years lurk in the collective memory, and the significance of the grave remaining close to the family is a long
held tradition.

The second thing was my proposed trip to the Ukraine.
This trip. The end of which was bringing me to Kraków, to
Antonina, who had told me that no Ukrainian could ever cross
her threshold. So I was approaching it with trepidation. When
she opened the door to me all my apprehension disappeared, I
knew straight away everything was going to be fine.

I show her the photograph I copied in the Ukraine of the
group of children clustered around her Uncle Michał.

'Ah tak, yes, I remember.'

'You can keep this one, Antonina. I will get another one
printed.'

'But I have this photograph already.' She gets a shoebox of
pictures from her room. We sit in the kitchen and she finds
her copy among the other black and white memories. 'Hanusia
also has it, and maybe Bronek. I don't know.' I have my own
copy now, the one I went all that way to get, which in fact
may have been at home all the time. I give her the address of
Jadwiga Wołosynowicz, whom she remembers.

'Why you go in there, Ukraina?'

'To see Lwów and Różniatów. To see where he was in prison,
in Tarnopol…'

'Dolina, he was prisoner in Dolina.'

'But, he told me he was in prison in Tarnopol.'

'No, Dolina.'

'Are you sure?'

'Sure. Yes, sure.'

Oh God, the most dreadful feeling of not being sure. I know I have made leaping assumptions about his story and yet, so many of the details about the town hall seemed to fit. I rack my brains trying to remember how and when he told me about being taken prisoner and the details of it. Had I superimposed the story on to the town I had just visited or did the place confirm the truth of it? Under my concentration the whole thing evaporates; I think I must have made it all up. I have rehearsed and repeated it so many times, it no longer feels like his story but mine. I was in prison in Tarnopol, even if he wasn't. But, if he was not there, why was I? Why was I there in prison and not in Dolina?

'Antonina, are you positive? Could he have been in Dolina and then in Tarnopol, or the other way round?'

She shrugs; it's possible. 'I remember in Dolina, only.' She waves a hand at it, who cares, he survived. 'Tarnopol, Dolina…' Something in Polish I don't understand but take to mean, 'What's the difference?'

I didn't go to Dolina, I don't know.

She turns back to the box of pictures, digs her hand down one side and lifts out a slab of them. Black and white, old, dog-eared pictures.

My journey slows to a stop in Kraków. My plan to stay only a few days and then continue on to Warszawa do not fall into place, and I begin to feel at home in the flat. Antonina's family, three generations of them, shift their lives a little this way and that to accommodate me in their big appartment. I remember Anna, her daughter, in 1972 as an inconsolable teenager too young to go with her brother Zbyszek and I to a party in the Rynek. Anna now has a husband, Jan, and two children: Paweł, in university, and Przemek, still at school. During the day I have the flat and Antonina to myself. Jan lends me his new computer and I settle down to make notes about the trip before they sink too deeply back into the past, and when my eyes get too sore, I wander in the city.

Kraków is regenerating and it regenerates me, too.

I was looking forward to going back to Warszawa. The time Bronek and I had spent there two years before was a lightning strike for me. The seed of this story started there in the street watching the crowds throwing flowers on to the railway truck monument, pouring out their grief. Flowers of steel and blood fell straight into me, red and white carnations strewed themselves over my view of Poland and my memory of that trip. When I started to write, that was the first story I wrote.

I wanted to see Marylka. She had been present, a midwife to that moment and I hoped there would be others. We had spoken on the phone about this trip and I had unfairly placed the responsibility for this last part of it on her, depending on her to be there and guide me through Warszawa. She protested that she knew nothing about history or culture; I protested that she did.

But it didn't work out that way, and in Ulica Szewska I meet Marylka again. She is at home in Kraków because her father, Edmund, is ill. He's dying. When we do meet, she tells me two interesting things. First, Warszawa is becoming a highrise city. 'Go there and see it now because soon it will not be as it was.' Second, they are going to build a museum in the garden of remembrance where another monument stands to fallen Poles. Polish Jews that fell in the Ghetto Rising. That was the first rising in Warszawa, the second was the Warszawa Rising of 1944 and the third seems to be the rising skyline of the city and the raising of Polish eyes to it.

I didn't go.

I see her for an hour in a café and the first thing she does is cry.

I say, when she comes back from the girls' room, 'Marylka, can I just say this, then, if you like I won't mention it again. Bronek died a year ago; I have been through this, I am still going through it. If you want to talk about your father, please don't worry about what I will think, I would be honoured, you know that.'

'No, really Mark, it's too much, it makes me too upset. Please, can we talk about something else? Tell me about your work.' I take her at her word.

We British are too bland, we are at a cultural disadvantage. People of the province of Hunan, when offered something they would die for, politely refuse three times and only accept on the fourth repetition. This convention contains within it all the combinations of acceptance, refusal and withdrawal of the offer needed to indicate a thousand nuances of the generosity, obligation and need. We have no such arrangement and I can't tell if I must press her or not.

I don't.

I think I should have because she tells me off.

'How can you not speak Polish yet?' This same question, 'Your father would have wanted you to.'

'I know, I know.'

'Have you not ordered yet? I would like mineral water, French, with gas.' She calls the waitress over to our table then looks at me and remains silent. I deal with the waitress quietly in English.

'Mark, even my mother, who has never been out of Poland in her life, has to talk to you in English on the telephone.'

'I know, I know. I must learn.'

'Mark, she likes you but...and your father's Polish was so beautiful.'

Bronek's Polish was beautiful; people often said so, older people especially. People of his generation. But I saw children and teenagers look at him strangely when he asked them questions and I saw him look at them strangely when they answered in the modern tongue. His was a pre-war language as strange to modern Poles as 'wizard pranks' and 'jolly good shows' are to us. His Poland was like that too; he had a Piłsudskian view, romantic and out of date but irresistible to his generation of Catholic Poles. Sometimes real Poland didn't measure up to his expectations or match his memory.

And we talk about the rising: 'Go there because soon...' but I do not go. I am tired and in tiredness cannot adjust my hopes and do it alone. But I will go, soon.

When we leave the café, she says, 'I go this way.' Pointing down the narrow street. I don't know which way I go but this is the moment of parting, so I point the other way. Having family in other countries is a painful business; I hate to say goodbye. 'I hate saying goodbye to you.' 'I will call you.' But she won't. The disappointment of this meeting knocks the stuffing out of me, what little there was left. The last leg of the journey, which I was looking forward to, is still to be taken. It has become another of the loose ends which I may never tie up in relation to Bronek's story. I tell myself it is not important: Warszawa was not his city in the way that Kraków was. Kraków was not in the way that Lwów was. Perhaps Poland was not his country in the way that Galicia was.

Walking back along Szewska, I want to cry. I feel weary with the weight of the disappointments the day has landed on me. I tell myself this happens on all journeys. There are times when things do not happen as they are planned, when you feel so lonely and homesick you wonder why you put yourself through such torture, and the emotional fatigue and loneliness are overwhelming. In a bar with a beer in front of me, I give myself a stiff talking to. I tell myself that disappointment is the hardest of emotions to accept. Like grief. And Bronek slides into my reflections through this channel. He reminds me of his disappointment at being unable ever to go back to Lwów or Różniatów and I start to feel sorry that I didn't try harder for him. I don't understand why I didn't, as so often is the case, I had all the information but for some reason didn't realise the significance of it. It would have been better to have been there with him, but I still would have wanted to go alone, somewhere if not there. The old man, I miss him.

Much later in the year I discovered that Edmund Jakubowicz died the next day.

I was worried that the day we left Kraków and headed south to the Tatras and the border would be a difficult one for Dad. This was the last goodbye to Poland; there would be no more visits between here and Hanusia in Poprad, Slovakia. I try to remember if I have ever seen him in emotional difficulties. I haven't and I can't imagine it.

He takes leave of Antonina and her family quickly and without ceremony, but he's very quiet in the car as we leave the city. He sniffs and exhales one or two loud sighs but no more than that. My attempts at conversation on the road to Zakopane are unsuccessful, and I leave him to his own thoughts. Whatever they are, he seems in control of them.

We wander the streets of Zakopane out of duty. It was a beautiful little highland town of wooden houses and narrow alleys, now invaded by the tourist industry, and seems constantly overcrowded. Every old house has been made into restaurant or guesthouse of uncertain and self-conscious alpine style and the old town is surrounded with new building. The whole of the countryside around Zakopane follows the same rule it seems. As Poland gets richer, and the rich want to spend their time in beautiful places, the population of this area swells and there is new building everywhere. In some ways the obvious lack of any planning in these expansions is refreshing, coming as we do from a country where the planners have the domestic building industry by the throat. However, the sight of these wooded hills and valleys around Zakopane now peppered with new concrete houses thrown up anywhere and everywhere is enough to make me reconsider the benefit of planners. It's a mess.

In the few kilometres from Zakopane to the frontier our conversation revives and Bronek begins telling me about the first time he clapped eyes on Prudence Wood, also known as Jinks, his future wife.

He watched from the window of her parents' house, where he was billeted in 1941.

'A taxi pulled up outside the house and when your mother got out I realised I had never seen anyone so beautiful in all my life. She was a land girl, posted away from home to Suffolk or Cambridge, and I had been there for some time before I first saw her, before that day. I had heard all about her from Alison.

"I know you'll like her, I know you will," she used to say, and I thought I knew what she would be like. But the woman who got out of that car took my breath away. The summer sun was still in her face and she seemed to be golden, she was shining. I fell in love at that moment. She took a little longer, I had almost given up...' The sight of the frontier point stops him mid-flow and we cover the last few hundred yards to the border in silence.

On a level area on a mountainside cleared of trees we come to the frontier post. In preparation we have filled the tank with diesel and tried to spend all our remaining złoty before driving up from Zakopane. Once out of the country the currency is worthless. We are alone at the checkpoint, the car parks are empty, and, apart from the three officers in their separate cabins, it would be completely deserted. The customs cabins look like little sausage-shaped sputniks adrift in space. The place has the atmosphere of a 1960s spy film. A breezy sunny day, innocence meets ruthless authority in the picturesque mountains. A blonde girl in a white dress and a strong dark type in a tight suit.

We stand at the window with all the documents, Bronek bouncing from one leg to the other, shoulders hunched up and with his hands clasped over his genitals.

'Paszporty.' He shouts at us through the glass partition. I hand them over.

Flip, flip, flip.

'Okay, car documents.' His voice is muted by the glass, he is miming at full volume.

Flip, flip,... 'Green card.'

'It's there.'

'It's no good, finished.'

'What?'

'Green card is finished; you have no insurance.' He raises his voice another notch. I shuffle through the documents still in my hands, I find another green slip from the insurance company which I slide under the glass to him. He studies it, then thumps it on the desk. 'No good,' he bellows, 'Finished.'

'Now what's the matter here, Mark? Didn't you buy insurance?'

Yes, I bought insurance; there's a mistake somewhere. 'Ask him to give me the green card to look at.'

The officer slides the vile paper under the glass again. He's right: it expired four days ago. I had bought three weeks' worth of insurance for our stay in Poland, the only country in Europe where it is still obligatory, to more than cover our planned itinerary. We have overstayed our schedule, and our insurance by four days.

'Dad, tell him we stayed longer than we planned. We didn't realise it had expired.'

'Oh, no Mark. That will never do. We cannot go without insurance.'

'We already have. Just tell him; what else can you say?'

The officer is already shaking his head when Bronek starts the story. 'Driving in Poland without green card is criminal offence,' he shouts. 'You will have to pay fine.'

'A fine?'

'Yes, you must pay me fine.'

'How much?'

He consults his calculator and yells the total to Bronek, who is trying to smile at the glass. His face falls, 'Millions of złoty!'

'How many millions?'

'Now, Mark, we are in trouble here. He wants millions of złoty!'

'Dad, old złoty, new złoty, what złoty? Ask him how many dollars it is.'

He goes back to his calculator. Click, click, click, 'Nine thousand dollars.'

'Nine thousand dollars! He's joking.'

'Not joking.' He's shouting.

'Now, what are we going to do, Mark. Nine thousand dollars.' I look through the screen at the officer in the cabin, a man still yelling in a glass box. I start to laugh at the hopelessness of it. If he had demanded one thousand dollars, it would have been much worse. It's not impossible that we could have scraped it together in traveller's cheques and currency, but nine thousand is out of the question. 'It's more than the car is worth.'

'Mark, this is not a laughing matter. What are we going to do?'

'Nothing, we cannot pay. Tell him we can't pay.'

In the sunlight we stand outside the kiosk, a wind stirs the dust off the car park surface and moves it in curved fronts twenty yards at a time. The guy shouts again and the same muffled noises emanate from the glass skin of his box.

'He wants to know how much we can pay.'

'Is this a fine or what? We can't pay the fine.' Dad looks at me as though I'm mad. I'm not mad, I'm stupid, and it isn't until we have driven away into Slovakia that I realise how lucky as well.

After shouting himself hoarse, the officer asked if we were coming back to Poland because he could let us out but not back in with no insurance.

'No, we are not coming back.'

Exasperated, he loses patience and tells us to go.

Getting back into the car, Bronek says, 'I hate these border crossings; there is always something. You should have given him few dollars: he would have let us go straight away.'

'What?' I had no idea. 'I'm sorry, Dad. I'm so stupid, I didn't realise. It never crossed my mind he wanted a bribe. He should have been more explicit, if he'd said, "I'll let you go if you give me fifty dollars." I'd have paid straight away.' I think of the poor man in the glass box trying to shout his subtle message through the screen. 'Anyway, why didn't you do it?'

'What? I wouldn't give him fifty pence.'

'But... I thought you...'

'No, no, you were doing fine.' He pats my arm.

'Thank you very much.' He's a dark horse, 'What about at the police station in Kraków, should we have offered them a few dollars too?'

'Maybe, I don't know. If you offer when you shouldn't, you are in the deeper shit.'

The last short distance to the col before starting our descent into Slovakia takes us out of the trees. The natural frontier is bare and we are hungry by this time, so we pull off the road for the last of our Polish picnics, in Slovakia. This is a meagre snack in comparison to some of our earlier outdoor meals, a couple of tomatoes, some sandwiches made by Antonina that morning, and some chocolate I bought in Zakopane. I'm all for eating it sitting in the car but this seems to offend him, 'Picnics are eaten outside, Mark. You know that.' I see old family shots of us sitting on some windswept Welsh headland, huddled together like the survivors of a disaster, enjoying Wonderloaf and corned-beef sandwiches in a force eight. The empty car in the background is a white Zephyr. An inappropriate name.

I am aware of something having fallen away now that we have crossed out of the country and started on our way back. We are in fact still moving away from home, but the feeling is that we have been to the extremity, and, having left Poland, our direction is homeward. I am having a piss with these thoughts. When I return to the car, Bronek has already spread the rug out to the leeward side and is sitting with a wheel between him and the draught creeping under the car body. I take the back wheel, a sandwich and look south over a very hazy Slovakia.

'Right, Dad, what about the night you left Poland in 1939? This seems like good place to hear this.'

'There is not much more to tell you: we just walked over the top into Hungary.'

'Come on, Dad, tell it like it was.'

—18 —
Hungary

With difficulty he starts, 'As we got higher up the mountains it got more difficult. There was no real climbing, it was all walking but some of it was quite steep. Once we got high enough to be out of the trees I began to find the going very difficult and as the snow got deeper, out of the shelter of the woods, I began to fall behind and hold the others up.'

'Why? You were a fit young man, you were used to the outdoor life.'

'Well, I told you my boots were not the right ones for the job. Ski boots with little or no grip. I had none of these things you lace to the soles with metal spikes,'

'Crampons.'

'Yes, I had no time to prepare.' He is defensive; these boots are still pinching. 'The other men were properly equipped and I felt terrible to be holding them up. You know, on a walk like that you must pace yourself, find a rhythm common to everyone and steadily keep to it. I was a nuisance to them because they could get no rhythm. They had to keep stopping for me to catch up or I would be sliding into them when we were going downhill. We tried tying some cords round the boots. It was better but they would come off and have to be retied, it was awful. One of the men cut me two staffs and that also helped, but the worst thing was that I became exhausted. On steeper parts, even with the sticks, I fell so often and sometimes so painfully that after a few hours I was completely soaking, half with sweat, half from the snow, and badly bruised. My feet were the only dry part of me; I would have given anything for them to be cold and wet so long as they would grip.'

I recognise the signs of exhaustion as soon as they appear. We had been on manoeuvres last winter in preparation for a winter campaign and I had seen other men get like this. I know straight away that I am in a dangerous state. It gets harder to haul myself out of the snow each time and more and more comfortable lying there. I am aware of the split, the dialogue between the will to go on and the feeling that it just doesn't matter. The rational part of my mind argues that this is the very thing to fight against, but it's there with every footfall, and it won't go away.

I climb out of the snow and totter up to the waiting group. As I approach, they turn and resume the walk, I get no rest. I stumble through the nights of our journey like this. On my own with the argument, I follow their tracks trying to keep them in sight. It is so much easier to win it when they are there ahead of me, a darker shape moving against the grey night. I become less resolute the further behind I fall. My rest is the time I spend lying in the snow, slowly chilling, gradually weakening, taking longer to get up. Then, as I get worse, someone comes back for me, 'Come on, Bronek, get up. We must go on.' Lubaczewski, always Lubaczewski. He pulls me up and walks to the others with me. Inside I am saying, leave me here, what difference does it make? And I am ashamed.

So we go on like this, walking during the night and finding somewhere to sleep in the day. We use the shepherds' huts in the high pastures, deserted in the winter, although I always thought them conspicuously dangerous. If a patrol came our way they would be sure to look in the huts, but, by dawn, at the end of a night of falling and rising I am too tired to care, I leave that to someone else. I flop down in my wet things and sleep. Once or twice we find a sheltered place outside, out of the wind and sleep for an hour or two in the sun. At night we keep moving in the security of darkness and because of the cold. To sleep somewhere in that cold could be fatal; you soon become hypothermic and then you are finished. You just want to sleep, as I do. Then you die.

The second or the third night of the walk is particularly bad. We are crossing the main high part of the range; it is steep and I am by now very tired. The night is filled with falling down and struggling up again, and I fall a long way behind the others. There is no chance of my getting lost so long as I follow their track; the night is fine and the sky clear, beautiful but cruelly cold. I view each new stretch of the terrain with depression, calculating how many slips I will make, how many hard objects are hidden under the snow waiting to bruise me when I land and how many battles to get up I will have to fight. I am in a bad way. I try to estimate, taking my own height and the number of my falls and rises into the equation, how many extra mountains I have climbed, but the calculation becomes confused. I am caught in a syndrome of repeating the same line, falling, rising, repeating the same line and then forgetting some part of it. Eventually I fall and do not rise, I cannot move. All my strength is gone and my will has collapsed; defeat comes instantly. I just don't care any more. I wish they would go on and leave me where I drop. I begin to wish I was dead.

Lying there in my stupified state, a beautiful calm comes on me, a serene clarity rises over my confusion. I feel myself exquisitely stretched, a string of a perfectly tuned instrument in an excruciating tension, yet I feel the total absence of any pain. In this man-shaped depression of snow I lie in sublime comfort and in perfect balance between my diminishing will to live, to get myself up and survive, and the total insignificance of whether I do or not. I am poised on the edge of life and death, between presence and absence, of significance and insignificance. Indifferent.

From a great height I look down again on that last view of our country. Passively, I am drawn to a closer scrutiny of the peaceful scene far below and it reveals now a process of constant modulation. A thin film of life covers the ground like moulds growing on the surface of a cheese. From here their progress is infinitesimally slow, the expansions of their competing colonies hardly discernible. Neither their over-lapping, mingling and coalescing, or their territorial strangulations can be seen, so gradual are they. But even from a little nearer this fragile layer becomes an agitated granular fluid. The nervous

and twitchy movements of the constituent individual creatures
together form the waves, the flickerings and bursts of activity
perpetually flaring up here and there, then dying away finally
to no lasting effect. I see that it is decipherable only as stochas-
tic, apparently random and ultimately irrelevant.

'Bronek, Bronek.'

A name is sounding in my head, vaguely familiar but so distant it has no meaning, no resonance. It is a far-off sound like
a lost sheep bleating alone in a landscape. Yet it persists, breaking into the dream of millions of black insects scurrying over
the ground. It drains the strength away from it, desiccating it.
A honeycomb pattern cracks the parched earth; insects tumble
into the crevasses, falling, glinting into the profound blackness
of the void behind the crazed shrinking fragments of my vision,
tiny now as stars in a frozen sky.

'Bronek, come on.' A shape, darker than the darkness,
descends over me. It is hollow, defined only by the absence of
stars within it.

'Bronek, come on, Bronek. Can you hear me?' I dimly understand, there is urgency in the bleating.

'Bronek, can you hear me?'

I hear it.

'Look at me.' But I want to see past. It is in the way, making
me uncomfortable.

'Jesus, hypothermia. Bronek, you will have to try. Bronek,
can you hear me?'

I hear you, I hear you.

'How long have you been lying here? Bronek, say something.
Can you hear me? Bronek.'

My name, it's my name. Some sluggish memory stirs and
congeals into my name and I look at the voice, I look into the
darkness. Lubaczewski.

'Bronek?'

'Bronek.' Mouthing more than speaking, such a feeble small
sound.

'Yes. Bronek.'

'Yes.' I agree, I understand.

'Come, Bronek. I promised your mother I would get you to Hungary and I will. I will carry you there if I must.'

'Must.'

He does carry me. He keeps me on his back until the discomfort for me and the effort for him become too much, then I walk frog-marched between two men where the going is easier, until we find a hut. I am cocooned by the other walkers and in my sleep I return to the living from the moribund.

Shouting wakes us all in the early afternoon, even those who were on watch have fallen asleep, so great is our fatigue and our hunger by that time. The sound of raised voices and the terrifying barking of big dogs comes from the outside, not far away. We make the assumption that they are Germans because of the dogs. Have we strayed too far to the west on our walk and run into a German patrol? But that means we must be in Czechoslovakia and that is not possible, we never could have got that far away from our route. I imagine that one of the older men must have been guiding us, though I don't know which of them. From almost the beginning of this journey I have been out of touch with the others, too far behind to have seen how the route was planned and too exhausted to care when I was with them.

With the others I drag myself towards the window and between their heads, black against the shining snow outside, I see the dark figures of soldiers and dogs moving towards the hut.

'German or Russian?' Impossible to tell, they are black cartoon shapes moving on a white background. They have us, they know we are here.

'Who are they?' Ruski or Niemcy, Bolshevik or Nazi, barbaric children or dumb automata, what's the difference? It is the hammer or the anvil. We are done for.

I turn from the window with an odd sensation of the peace and comfort I felt lying in my bed of snow the night before, the residue of my treacherous desire to give up still lurks inside me. Behind the physical fear of the present moment, there is a kind of relief that it is over. I turn away, ashamed of it.

A figure, solid black against the glare from behind him, stands still and silent in the doorway for what seems an interminable length of time. Later I realise that coming in as he did from the snowy landscape to a darkened room, he would have been more or less blind. The interior would have been a shimmering dark pink or orange until his eyesight adjusted. Only when he moves away from the doorway into the room does his silhouette become a three dimensional officer of the Hungarian Gendarmerie.

'Welcome to Hungary. You are under arrest.'

'We are Polish nationals. We claim the rights of refugees under the Geneva Convention.' Lubaczewski has done his homework.

'Of course.'

'What happened then?' I have to break into his silence. He stopped and for a long time ruminated on his sandwich, looking blankly ahead from the top of another hill, further to the east but in the same range.

'What?'

'What happened to you after the Hungarian patrol found you?'

'They led us down to the railhead and from there we went by train to Budapest. There were thousands of Poles streaming across the frontier, trainloads of us being taken down from the mountains to Budapest. On Christmas Eve we arrived and made camp in a huge compound for internees. Then, in January, I managed to get to France.'

'How did you manage that?'

'I did the same as I had done in Tarnopol: I volunteered to carry the water every day. That way I got out of the main compound of the camp and found out what was going on. I applied for a passport to travel to France from the Polish Embassy in Budapest, and they gave me one. I was always young looking and I was given the passport of an eighteen-year-old travelling back to my family in France. In the middle of January I went by train to Yugoslavia, Italy and then to France, and I joined the Polish forces in Paris. General Sikorski's army.

'What about Lubaczewski, did he go to France too?'

'Ah, Lubaczewski. I don't know what happened to him then. Later we made contact in London. He had managed to find his family after the war and bring them to London. We kept in touch. He is dead now, of course. His son Ryszard, who was a little boy when we left, came to stay with us when we first came to New Moat. We used to keep in touch, but I haven't seen him for years.'

'I don't remember him.'

'No? You must have been three or so.'

'Funny what you do remember and what you don't.'

'Yes. Very funny.'

He sniffs and takes in the view down over Slovakia. I eat my sandwich.

'If it wasn't for Lubaczewski, I wouldn't be sitting here now. Nor would you.'

'Because he carried you over the mountains?'

'Yes, he carried me. He was the last one to carry me.'

'What do you mean?'

'Ach, never mind.'

'What about coming to England?'

We came back from Norway in June 1940 after the battle of Narvik. It seemed then that the Germans were unstoppable. We came from one defeated nation to another in the last throws of defending itself. In the middle of June, when we arrived back at Brest, the German tanks were sweeping across northern France. They had already entered Paris and the French government was suing for peace. It was demoralised. At our barracks, we were greeted with the order that our brigade, The Polish highlanders, had to surrender its weapons. We were under French command and this was one of the conditions for their peace with Hitler.

You can imagine the way the men felt about this; it's true we were under French command but surrender was the last thing we wanted after escaping from one occupation already. The bulk of the Polish army had been recruited in France from the migrant population in the mining areas like Alsace, but there was a significant number of escapees, men like me, who had come a long way to fight. Among this group particularly, there was almost a mutiny; these men had already lost or given up everything to get to France, and many were already battle hardened from the Polish campaign. They couldn't believe it: how could they give up now without a fight?

I had been commissioned before we went to Norway, I was now second lieutenant and I had some men I had to look after. It was the junior officers who were meant to keep the men in order, but I felt as they did. I had staggered out of Poland, crawled and been carried over the mountains to Hungary like an unwilling child. I had to be pushed, encouraged and helped by men like these, whose surrender I now had to enforce.

On the parade ground of the barracks we formed up in companies and one at a time had to advance, throw down our rifles and retire. There was a growing heap of weapons guarded by the French who were supervising this. Behind them, our top brass, mounted on their beautiful horses and dressed in their hand-made uniforms chatted and joked. These were the last of their kind, the old aristocrats who bought their commissions. They were dinosaurs, anachronisms, and this was the last time they appeared. In the old days they would have provided soldiers from the peasants on their estates and, naturally, you might say, commanded them as they always had. Some were courageous men and natural leaders, but some were not; some were foppish and dangerous to the men in their command. These were the same privileged types I had fallen out with at college over working with a Jewish student.

There is a final parade; the companies march past the pile of arms and then the group of officers. As we approach them, there is no order to salute and the men march eyes front, back to the barracks. After that it is every man for himself. The French residents leave and return to their families, some of them behind the lines. Our gallant commanders evaporate leaving a group of us with nowhere to go, supposedly waiting for the Germans to arrive and take us prisonner.

I got together with a few other men, about half a dozen who had nowhere else to go, and we left the barracks to look for some way to get out of France while we still could. Our best hope, we thought, was to try the Channel ports for any kind of ship that could take us to England before the Germans arrived. We had missed the Dunkirk evacuations and there was a lull before the Nazis arrived in this part; we knew they had got at least as far as Rouen and it wouldn't take them long. Some of the French were welcoming them, and the rest, well, peace would be signed any day now, so their fight was over.

I had fought alongside the French Foreign Legion in Norway. Of course they were not all French, there were even some Poles in it. They were fierce fighters, and absolutely reliable.

It was chaos. You cannot imagine it. The British Army had abandoned everything in their scramble to get off the beaches. Along the Brittany coast there were convoys of equipment left on the roads, lorries, cars, all sorts of things; most of it not even disabled. This became our scource of transport. We would search the lines of vehicles until we found one that still had some fuel in it, get it going and drive until it ran out, then look for another. I myself liked the big Humber staff car best, but there were Rovers and Rileys. For a few days we lived in whatever vehicle we found, travelling up and down the coast looking for a ship or even a fishing boat that we could persuade to take us off. It was amusing in a way, but it was becoming more and more dangerous. Reports that the Germans were coming closer made the French nervous of us; we never knew if someone would inform on us or if the police would be friendly or not. We never managed to persuade a fishing boat captain to take us, we had no money to pay for the trip, but some gave us food and wine. Once or twice we heard of a ship somewhere and we would race to the port, say Douarnenez or St Pol de Léon on the north coast, but by the time we arrived it had gone.

Eventually we did find a ship, in Brest. As we approached the town in our stolen car, we could see columns of smoke rising from the dock area and then the sound of explosions. We thought perhaps there was some kind of bombardment going on. That might mean there were British troops in the area and we could join up with them. When we got a little nearer we saw there was a British destroyer in the port, the *Galahad*. She had come with a demolition crew to destroy the ammunition and fuel dumps left there by the army after the landings. We made contact with the crew and she gave us a ride to Portsmouth after watching the fireworks. We arrived on 23 June.

A few years ago I went to a lecture given by Sir Peter Scott, the naturalist. Recounting his war experiences in the navy, he mentioned that he had been a first lieutenant on the destroyer *Galahad* at the beginning of the war. I asked him later if he had been on the ship in June 1940. He had, and he remembered picking up a party of stray Polish infantrymen while on their demolition run to Brest. I don't think we met at the time.

'Now Mark, we better get on because Renia will be waiting for us.' Down there in the haze below us. He gets up stiffly and helps me repack the boot.

'What did you mean, Lubaczewski was the last one to carry you?'

'Oh, never mind now.'

'No, go on. What did you mean?'

'When they came to the hut, I thought it was all over.'

'It is never over, Bronek, until you are dead. And you were nearly dead the night before.'

'I thought it was over then too.'

'You sound as though you would like it to be over.'

I lay in a dream of insignificance with no distinction between life and death.

'What difference would it make?'

'None, Bronek. That is our great strength.'

'He was a clever man, Lubaczewski. He helped me when I couldn't help myself, and, after that, I was able to.'

'What?'

'Help myself.'

'How do you mean?'

'Ach, Renia is waiting. I'll tell you another time.' He probably won't.

On the way down the hill another question occurs, 'Did you ever find out how Granny got you out of prison?'

'No idea.'

'You must have some idea; you know she paid someone. Who was it?'

'Mark, she never told me. Many times I asked myself that question. Many times I had to say something, but I was never sure.'

— 19 —
Bronek

We sit down in the sitting room of their new house at the beginning of a Rugby international, Wales v. France. I have taken a break from putting up shelves and new locks on doors to watch the game with Dad. They are singing the national anthems and I settle next to Bronek with a bottle of beer. He puts his old hand on my arm, 'Now, Mark, fetch me a beer.'

This is a real problem, he has been expressly forbidden alcohol as it upsets the effect of the frusimide, which we are still confused about. I try to avoid refusing by saying I'll make him some tea. He still wants beer.

'What about orange juice?'

'Can't I drink a glass of beer in my own house?' I start to try to explain but he's pushing himself out of his seat, shaking, propelled upwards mostly by anger. The effort buries his head between his shoulders. He knows all the explanations. I watch his back waver along the corridor to the kitchen, his socks over his pyjama legs, dressing gown hanging off his rounded back and collapsed shoulders, one arm hanging lower. While he is out of sight in the kitchen, I stare down the empty passage. Through a receding series of doorways, frames around the picture of a picture of the yellowy telephone, half a table, red-topped stools, the end of the worktop. Full, but the subject temporarily absent, a still life.

How much of what he was is left now in his last moments? He is always the accumulation of all his previous moments but now apparently innocent of them. He appears to be independent of his past, of his memories and to be sometimes lost, as he was in Kraków. I sense that his memory is already carried in those around him, those like me who will mix his related memories with my own. Not only the stories, but our image

of him will maintain his identity; our expectation will remind
him of who he is now that he is forgetting. There are times
when he is as clear as ever, engaging in conversation about the
subjects that always fascinated him, history first, the classics,
music, painting. And there are times when he is lost.

In his last days, I wish I had taken more care to just sit with
him and ask, what is your favourite of all things? The spring?
It is March and almost spring. I pick an abstract answer as I
think he might, one that is a clue. He is a master of not saying.
When he first told me he loved the spring before all other seasons I was young enough for this idea to be new; I had not yet
made the distinction and the act of choosing had not occurred
to me. Then for a while it became a trite remark, obvious. But
obvious things can be true and have a meaning beyond the
obvious, connected to the personal, like my own feeling for the
spring now. But I didn't ask him, it is a busy time in a new
house and we all buzz around him trying to get everything into
some kind of order as quickly as we can so that we can then
take the time to be with him. We pursue this as the logical
course, which of course it is not, as if the energy invested in
the pursuit will make it so and put off the thing we cannot yet
name until we are ready. In a year's time the house will be still
unfinished, but he has only a matter of days left.

He returns from the deep, marching up the corridor towards
me with the beer I made him get for himself, not looking at me.
His back towards the chair, he controls his weight as long as
possible then lets go and falls the last few inches with a sigh
of fatigue. For a while he remains frozen with the beer bottle
raised in his left hand, eyes shut, as if trying to recall some
name or thing from his obstinate memory. Finally he exhales,
opening his eyes and tries to twist off the cap of his beer bottle.
His grip is not what it was and he shakes with the strain but
cannot shift it. I am embarrassed to interfere having already
caused so much unnecessary exhaustion. I think of it as minutes of his remaining life, so significant now that those left are
not innumerable.

'Shall I have a go, Dad?'

'You better, I have no strength left.'

Two and a half tons of Welsh and French strength hurls itself at itself for an hour and a half. He swigs shakily with exaggerated satisfied aaahs after each mouthful and we root for the Welsh together, unsuccessfully. He nods off in the second half and I can't cheer very loudly on my own: it sounds too lonely.

We moved them to the new house while he was in hospital, and he more or less discharged himself the next day, determined not to miss a moment he didn't have to in the new house. He was spared the trauma of the actual move, of stripping their lives out of the old house, leaving it bare and awkward, doors flapping into empty and dowdy-looking rooms. It doesn't seem like anyone's home.

Aunt Alison sits down next to me on the bed in my old bedroom as I'm emptying the cupboards. She has a tissue-paper package in her hand, 'I wanted to give you this now, before I forget, and 'cos I know you're interested.' It's dark blue, the outer layer of paper, a flat, hand sized thing. It looks heavy on her hand as she looks for the edge of the tissue.

'After the war I went to work in Germany with the Jewish Committee for Relief Abroad organisation. We traced families that had been split up, survivors of the camps and helped refugees returning to Germany to find their families again.' She turns the package over and removes the first layer revealing white paper underneath. 'A young boy who said he was sixteen came to me from Auschwitz, no family left at all. He was determined to go to Israel. He looked too young to travel alone but it was hard to tell how old the children from the camps were. Some looked dried up and old before their time, others didn't grow and looked like children when they should have been adolescent. He also knew he was going to be an engineer, even though he had no idea what it was.' She weighs the parcel, turning off another layer of its wrapping. Through the paper I see a dark shadow. 'I found him a place at an engineering works for a few days while his passport and papers were prepared. I never expected to see him again but he turned up a few days later to tell me that he was leaving: his papers had come. And he gave me this.' She unwinds the last layer from a dull steel Star of David milled out of solid plate half an inch thick. ' "For you," he said, "the first thing I ever made." '

I leave for a few days but return to find Dad back in hospital and much weaker. He is in a private room in the same ward as before. I am shocked at the deterioration in his condition in such a short time: a few days seems to have cost him dearly. He is restless and very breathless and has to wear a mask over his face or a tube which passes under his nose to give him oxygen. His lungs are filling with water; he is secretly drowning again. He breathes in pants accompanied by sighs and bubbling rasps; the mask infuriates him and increases his restlessness, and with enormous effort he tears off the plastic cone that covers his nose and mouth to get more ordinary air. He also tends to kick off his covers and lie as though drunk, dishevelled with his pyjama jacket hitched up behind his neck and his trousers pushed off altogether. I never see how he accomplishes this. We try to make him comfortable and decent, but left alone for a moment he transforms the scene into the aftermath of a drunken brawl, even rolling his yellow eyes and forgetting where he is.

I arrive to see him alone, Thursday evening, 27 February. He tells me he has to be at home. He knows he is dying now; there is no way back from this. The fact that he's in hospital seems to rob me of normal reason; I feel guilty about his being here, which he obviously hates, but still somehow I think that it must be the best place for him. Doctors confuse the matter further by wanting to try just one more thing, or, leave it till after the weekend and we'll see how he is then. Bronek gets more despondent. 'I want to die in my own bed.' I sit by him, numbed with this thought, and he drifts back into sleep. I'm still staring at the same spot on the bedclothes when he opens his eyes again.

'Now, Mark, I have a serious question and I expect an answer. How much beer do we have in the house?'

Pete, Marie-Jeanne and I arrive at the hospital on the following evening, Friday. They have just come from France and Pete hasn't seen Dad in this bout of illness. We think we will stay with him until he goes to sleep and then maybe go for something to eat or a drink. He is in a room on his own behind the reception desk and next to the office. Through the half-open door as we approach, I can see him propped up by pillows into a sitting position, his pyjama jacket ridden up under his armpits the buttons straining to hold it together across his chest, but otherwise naked. He has managed to kick off everything else. The skin of his abdomen is so clear and soft in contrast to the motley stained and ancient skin of his face, hands and forearms. We lift him back into his pyjamas, Pete helps him through the performance of urination, we try the oxygen mask on him but he tears it away. He's been a modest man all my life and I have never seen him naked until now. It's hard to imagine how this should be possible, but I felt pleased that I had, and pleased to be lifting him, dressing him. And surprise that he doesn't object to or worry about our intervention.

He drifts in and out of our company, dozing with his eyes almost shut then rousing himself to look at us or ask something. Sometimes he concentrates on his breathing which is becoming more and more difficult. He sighs heavily with every third or fourth exhalation and when he's half asleep his breathing occasionally stops altogether for an alarmingly long time. Our conversation stops and we all listen and wait for him to give a slight twitch and start up again. When I'm very near him sometimes and his breathing has stopped in this way, I can hear the faintest bubblings and gurglings from his abdomen. All outward stillness, the semblance of death. Will his body still bubble and gurgle inside after its death? These lapses of his respiration become a feature of his last few days: they become more frequent and longer, like rehearsals.

It doesn't take us long on this visit to agree that we cannot leave him here any longer. As though we were all thinking the same thought but not able immediately to bring it to the surface and decide. I talk to the nurse who runs the ward. We go through the routine about needing constant care and medical attention for a few minutes but, mid-sentence, he suddenly changes his mind and agrees that we should take Bronek home as soon as possible.

We were very lucky with Bob, the nurse; having him on our side made a huge difference to all our lives for a few days, and made Bronek's last few days into part of his life instead of part of his death. Who can say what might have been; in this case what was was wonderful.

We cannot move him immediately as by now it is late evening, but Bob arranges for everything to be done first thing on the following morning, Saturday. It is to our advantage that it is a weekend. On a weekday a discharge would have to be agreed and authorised by a consultant. All the social services would have to be involved because he would be regarded as needing nursing care at home, for which he would have to be assessed, Thursdays only, then their list of his needs, special mattress, oxygen cylinders and so on, would need to be ordered and delivered and checked prior to his discharge. By the book this could take a week. We could of course just have discharged him against the advice of the hospital but then it's doubtful that we could have managed. Without the provision of oxygen it would have been impossible, and without their support, particularly Bob's, it would have been very difficult.

I stay overnight with him on a camp bed. The room is airless and too warm and I struggle to resist sleep, reading to stay awake. I watch him on his high bed from my very low one, both of us sliding in and out of sleep, and I listen for his bubbly breathing. In Poland we always shared a room, we even shared a bed in Inowrocław and in Poprad. Here we are again, the last time.

He was a very tidy sleeper, lying always on his left side, with his left hand under his cheek, his right arm neatly laid along his side on to his hip and thigh, legs slightly bent but together one on the other. Compact and relaxed, he would stay in the same position all night. Now he is restless in a half-sitting position, if he lays flat the water in his lungs makes him cough. Paradoxically it sounds dry and dusty, mostly one or two barks at a time but sometimes an accelerating crescendo that threatens to shake the life out of him. I'm listening to the cough, this dry single report, realising that it's been there in some form for as long as I can remember. In still-dark winter mornings I would hear him cough once as he crossed the yard to start the milking. A night noise, like a fox. Now, his voice is weaker and less distinct; his teeth don't fit any more and his mouth hangs a little slack. But with my memory I fill in the clarity and the tension because there is still some indestructible intent: either he wants to know something or else he wants me to. When he wakes, he starts talking immediately while still half in a dream, or as if continuing a conversation. I try to pick up where someone in his head has left off, maybe me as well, but it doesn't always work.

In Poland he often woke in the morning and started a conversation with me in Polish, I would nod in imitation of his nodding, I'd say, tak, tak, and he'd keep talking for a while until something tripped it up, perhaps I'd say, tak when I should say, nie. He looks at me for a moment wondering who is being stupid. I liked it when he laughed at himself, a silent chuckle shaking his head, but I wish to God I really could have spoken to him in Polish, in his own language.

I try to keep him drinking as much as possible from a beaker rather like the ones that children use with a moulded spout on the lid. Everything now is exhausting. Our conversations are punctuated by draughts of orange juice and interrupted when he drifts off for a few minutes. Sitting on a stool next to his bed in my underwear, through the timeless part of the night I feel I should somehow be reviewing his life, or asking him things, maybe about the gaps in the stories he told me in Poland. I don't, instead I look at his old head and wonder how he managed to shave, I look at his old hands and see that his nails are clipped and clean. I study old age trying to see it objectively, trying not to hear his younger voice or see his younger face, stopping my memory from fleshing out the actual man dozing in front of me. It's impossible; I cannot uninvent him as my father, I can't remove the past from the present and, but for the moment of detachment looking at him sleep, I am sure I don't want to. After all, the past is true. 'I am afraid I have been a disappointment to you boys,' he says this out of nowhere. I'm holding the stupid beaker in front of his face wondering what he means, he won't say more, he shrugs and turns away. This is an interesting reversal: I always thought we had disappointed him. None of us has lived up to his academic hopes and the world has changed us into something he did not altogether approve of or understand. We are casual, untidy and appear disrespectful. But he was as full of contradictions as we are, and this he did understand. He was someone who worried constantly about what others thought but at the same time would not be told what to think. I suppose the Polish characteristic ability to be accepted anywhere is something they wish to be, rather than expect to be.

'Mark, I am very worried about champagne, have we got the champagne?' I offer him the baby beaker which he accepts automatically, sucking one mouthful only then turning away. He makes a face at the taste of it.

'What champagne, Dad?' But he's gone again. Drink seems to be a preoccupation for a while in the night, maybe he is confusing drink with drinking, wishing for something other than orange juice. We had our adventures with drink, Dad and I. He believed I had a very low tolerance for alcohol because on a couple of occasions, one notable, he saw me the worse for a hangover. On our first trip we had attended Renia's wedding in Czechoslovakia. I had been encouraged by my cousin Milan to enter in to the spirit of the occasion, keeping up with the outrageous drinking customs of the Czechs.

'Drink this tumbler of wódka, Mark, and look into my eyes while you do it. Don't stop, blink or look away.'

Yes, I drank them all, with severe alcohol poisoning as the reward. The way Bronek saw it, my life was saved the next day by Renia's friend, Dasia, a doctor, who injected my thighs with strychnine to stop the convulsions and then tried to drown me in mineral water while marching me round the village. She carried bottles of water in a plastic shopping bag and stopped me every few minutes to pour them into the general area of my face. I remember only the green copper onion tower of the village church, leaning on Dasia and listening to her musical voice chatting away to me in Czech and wanting to sleep at last. We saw her at the end of this last trip, in the Tatra on the Slovakian side. I say to her through Bronek, 'You are the only woman who has saved my life.' She smiles but doesn't remember.

He wakes with a worry about the house, but before he finishes asking me if something has been done he answers his own question. Nervous worries. I think of his mounting anxiety as we approached frontiers, a reaction I haven't fully understood. He is approaching the last one now, all previous crossings done in preparation for this one. The human obsession with borders, with a line which marks the difference, the place beyond which you cannot go. Borders and death. Are we so concerned with borders because we fear this final line through our lives, this final crossing out? Within our own territory our identity is reaffirmed as distinct from our neighbour, and from without we are recognised by the markings of our shell. Stalin moved hundreds of thousands of people from the centre of Russia to the edges of the Soviet Union to reinforce this point; within these frontiers we are different, and as if to underline the morbid fascination and his fear, he made the crossing of it fatal, a mortal sin.

At home, in their bedroom at last, we assemble for an impromptu party, four generations gathered to welcome him. His hands like paddles scoop in his great grandchildren, Craig and Holly, to the bedside. These two have charmed him in the last few years. All the responsibility of parenthood gone, he has allowed himself to be uninhibitedly emotional with them, delighting in their visits, standing in silly hats to be photographed holding their hands, cuddling them and listening to the streams of questions and stories they tell him. Pete produces the pink champagne and, with the popping cork, releases the tight grip of worry we've all been holding in. Brows unknit as the champagne is passed around; we let go of the forgettable problems in our pleasure at his arrival. His weak smile, shaky hands balancing the glass on his belly. He would say, 'Cheerios', as a toast. He always got this wrong. He doesn't say it now but I am thinking it.

Later, the same day or the next, I find myself again trying to force orange juice on him, he tries too but half way through a suck on the beak he waves it away with a slow movement of his hand. Trying to clear his mouth of the thick taste of the claggy juice mixed with his own dryness, he says, 'Mark, this is a horrible stuff. Have we got some cognac in the house?' I have to admit that the thought that this might not be good for him makes the briefest appearance on the way to the drinks cupboard, what if it kills him now? So I get myself one too. I understand immediately I taste it what he wanted in asking for this. The strong solvent spirit cuts through all the stale heaviness and the medicated cotton wool of illness. He savours the fire and the heat, a naked and a clean sensation. And he likes cognac. Na zdrowie, Dad. To health. Cheerios.

On Monday morning Mike and I are still in bed in the boys' room. He arrived from Canada on Saturday and we've been sitting in with Dad on a constant rota. On Sunday night a nurse came in for the night to give Jinks a rest as she has taken the burden of the nights herself. We are talking about pigs, how Julian is getting on in Canada and God knows what else, laughing at the moment when Jinks comes in to ask us to help turn Bronek over for the nurse to give him a bed-bath. He is turned this way and that, sighing and smiling.

'How are you today, Dad?'

'Oh, not too bad. Not too bad.'

The nurse goes off at nine, I make some coffee and Mike and I resume our porcine conversation in the boys' bedroom. Pete and Marie-Jeanne, habitual late risers, haven't surfaced yet. Jinks goes to the bathroom.

Bronisław Zygadło dies.

Light. Choosing a time when there was no one with him to watch, no one's attention to hold him. I imagine one of those lapses in his breathing.

The final party scene, after the memorial service, is in the village hall. His absence the reason for it. It is exactly the kind of occasion he most loved, a gathering of good-hearted friends and their families. Voices buzz together in a kind of excitement, an enthusiasm for each other and for themselves. I look around expecting to see him sitting at a table bent in conversation, his fingers spread across his forehead or laughing with his head thrown back and his eyes shut.

As you look around you might see me doing the same.